GREAT
SEXUAL
SCANDALS

GREAT SEXUAL SCANDALS

4,000 YEARS OF DEBAUCHERY

SUSAN CROSLAND

ROBSON BOOKS

First published in 2002 by Robson Book
64 Brewery Road, London N7 9NT

A member of **Chrysalis** Books plc

British Library cataloguing in Publication Data
A catalogue record for this book is available from the British
Library.

ISBN 1 86105 556 0

Typeset by SX Composing DTP, Rayleigh, Essex
Printed by Mackays of Chatham Plc, Chatham, Kent

For Alex and Alistair

Contents

Introduction

At times my choice of scandals was directed by personal experience. Soon after I learned to read, I was given a child's version of ancient Greek history and myths. History had been shortened, but everything else was there: fearlessness, betrayal, honour, brutality, loyalty, jealousy. And, of course, lust and love. They set my fantasies for life, varying according to my age. At six, I named my turtle after my hero, Theseus.

In pre-puberty, I was Hippolyta, Queen of the Amazons, in single combat with King Theseus. I was thrilled when finally he pinned her to the ground and then carried her away. His habit after each battle was to take a girl-trophy, but in Hippolyta's case, Theseus was so fascinated by her that he declined to take her sexually by force, sleeping on the floor of his tent until she wanted him. This suited me, as at that time I was remarkably ignorant about the ultimate object of erotic sensations. I preferred being Hippolyta fighting the enemy, side by side with Theseus.

Then I entered puberty and my cousin told me the facts of life. Thus I could vaguely fill in the missing bit of Hippolyta's story in my fantasies.

King David, Israel's second and greatest King, also entered my life in childhood. Every summer was spent in Vermont, away from Baltimore's heat, on my uncle's isolated, derelict, poetic farm looking west over Lake Champlain to the Adirondacks. Cut off for ten weeks from other members of the human race, on Sunday afternoons my mother read the Bible to my sister and me. From the moment that the shepherd boy volunteered to duel with Goliath, I was hooked on David. He was brave, honourable, and all things admirable.

Then disillusionment. One Sunday, out of the blue, I learned that this King, born with every gift and venerated by his people, committed an act of calculated callousness so foul that it shocked me deeply. It was my first realisation that between good and evil we have every other quality in us. I suppose a psychiatrist would see my chapter on David as my 'coming to terms', today's vogue phrase, with childhood loss of innocence.

When I finished researching and writing my first chapter – about the grotesquely erotic Queen Pasiphaë at the Cretan Court of King Minos in 2000 BC – I thought: this makes twentieth-century licentiousness seem like kindergarten. I was mistaken. Debauchery during the last 4,000 years has frequently been bizarre, but often deeply moving as well.

I have set each sexual scandal in the history and culture of its day. In several instances, myth has attached itself to real events more than usual – notably in the courts of ancient Crete and Athens and King Arthur. The Athenian Court bore witness to the danger in believing that any woman who cries rape is a victim. Phaedra, the Cretan wife of Theseus, became obsessed by love for the King's favourite son, Hippolytus. When the youth honourably rebuffed his stepmother, her frustration turned to vindictiveness, and she claimed Hippolytus had raped her. Familiar?

Some 'experts' argue that Arthur and Queen Guinevere and the stunning knight Launcelot never existed. For me the influence of the Round Table and the Holy Grail on historians such as Geoffrey of Monmouth and Sir Thomas Malory and composers (Wagner wrote *Parsifal* thirteen centuries later), not to mention the Kennedys' failed claim to have created a second Camelot, makes it real enough. All reality attracts myth (see our current tabloids), and I admit that this chapter, unlike the others, contains much that is legendary about one of the most famous characters in British history.

A number of the subjects and the attendant characters – the Duchess of Windsor, Gore Vidal, Lord Boothby, Jeremy Thorpe, the actor Peter Lawford who pimped for Jack Kennedy – I interviewed when I wrote profiles for the *Sunday Times*. I plundered my own work ruthlessly, now seeing them from a later perspective.

General truths recurred. During Secretary of State for War John Profumo's infatuation with a Mona Lisa-faced prostitute, Christine Keeler, two common traits of errant husbands appeared. One was the desire to 'defile' the marriage bed by taking his mistress to his home in his wife's absence. And, as is common for caught-out husbands, in the War Secretary's fatal statement of lies to the House of Commons, he referred repeatedly to his wife as having been present on occasions when he saw Christine, thus attempting to cloak his infidelity. You may well ask how his distinguished actress wife, Valerie Hobson, felt about the role foisted on her.

Johnny Hyde, one of the biggest agents in Hollywood, was regularly unfaithful to his beautiful wife, Mozelle, but neither he nor Mozelle allowed this to damage his being a good husband and a good father to four sons. Then disaster. Hyde fell in love with the thirty-years-younger Marilyn Monroe. When his wife heard that he was obsessed with a girl who seemed to Mozelle to be a slut, she confronted her husband who made the classic remark of older men who fall for younger women: 'It's happened and I can't do anything about it.'

Lord Byron and his half-sister Augusta illustrated a sometimes unconscious (in Byron's case, conscious) reason for humans' deep attraction to incest: narcissism. The close blood relation provides a reflection of oneself.

The frequent ease of 'seduction' was seen in the life of the most celebrated medieval philosopher, Peter Abelard. At 38 he was invited by the Canon of Notre-Dame to move into his home, where the philosopher was to tutor the Canon's seventeen-year-old niece, Héloïse. In anticipation, Abelard wrote in his journal, 'It was like giving a tender lamb into the care of a hungry wolf' – only to discover that his virginal quarry was at least as lustful as he was.

In writing about the then Prince of Wales and Mrs Simpson, I thought frequently of the Prince of Wales in our time. The behaviour of Charles and Mrs Parker Bowles has always been a thing of blameless discretion compared with the public relationship of his great-uncle and Wallis. As for Charles's problems with Diana, he should count himself lucky that he was not his ancestor George IV, whose wife Queen Caroline had endless liaisons on the Continent, at one time residing with an Italian lover who had been her servant.

Two other distant relations in my series are Lady Jane Digby and Pamela Churchill Harriman. The first was a notorious nineteenth-century sensualist and adventuress, the second was the last of the great courtesans. Pamela liked to think she modelled her life on her amoral great-great-aunt, but both chapters make it clear that she was kidding herself.

Because I had a ringside seat in the world of politics, this book's evidence of betrayal and dissimulation, the link between power and sex hardly came as a surprise to me. But the variety of sexual antics was a good deal more extensive than I had previously observed – even at Westminster.

The only thing really new about John Major's affair with Edwina Currie when both were MPs was the excessive vulgarity of much of the style and substance in Mrs Currie's diaries. Curiously, she complained bitterly to the media that she was being vilified for her money-spinning revelations because she is a woman. Oh, pur-lease!

My feelings about my subjects seldom ended in active dislike, however rotten their behaviour. Even the calamitous betrayals by Colonel Alfred Redl, the greatest pre-First World War spymaster, did not remove a lingering warmth towards him. I found it difficult to study the characters – and discover why they acted as they did – without feeling a certain sympathy, though there were exceptions.

Readers will observe in my collection that justice too often was belated. But such is reality.

1

Queen Pasiphaë

TWO THOUSAND BC

The centre of power in Greece in 2000 BC was the island of Crete. The King of its sea-empire was Minos. Excavations of his palace at Knossos have revealed his vast wealth and the sophistication of architects, stonecutters, painters and goldsmiths.

When the hereditary kingship of Crete was disputed, Minos prayed to Poseidon, Greek god of the sea, to help him win the throne. The King promised that in gratitude he would sacrifice the most majestic bull in the land to Poseidon. But the gods knew of mankind's greed. Having granted Minos his prayer, Poseidon tested his good faith. Not far from Knossos, a great bull appeared suddenly on the shore, pure white except for a black spot between gleaming horns.

Minos directed the beast's capture, exhorting the bull-catchers that any injury to the glorious creature would cost them their lives. They netted the bull, and it was led to the altar to be offered to Poseidon. Then, before the priests could strike, the King halted the sacrifice: the bull was so beautiful he could not bear to kill it. He wanted it for himself.

Close to the palace, a large tract of land was barricaded, and there the living symbol of brutish, untamed strength could be gazed upon by the royal family. The King, Queen Pasiphaë, their young daughters Ariadne and Phaedra, all were fascinated by the white bull. Disastrously, the Queen grew obsessed by it. Frequently she left the palace at night to stand by the enclosure fantasising about the beast she craved. She yearned to put her bare arms around the great neck swollen with muscles. Yet she knew the bull would savage her. She could face being destroyed by it if first it possessed her. But how?

The Queen summoned the master craftsman Daedalus, known far and wide for his creations, to her rooms in the palace. Pasiphaë told Daedalus what she wanted him to build. She would assure secrecy from her closest attendants. Should Daedalus himself ever reveal that she had ordered his bestial creation, she would claim he was lying and accuse him of raping her.

The night came when the barricaded gate was stealthily unlocked and a hollow wooden cow, covered with cowhide, rolled in. Within it Pasiphaë arranged herself, unspeaking, her gown pulled up to her waist. In terror for themselves, the attendants pushed the cow only a short way into the meadow of Gortyn where the bull was grazing. Just before they fled back to the gate, one of them daubed the replica's open vagina with discharge taken from a real cow in heat.

In the moonlight, the bull lifted its head to sniff the new scent on the air. Pasiphaë heard the bawling begin, then the pounding of hooves. She shuddered with desire. The approaching bellows grew more frenzied. She opened her legs. The beast's front hooves crashed on the wooden haunches above her, and the bull's wild cries covered her own.

The offspring of this obscene rapture was a boy with a bull's head and a man's body. He was called the Minotaur. Ovid described the King's horror.

> The palace blazed with trophies; but within
> Was scandal dark and hideous fruit of sin,
> The household shame, full-grown and foul to see,
> The illicit half-and-half monstrosity.
> To rid his roof of such a strain, the King
> Commissioned Daedalus to house the thing;
> And he, the world-famed architect, designed
> A multiplex of courts and cloisters blind
> Where misdirections led, in mazes long,
> The cheated eye circuitously wrong.

Into the depths of the labyrinth the Minotaur was consigned. Daedalus himself was imprisoned at his workplace lest he flee Crete and tell abroad how the Minotaur came to be born. The master craftsman had the arrogance of a genius. Resentful at being confined by the King, he made wings for himself and his son Icarus to escape the island. 'Minos possesses the earth and the sea,' he told Icarus, 'but he does not control the air, and that is the way we shall go if Jupiter pardons the enterprise.'

It took him many months to achieve the right balance with feathers and linen-fastenings and wax. Then father and son donned their wings and flew away from Crete. But Jupiter could not pardon this enterprise, which rivalled a creation of the gods. He filled young Icarus with reckless pride. Against the warnings of his father, the boy ascended higher and higher, and when he felt a change in his wings and saw the sun was melting the wax, it was too late. Daedalus heard the screams as his son plunged down until he hit the sea and disappeared. The heartbroken father flew on to Sicily.

At Knossos the horrors continued. Queen Pasiphaë felt no remorse for her monstrous act, but the birth of the offspring blighted any chance of fulfilling her bestial lust again. Driven mad by her desire, she hanged herself.

King Minos, having defeated the Athenians, exacted a gruesome annual tribute: six youths and six virgins whose blood would feed the Minotaur. The ship carrying them from their homeland bore a black sail. Once within the Cretan labyrinth, they became hopelessly lost. Sooner or later their smell attracted the Minotaur.

Tribute followed tribute, and when the dreaded next one came due, the city of Athens went into mourning. This time the twelve unfortunates chosen by lot were joined by a volunteer who put himself at their head, Theseus, then sixteen, son of King Aegeus of Athens. He organised them, girls and boys, and on board the ship they practised endlessly, leaping over one another. For all knew that bull-dancing was the favourite game in Crete, the dancers grabbing the horns of the charging beast and vaulting over its back until one of them was in position to slip in the short sword worn at the hip. None spoke of the fact that even if they could evade the

Minotaur's horns, they would be unable to find their way out of the labyrinth.

When the ship reached Knossos, it was met by palace officials and guards. Before the prisoners entered the labyrinth, they were to enjoy Minos's hospitality for three days and nights. In the evenings Prince Theseus sat at the same table as the King and the two princesses, Ariadne in her teens, Phaedra still a child. Theseus wore his hair short in front so no one could grab it in a fight, the rest twisted into a handsome plait behind. In the daytime he took part in the Cretan games, and both young princesses watched the grace and skill with which he overcame all adversaries.

On the final evening, love-crazed Ariadne took Theseus into a darkened garden of the palace. She adored him. She was revolted by her half-brother. And Minos's family had bad blood: each of them would betray easily. She gave him a ball of thread to unwind when he entered the labyrinth and a dagger to kill the Minotaur.

Within the entrance to the labyrinth, Theseus fastened the end of the thread. The group moved forward together. Before they got far, they heard the blood-chilling sounds of the beast, but in the twisting maze it was impossible to judge how far away the Minotaur waited. Theseus knew he must find the monster before he himself grew weak from hunger. One of the youths, to impress his male partner, slipped ahead in hopes of sighting the Minotaur and then returning to warn Theseus. Almost at once he became lost. An hour later, his beloved and the rest heard the vicious bawling and the cries.

Halfway through the next day, the prisoners realised the snorting breathing was close by. Handing the ball of thread to one of the others, Theseus took the dagger from under his tunic and advanced alone. Within minutes he confronted the Minotaur, its mouth and horns smeared with gore. At its feet lay the torn body. The half-man lowered its bull head and charged. With the dagger in his belt, Theseus grabbed the horns and vaulted over the monster's back. The Minotaur turned, and this time its human body threw itself upon Theseus and seized him by the throat. With a single thrust, Theseus plunged the dagger into the monster's heart.

The prisoners retraced the route marked by the ball of thread, and at last emerged into daylight. Their ship's crew, never expecting to see them again, had made ready for departure, the black sail raised with Theseus and the prisoners on board, they sped from Knossos. What King Minos did not yet know as he watched the sail grow smaller was that within the vessel was his daughter Ariadne. For love of Theseus, she betrayed her father, her half-brother and her country.

The ship made for Athens, passing near a small uninhabited island called Naxos. Theseus bade his crew drop anchor for the night, and on the shore beneath the stars he lay with Ariadne in his arms. Some time after dawn, she woke to find him gone. In the distance she saw the black sail.

His desertion of Ariadne was what every trophy girl of that day might have expected. What was uncharacteristically cruel was abandoning her on a deserted island. She was prepared to serve him in any way. He simply forgot about her: his mind had moved on to other things.

In Athens, King Aegeus was keeping watch from the Acropolis when the black sail at last came into sight. He and Theseus had agreed that the sail would be changed for a white one if the mission to slay the Minotaur was successful. When the King saw the sail was black, he flung himself on to the rocks below.

Did Theseus forget the sail's significance for his father, just as he forgot Ariadne? Or was he, perhaps unconsciously, hurrying his father's death? *Some* time the King must die. When the returning Prince landed at Piraeus, he was led jubilantly into Athens: 'Long live the King.'

2

Queen Phaedra

TWO THOUSAND BC

Loved by his people for his fearlessness and just governance, King Theseus extended the rule of Athens over Attic principalities. From each victory, Greece's greatest hero always took a girl-trophy. Battles, however perilous, had an erotic aura. He fought the Amazon Queen, silver-haired Hippolyta, in single combat. But unlike his other trophies, Hippolyta fiercely resisted capture. When he defeated her, such was his respect for her courage that in the privacy of his quarters, he declined to force himself on her. Not until she was ready to submit did he take her sexually.

Their love was the grand passion of both lives. Whatever the battle, they fought side by side – even against the Amazons, who now saw their former Queen as a traitor. Except when she gave birth to their son, Hippolytus, she and Theseus were parted only for brief intervals when duty required him to treat his young wife, Phaedra, with honour.

The second daughter of King Minos, Phaedra, was a child in the Cretan Court when she first saw Theseus, then a prisoner, and fantasised about him. When she reached her teens, a political marriage was arranged with the Athenian King. The Princess with her entourage disembarked at Piraeus and was escorted into Athens, elaborately painted, her hair dressed in ringlets, a bare-breasted doll bedecked in gold.

Theseus performed his marital obligations with kindness, though wanting only to return to his silver-haired warrior. Phaedra knew, but could do nothing to make him truly desire her, let alone love her.

When the Amazons launched a siege of the Acropolis, in their bedchamber Hippolyta and Theseus donned their armour with a sense of foreboding. He asked her not to wear her distinctive golden helmet, but she refused to be intimidated by the avenging women she once had led. It was the one who had loved her best who got Theseus in her sights and let her arrow fly. Hippolyta, at his side, saw it coming and stepped before him to take the arrow. She died as he bent over her.

Theseus directed some of his men to lay her on her shield and carry her behind the front line. Then he went mad, advancing on the Amazons, his sword rending anyone who crossed him, finally reaching the one who had slain his beloved and hacking her to pieces.

In the years that followed, the King governed, fought, took his trophies and spent the least time possible with Phaedra. His and Hippolyta's son. Hippolytus was by now a young man with medical gifts. Phaedra became ill and peevish, claiming that only Hippolytus could cure her. Theseus was puzzled that the gentle Hippolytus was loath to go to his stepmother's bedroom to attend her. Fretting on her pillow, Phaedra still called for him. When the youth fled to the countryside, she left her sickbed to seek him.

Farmers heard screams. Then they beheld a woman, her dress ripped open, hair dishevelled, breasts bleeding from deep scratches, stagger out of a copse. They recognised the Queen. She cried out that she had been raped.

She was borne back to the palace, where Theseus came to the darkened room where she tossed, weeping, on her bed.

'Who did this?'

Phaedra buried her face in the pillow and didn't answer.

Growing angrier, he repeated the question.

Again his wife refused to speak.

She turned to look at him, and he shook her until she answered: 'Hippolytus.'

What happened next was like a nightmare. Theseus searched the countryside, noticing that the cattle lifted their heads to listen to what as yet he could not hear: the distant rumbling of the earth gathering force to split. On finding Hippolytus at last, the father disowned the son for his treacherous villainy, banishing him at once and invoking the god of the sea: 'May Poseidon avenge me.'

Returning to the palace on the Acropolis, Theseus looked down on the coastal road and saw dust rising from Hippolytus's chariot as, urging his horses faster, the reins tied around his waist, he galloped away from Athens. The air was strangely still, birdsong silent, and the sea drew back from the shore, further and further, stranding shellfish on the rocky bed. Cattle in the fields above were lowing. The earth began to shake, and peasants ran from their homes, carrying what domestic animals they could. Then the sea gathered itself into waves as high as houses, which crashed one upon the other as they swept to the shore.

The chariot reeled from the first onslaught of water, and the horses whinnied and strained at their harness. Hippolytus whipped them on, making for where the road turned inland. He was never to reach it. For in the next instant, the bull from the sea was upon them.

Afterwards, some said that the bull must have been washed away from the shore when the water withdrew and then thrown back on the waves. Horns, limbs, chariot wheels, horses struggling in panic, reins entwining the youth, all were entangled in the massive banks of pounding water.

Then it was over. The sea settled. Cattle on the hill ceased their lowing. Farmers looked down on the wreck by the shore, the bull wreathed in seaweed standing over the smashed chariot, horses trapped in harness, their legs broken, striving frantically to stand, the driver still tethered by his reins to the havoc, his helmet lying at the water's edge.

Men ran down the hill to help. On reaching the wreckage, they recognised the King's favourite son: he had his mother's silver hair. One of them set off to bear the news to the palace. Another took a knife from his belt and cut the thrashing horses' throats. Hippolytus, groaning, tried to lift his head from where he lay twisted, but he was helpless. His back was broken. Tenderly the men tried to straighten his limbs.

In the palace, built to withstand earthquakes, the ferocious short tremor had caused little damage. The young son of Theseus and

Phaedra was with his father. Gossip spreads rapidly in a palace, and when the boy heard that his mother had been raped by Hippolytus, he had asked to see Theseus. The boy idolised his half-brother. Now he told his father what he had overheard from his own bedroom on previous nights: Hippolytus repeatedly resisting his stepmother's attempts to seduce him. She had accused him falsely.

At that moment the messenger was shown into the room to tell his dire tidings. The boy began to weep. Theseus called for his chariot to be readied. When he reached the disaster, he leapt down without his helmet and knelt by his son. 'Forgive me.' He touched the silver hair.

Hippolytus opened his eyes. He spoke in a whisper: 'I didn't do it.'

'I know.'

Hippolytus closed his eyes, shuddered and was still.

His body was carried home on his shield. Theseus rode ahead. At the palace he went directly to Phaedra's bedchamber, dismissing her attendants. When he had bolted the door, he turned to his wife whose face was defiant until she saw his eyes and knew he knew. Falling to her knees she grovelled before him.

'Like a Cretan,' he said contemptuously. 'Get up.'

With one hand clamped on her wrist, he half-dragged her to a writing table and spread the writing materials in front of her. He pushed her on to the chair and kept a hand pressing on her shoulder.

'I didn't know what I was doing,' she whimpered.

'Write what I say,' he ordered. "I tried to bring Hippolytus into my bed."'

Phaedra struggled to rise. Theseus placed both his hands around her throat. '"To avenge my humiliation, I falsely accused him of rape. This is the truth."'

Theseus tightened his hold. 'Sign it.'

She put up her hands to his, but she knew she could not loosen his grip.

'You are hurting me,' she said in a strangled voice.

'Sign it.'

Looking coldly at the Cretan handwriting, he took the paper and turned from his wife. Again she fell to her knees, cowering, mewing like a kitten.

He strode to a window and wrenched a woven curtain rope from the wall. Throwing one end over the intricate decoration of a rafter, he made a noose. Unspeaking he returned to his supplicating wife and hauled her from the floor. When Phaedra opened her mouth to scream for help, Theseus struck the back of his hand hard across her lips. That is when she went limp, accepting her fate, making no further attempt to evade the rope.

With the noose in place, he reached for a chair and lifted the Cretan doll upon it. He kicked away the chair and left her hanging there, the self-damning letter near her. Unbolting the door he departed, closing the door behind him.

3

King David

ELEVENTH CENTURY BC

Next to Moses, the most eminent of the Hebrew prophets was Samuel. He became the revered last judge of Israel, a people without a monarch until Samuel anointed Saul as the first King.

Throughout his reign, King Saul was beset by marauding Philistines, the uncircumcised. Bravest of his young warriors was his eldest son, Jonathan. But not even Jonathan would take on the Philistine giant who terrorised the Israelites. With the opposing armies camped on two mountainsides, a valley between, Goliath of Gath strode forth, a ten-foot-tall warrior clad in bronze from his helmet to the soles of his feet, his shield carried by a soldier walking before him.

'Choose you a champion,' the giant shouted to Saul's armies, 'and if he defeats me, the Philistines will be your servants. If I defeat him, you will be our servants.'

King Saul and his men were deeply afraid. But the Lord spoke to the prophet Samuel, 'Send thee for Jesse the Bethlehemite. I have provided myself with a King among his sons.' And when David, Jesse's youngest son, appeared, God told Samuel: 'Anoint him. This is he.'

When David was taken before Saul, he told the King, 'Your servant will go and fight with this Philistine.'

'You are but a youth,' said Saul. 'Goliath has been a man of war all his life.'

'I tend my father's sheep, and when a lion or bear drags a lamb from the flock, I go after it and smite it,' David replied. 'When I take the lamb from the lion's jaws and he attacks me, I grab his beard and slay him. The Lord who delivers me from the paws of the lion and the paws of the bear will deliver me from this uncircumcised Philistine.'

Saul armed David with his own armour and sword, but the young shepherd remained where he was. 'I cannot walk in these,' he said, removing them.

Jonathan, standing beside the King, looked intently at the fresh-faced youth, rapt, as David took his staff and chose five smooth stones from the brook and put them in his leather bag. His sling was in his hand as he approached Goliath.

The giant laughed when he saw his challenger. 'Am I a dog that you come to me with a stick?' He cursed David in the name of the Philistine gods. 'I will give your flesh to the vultures and beasts.'

David shouted back: 'You come to me with a sword and spear and a shield. I come to you in the name of the Lord whose armies you have defied. Everyone will see the battle is His. He will give you and your army into our hands.'

Whereupon David ran towards the Philistine army to meet Goliath, and putting a hand in his bag he took a stone and slung it at his brow through the opening just below the helmet. As the stone sank into the giant's forehead, cracking his skull, he crashed face first to the ground. Racing to where Goliath lay, David seized the giant's sword and cut off his head. It was over in minutes.

When the Philistines saw their champion dead, they ran away. The soldiers of Israel and Judah let out a great war cry and followed in hot pursuit, Saul, Jonathan and David in the lead. When at last they returned from the slaughter, David was summoned to Saul.

'Whose son are you, young man?' asked the King.

'The son of your servant Jesse the Bethlehemite.'

While Jonathan stood by his father and listened to David's words, he felt his soul unite with David's and he loved him as he had loved no other man.

From that time on, Saul had David at his own table, and let him go no more to his father's house. If the King was depressed, David was summoned to play the harp for him. The youth was already a master of lyric song.

When Jonathan and David were alone, the King's son stripped himself of his robe and belt and his sword and bow, and gave them all to David. Embracing, they made a covenant of love.

David succeeded in all that Saul sent him to do, and soon the King put him in command of a division. But after repeated victories over the Philistines, disaster struck. As the warriors returned from the latest rout, the women ran from Israelite towns to welcome King Saul, joyfully singing and dancing with musical instruments, chanting back and forth, 'Saul has slain his thousands! David his ten thousands!'

From that day Saul eyed David with suspicion. A black spirit came upon the King, and when David took his harp to soothe him, Saul hurled his javelin at the youth, who managed to dodge it. The longer David conducted himself wisely and did whatever Saul told him, the more the King feared him. He saw that the people of Israel and Judah loved David as he came and went amongst them. To some who served him, Saul said, 'My own hand shall not injure the son of Jesse. But let the hand of the Philistines be upon him.'

Michal, the King's daughter, was in love with David, and Saul sent officials to inform him that the King was happy for him to marry Michal. David told them, 'It is no light matter to be the King's son-in-law, seeing that I am a poor man.'

Whereupon he was told that rather than a conventional dowry, the King wanted a hundred Philistines' foreskins. David went out with his men; instead of falling at the hand of the Philistines as Saul had hoped, he returned with two hundred foreskins, and the King gave his daughter in marriage. But his mistrust of his son-in-law grew daily.

Finally Saul told Jonathan that David must be killed. Delighting in David, Jonathan warned him to flee, and that night Michal helped her husband escape through an upper window. David's years as an outlaw began.

Obsessively, Saul expended as much effort on trying to capture David as on fighting the Philistines. But Jonathan continued to meet David in the desert, because he loved him as he loved his own soul.

They kissed one another and wept, and together they renewed their covenant, 'The Lord bind you and me and bind my seed and your seed for ever.' Then David arose and departed, and Jonathan returned to the city.

When David and his band of men reached the city of Nob, he asked the high priest for bread and arms. The priest answered, 'I have only hallowed bread. You may have it if your soldiers did not sleep with women last night.'

'My men have not been with women for three days.'

The high priest gave them the sacred bread and then unwrapped a sword hidden behind a statue in the temple. 'You slew Goliath of Gath,' he said to David. 'Take his sword.'

David took shelter in the enormous cave of Adullam, near Gath. Men in distress, men in debt, men who were discontented gathered themselves under him, and soon he was captain of some hundreds of freebooters.

When Saul, grown half-insane in his pursuit of David, heard that the priests of Nob had helped the son of Jesse (he could not bring himself to speak David's name), he summoned them and instructed his bodyguards to slay them. But they would not fall upon the priests of the Lord.

Saul then commanded Doeg, who was from Edom: 'Smite them all!'

And Doeg and his men on that day slew 85 priests, and smote the city of Nob with the edge of the sword, killing men and women, children and babies, oxen, asses and sheep.

God told David to go to Keilah where Philistine armies marauded. With his men he went and slaughtered the Philistines and saved the inhabitants of Keilah. Yet these same people of Keilah then betrayed him to King Saul. Before the King's army could trap them in the city, David and six hundred men escaped into the hills.

There Jonathan found him and assured him, 'My father the King will never capture you. You shall become the next King of Israel, not I. I shall be second to you.' They went to David's quarters in the stronghold and lay together in each other's arms.

Still pursuing the son of Jesse, Saul entered a cave to sleep. Hidden deeper in the cave were David and some of his men. Silently

David approached the sleeping Saul, cut a piece from Saul's robe to show he had spared the King, and forbade his men to slay Saul, saying, 'He is the anointed of the Lord.'

The prophet Samuel died, and all the Israelites lamented him. At last, David accepted that the only way to escape Saul's pursuit was to go with his six hundred men and their households across the border into the land of the Philistines where he agreed to serve the King of Gath loyally. The other Philistine princes did not trust him, and refused to have him go into battle with them against the Israelites. So David and his soldiers returned to their base in Philistia, only to find that in their absence their wives and children had been carried off by the Amalekites.

In their initial despair, the soldiers talked of stoning David. He persuaded them instead to pursue the Amalekites, and by the end of the day's battle, the enemy were slain or had taken to their heels, and all the prisoners they had taken, including David's two wives, were rescued. Triumphantly the soldiers travelled back to their base.

At the same time, King Saul and three of his sons were fighting their last bloody battle against the Philistines.

At Mount Gilboa, the Philistines closed in. Jonathan and his brothers were slain. Saul was hit by archers but his wounds were not fatal. He cried out to his armour-bearer to run him through, lest the Philistines torture and mock him, but the armour-bearer was afraid to kill the King. Thereupon Saul fell on his sword, and his armour-bearer did the same. Yet life remained in the King. When he saw a soldier nearby, he called him over.

'Who are you?' asked the King in his agony.

'I am an Amalekite.'

'Stand, I pray, upon me and slay me.'

And the Amalekite did the King's bidding.

The day after the battle, the Philistines returned to Mount Gilboa to strip the slain, and they found Saul and his three sons. They cut off his head, stripped off his armour, and nailed his body and the bodies of his sons to the wall of Beth-shan.

When the inhabitants of Jabesh heard what had been done to Saul, brave men travelled through the night to Beth-shan. They took down the bodies from the wall and carried them back to Jabesh and burnt them there, burying the bones.

On David's return from the slaughter of the Amalekites, a man with his clothes rent came to him, telling him he had escaped out of the Israelites' camp.

'How went the battle?'

'The people are fled from the battle. Many are fallen and dead. Saul and Jonathan his son are dead also.'

'How do you know Saul and Jonathan are dead?' David, demanded, aghast.

The young man replied, 'I am an Amalekite. The King was grievously wounded. He asked me to kill him so the Philistines would not capture him alive. After I had slain him, I took his crown and bracelet, and I have brought them to you, my lord.'

David drew back in revulsion and wept. Then he turned on the Amalekite. 'How dared you destroy the Lord's anointed?' He called to one of his soldiers, 'Kill him!'

The soldier drew his sword and ran the man through.

Crying aloud his lamentation over Saul and Jonathan, David ended his song of grief with the lines:

How are the mighty fallen in the midst of the battle! O Jonathan, thou wast slain in thine high places.

I am distressed for thee, my brother Jonathan; very pleasant hast thou been unto me; thy love to me was wonderful, surpassing the love of women.

How are the mighty fallen, and the weapons of war perished!

Still an outlaw, David asked the Lord, 'Where shall I go?'

And the Lord said, 'Go unto Hebron in Judah.'

When David reached Hebron, along with his wives and his men, he was annointed King of Judah. He was thirty years old. At the same time, the commander of Saul's army made Saul's surviving son, Ishbosheth, King of Israel.

A long war ensued between the followers of Saul and the followers of David. David waxed stronger and stronger; the house of Saul grew weaker and weaker. When two men succeeded in stabbing

Ishbosheth in the stomach, they cut off his head and travelled with it to Judah and said to David, 'Behold the head of Ishbosheth, the son of Saul your enemy, who sought your life.'

But David would not tolerate the murder of one who was anointed. Instead of rewarding the men, he told them: 'Only the Lord rescues me from adversity,' and handed them over to his soldiers, who slew them, cut off their hands and feet, and hung their bodies over the pool in Hebron. Ishbosheth's head was buried in a sacred sepulchre nearby.

Then came the elders of Israel to Hebron and made peace with David. They anointed him King of Israel. He was 37 years old when he began his long reign as King of Israel and Judah.

Determined to take over the independent city of Jerusalem, he and his troops attacked the fortress on Mount Zion, captured it and renamed it the City of David. He moved there from Hebron with his wives and began his – largely – glorious rule. King Hiram of Tyre sent carpenters and stonemasons to build this former outlaw a palace in Jerusalem. When it was complete, David brought the ark, the cupboard that houses the Torah scrolls and is the most sacred symbol of God's presence among the Hebrew people, to Jerusalem.

Soon afterwards, the prophet Nathan had a vision in which God said he would establish David's line for ever. 'If he commit iniquity, I will chasten him with the rod of men. But I will not withdraw my mercy from him as I did from Saul.' And Nathan told David all that the Lord had said.

David asked, 'Is any left of the house of Saul, that I may show him kindness for Jonathan's sake?'

And he was told: 'Jonathan had a son who is lame.' The child had been dropped when his nurse was fleeing with him after the Philistines killed Saul and Jonathan. His name was Mephibosheth.

David sent for him and told him: 'I will restore to you all the land that would have been your father Jonathan's. You will eat at my table and be my son.'

In Jerusalem, David took many more wives and concubines and his line grew. He delivered judgement and justice to his people. Though the wars with the Philistines never ceased, Israel's generals kept their enemies at bay. The King of Israel and Judah had all that most men could want. And yet . . .

One evening, having returned from battle to Jerusalem, David was relaxing on the flat roof of his palace when he saw a woman down below washing herself. She was exceptionally beautiful. He sent a servant to find out who she was. The man returned with the answer, 'Her name is Bathsheba. She is the wife of Uriah the Hittite.'

Uriah the Hittite was one of David's finest generals. He was away, fighting the Philistines. David sent messengers to bring Bathsheba to him. He took her into his bed, and afterwards she returned to her home. Some weeks later she sent a message telling him she was pregnant.

Immediately David plotted to conceal their adultery. He recalled Uriah the Hittite from the battlefield so he would lie with his wife and believe it was he who had impregnated her. With a great show of concern, David asked Uriah how the battle was going, and how was Joab, the commander, and about other battlefield matters. Then he told Uriah he must go home to his wife for a few days' relaxation. It was only when he sent a feast down to Uriah's house that he learned the captain was not there. He had washed and rested with the King's guards.

Summoned again to the King, Uriah explained that his men were still in the battlefield. 'Shall I then go to my house to eat and drink and lie with my wife? I will not do that.'

In the morning, David – this man famed for his honour and integrity – ordered Uriah's murder. He wrote a chilling letter to Joab. With exceptional brutality, he gave the letter – Uriah's death sentence – to Uriah himself to bear to the commander. When Joab opened it he read: 'Send Uriah into the forefront of the most hard-fought battle. Then pull back your soldiers from supporting him, so that he will be killed.'

Joab carried out the order. A messenger was sent to the King, telling him Uriah the Hittite was slain.

King David sent back a further impervious message to Joab: 'Do not let this thing distress you, for the sword devours one as well as another.'

When Bathsheba learned that her husband was dead, she mourned for him. Once the mourning period was passed, the King sent for her to be brought to the palace. She became his wife and bore a son.

A day or two later, Nathan the prophet came to the palace and told the King a parable about a rich man and a poor man. The rich man had many flocks and herds. The poor man had one ewe lamb, which grew up with his children, and drank from his cup and lay in his bosom. A traveller came to visit the rich man, who did not want to kill one of his own lambs, and instead took the poor man's lamb to serve at his table.

David's anger exploded against the rich man: 'He shall be punished! For this he shall die.'

'You are that man,' said Nathan.

Appalled, David acknowledged his sin and was deeply ashamed.

Then Nathan told him: 'The Lord has not withdrawn his mercy from you as he did from Saul. You shall not die, but you will be punished. The sword shall never depart from your house. And the Lord will take your wives and concubines before your eyes and give them to your neighbour. He shall lie with them in the sight of all. You lay with Uriah's wife secretly, but all Israel will be watching when your neighbour lies with your wives. And your son born to Bathsheba shall die.'

That night the infant was struck down. Beseeching God to spare the child, the King lay on the ground beside the sickbed and fasted. On the seventh day, the child died.

David arose, washed and changed his clothes, entered the Lord's tent and worshipped. Then he went to the palace and ate.

'While the child was yet alive,' he told his puzzled officials, 'I fasted and wept, for I said: "Who can tell whether God will be gracious to me and let the child live?" But now he is dead, why should I fast? I cannot bring him back again.'

He comforted Bathsheba his wife and lay with her and she conceived. The child she bore was called Solomon, and the Lord loved him.

The punishments prophesied by Nathan were far from ended: within David's family, violence bred violence. One of his sons, Amnon, fell in love with his own sister, Tamar, and raped her. As soon as he withdrew from her he hated her more than he had loved her. 'Arise and be gone,' he told her, and called his servant: 'Put this woman out and bolt the door after her.'

Tamar went weeping to the house of her brother Absalom. He bided his time, and then had Amnon killed for forcing himself on their sister. Absalom fled the city for two years before his father sent word that he could return. For King David loved Absalom dearly.

In all Israel, none was praised so much for his beauty as Absalom: from the soles of his feet to the crown of his luxuriant hair, there was no blemish on him. But in his heart was the deep desire to supplant his father as King. Cunningly he intercepted supplicants on their way to David for judgement and lied to them: 'The King has no one to hear your kind of complaint. If I were made judge in the land, I would give you justice.' In this way Absalom stole the hearts of the men of Israel, and David was forced to flee Jerusalem.

Some of his concubines were left behind to look after the palace. To disgrace his father in the eyes of Israel, Absalom had a tent spread on the flat roof of the palace, and there each of his father's concubines came to his bed. The rebellion reached its climax in the wood of Ephraim, where Absalom's forces lay in wait for the soldiers loyal to David. Joab was one of three captains commanding David's army, and as they marched forth for the conflict, David called: 'Deal gently for my sake with the young man Absalom.' All the people heard him charge his captains with Absalom's safety.

Twenty thousand men died that day in the wood of Ephraim. As Absalom rode upon a mule to meet his enemy, his splendid hair became entangled in the branches of an oak. The mule ran from under him, and Absalom was left hanging between heaven and earth. A man who saw him told Joab.

'Why did you not smite him to the ground?' Joab asked.

'I heard the King charge you not to harm Absalom. And there is no matter hidden from the King.'

The captain turned away impatiently and sought out Absalom, still hanging in the oak. Joab thrust three spears into the King's favourite son, and his armour-bearers finished the killing. They took down Absalom's body and threw it into a deep pit, where they heaped stones upon it – after which all the soldiers fled to their tents.

David waited by the gate for tidings. At last a messenger arrived: 'The Lord has avenged you this day against all who rose up against you.'

'Is my son Absalom safe?'

'May all your enemies be as that young man is,' the messenger replied.

The King withdrew to a room above the gate, and as he went he wept bitterly. 'O my son, Absalom, my son, my son Absalom! Would God I had died for thee, O Absalom, my son, my son!'

The people below listened as David cried in a loud voice again and again, 'O my son Absalom, O Absalom, my son.'

Victory that day turned to mourning. Joab confronted the King: 'You have shamed those who saved your life, and the lives of your sons and daughters, and the lives of your wives and concubines. If Absalom had lived and all of us had died this day, that would have pleased you. I swear by God, if you do not go forth and thank your people, none will be here in the morning.'

David went down and sat at the gate. And the people left their tents and came before him. At last a message was delivered to David: 'Return with all your soldiers.'

He rode back to Jerusalem and once more he ruled justly. When he lay dying, neither clothes nor blankets could warm him. His servants searched the city for a beautiful young virgin and brought her to lie with him. She warmed him, and cherished him, but he was too weak to enter her.

In his final days, another of his sons, Adomijah, tried to usurp the throne. Nathan the prophet informed the King, and David sent for Bathsheba.

'I swear to you by the Lord God of Israel,' he told her, 'Solomon your son will reign after me. Let Nathan the prophet now anoint him King over Israel.' To Nathan he said: 'Have the trumpets blown and cry: "God save King Solomon."'

The death of the greatest King of Israel took place some time between 1018 and 993 BC. Not only had his rule united the Israelites. 'The sweetest singer of Israel' had also created the most sublime lyric poetry of his people, for centuries used in the Christian faith as well. (On 9/11, Todd Beamer, a passenger aboard United Flight 93, could only get through on his cellphone to an operator. She told him about the World Trade Center. He said that he and other Americans had a plan to jump the hijackers and asked her to pray with him.

Together they recited David's 23rd Psalm: 'Yea, though I walk through the valley of the shadow of death, I will fear no evil: for thou art with me . . .' Then she heard him shout, 'Let's roll!' He and his ad hoc platoon rushed the hijackers, crashing the plane into a Pennsylvania pasture instead of the Capitol.)

David was buried on the highest hill in Jerusalem, Zion, city of David – a hero tragically flawed by lust.

4

King Arthur

REIGN *C.* AD 520–542

When the Romans departed from Britain early in the fifth century, society grew fragmented and power devolved upon local chieftains, who became petty kings. Soon afterwards the Saxon tribe in north Germany invaded and colonised southern Britain. The Britons they conquered, who had lived there since before the Roman conquest (AD 43–410), were precursors of Britons throughout the ages whose fighters were at least as ferocious as any of their sometime conquerors. They took no prisoners. In the sixth century, the greatest of the warrior kings was Arthur – legendary King of the Britons.

In Wales, a sword had been driven into a stone up to the hilt. It resisted all attempts to pull it out until at the age of fifteen, Arthur achieved this feat. With the sword, Excalibur, he made himself King. A military genius, he kept the Saxons at bay and conquered the Picts and Scots, and invaded Ireland, Iceland and Orkney.

To pay homage to him, lords from the conquered tribes rode to Arthur's Court, Camelot, in the west of England. King Lottis of Orkney sent his wife and their four sons to represent him, bringing gifts. (The eldest son was Gawain, destined to be a key figure in Arthur's life.) The Queen interpreted her husband's wishes more liberally than he perhaps intended: Arthur, on seeing her, desired to bed her, and she at once acquiesced and became pregnant with his child. After resting a few days at Camelot, the Queen departed. On later discovering the identity of his real parents, Arthur realised that Lottis's wife was his sister. The son of their incest, Modred, was born on May Day.

When Merlin, a seer, told the King that he would be killed and his knights destroyed by a man born on May Day, Arthur ordered such children to be taken from their parents and put on a ship bound for Ireland. When the ship foundered on rocks, only Modred was saved. It says something for the Britons' adulation of Arthur that the bereft parents blamed Merlin for the tragedy.

When first Arthur saw Guinevere, he fell deeply in love with her. A Roman lady of exceptional grace and beauty, she was brought up in the household of the Duke of Cornwall. Whatever later befell them, Arthur never ceased to adore her. With their marriage, he proved the most uxorious of husbands, and Camelot became renowned for its elegance. 'Courtly love' was born, and knights jousting for honour fastened the scarf of the lady they most admired on to their chain-mail armour.

King Arthur was repeatedly absent from his Court, leading twenty thousand knights in battle against other chieftains. Some of the most savage engagements were settled by single combat on horse or on foot; however many wounds were inflicted on Arthur, he emerged the victor. He and Excalibur were famed as far away as Rome.

When he returned to Camelot, the King joined his knights at the Round Table, devised to avoid disputes about precedence. The Round Table knights were spiritually inspired by their quest for the Holy Grail, a cup associated with Christ's crucifixion. Brought to Britain in the second century and later lost, it was the symbol of purity.

The reputation of one knight, the twenty-year-old Sir Launcelot, who had lately presented himself at Camelot, shone above all others. When Guinevere and her ladies watched the jousting tournaments, all were eager to see Launcelot ride into the lists, for his courage and skills matched Arthur's. To mark one of Launcelot's victories, Guinevere presented him with her scarf. Thenceforth when he rode out for a contest, her scarf was tied around his arm.

Like the King – the ideal Christian knight – Launcelot was a man of honour, and Arthur regarded his open admiration for the

Queen as natural and proper. He had the utmost trust in his knight and his wife.

Guinevere was less tolerant. When she discovered that Launcelot was having a casual affair with another woman, she was beside herself with rage. Her possessiveness grew, and her anger was further fanned by the birth of Galahad, the son of Launcelot and his lover. To allay Guinevere's wrath, Launcelot put aside what for him had been a mere sexual dalliance, for he venerated the Queen.

As time passed, her ladies observed her radiance whenever she saw Launcelot. The Court began to whisper. Yet no suspicion troubled the clear face of the guileless King.

At last, fearful that the scandal would break wide open and tear the Court apart, Guinevere told Launcelot they must part. Kissing and weeping, they said goodbye, and he mounted his horse and rode away in penitential search of the Grail. Soon, however, his obsession with earthly rapture prevailed and he abandoned the quest and returned to the Court, where once again, in secret, the lovers met and met.

Launcelot's imperfection – his courtly love, which had become physical passion – set events on a devastating course. Arthur's illegitimate son, Modred, exploited the affair to stir up trouble at the Court. Sir Gawain, a leading knight of the Round Table and Arthur's ambassador to Rome, returned for a short visit to Camelot and chanced on the Queen and Launcelot ecstatic in each other's arms. Overnight Gawain changed from a generous, amiable man to a harsh, embittered one. His anger at Launcelot turned to cold hatred when the knight accidentally killed Gawain's beloved youngest brother in a jousting tournament. Gawain betrayed Launcelot and the Queen to Arthur.

In expiation, Launcelot embarked again in quest of the Grail. The King at last recognised that the two people he loved and trusted most were bound together in enduring sexual intimacy. Vowing revenge, he and Gawain set off in pursuit of Launcelot, but before they could overtake him, Arthur was summoned to pay tribute to the Emperor Lucius of Rome. Instead, the King declared war. Gawain went ahead to Rome and fearlessly threw down the gauntlet.

Leaving Modred in charge in Britain, Arthur rode off with his knights to Rome. He had just reached the imperial city's gates when he was warned that Modred had seized Queen Guinevere and the kingdom. At once, he and Gawain returned with the army to England.

When they landed at Dover, they found Modred waiting with his own men. The two forces met. In the vicious combat that followed, Gawain was killed. Modred retreated to Cornwall with Arthur in pursuit. In the final battle in Cornwall, the traitor was slain with all his followers, but not before he dealt the King his death blow. Arthur was borne by boat to the island of Avalon in the vain hope of healing his wounds. He was 37.

Launcelot, having abandoned his quest for the Grail in order to return and help Arthur, arrived too late to save the King, and too late to stop his beloved from entering the convent at Amesbury in penance. He went there to bid her a final farewell. Then he became a priest.

Had Gawain not betrayed Launcelot and Guinevere to Arthur, Launcelot would have been fighting alongside the King, and history might have taken a different course. The only silver lining was that Launcelot's illegitimate son Sir Galahad, the Pure Knight, would one day find the Holy Grail.

Of course, there are always 'experts' who claim that King Arthur never existed. But there is no law saying I have to believe them if I choose not to.

5

Abelard and Héloïse

PETER ABELARD (1079–1142)
HÉLOÏSE (*c.* 1101–64)

'Is love lust?' asked Héloïse.

'Its root is lust,' Abelard answered. 'And marriage is the effort to make permanent what is in its nature transient.'

Unusually for a seventeen-year-old girl, Héloïse was already highly educated in philosophy. There was no shortage of teachers anxious to engage her mind. Radiant, beautiful, avid to learn, she came to live with her Uncle Fulbert in the precinct of Notre-Dame of Paris, where he was a canon. An orphan educated at the convent of Argenteuil, she quickly became known for her thirst for knowledge. Canon Fulbert was a man of exceptional innocence, his tonsure encircled by fluffy white hair, his benign pink face beaming with pride whenever his eyes settled on his niece. He adored her.

Peter Abelard lectured in the cathedral school of Notre-Dame, where his fame as a philosopher led to its becoming the medieval university of Paris. From all over Europe and beyond, young men flocked to Paris to hear the boldest theologian in the twelfth century. Born at Le Pallet near Nantes, he was the eldest son in a family of minor Breton nobility. He relinquished his birthright to become a true scholar.

Outspoken, handsome, supremely confident, with his extra-ordinary mind he ran circles around his learned masters, who based their teaching on canonical tradition. Abelard argued by reason alone, using his formidable powers of logic to draw a coherent relationship between faith and reason. Immensely influential, he was endlessly in trouble with the Church authorities. His students idolised him, carrying him in a chair on their shoulders after his lectures. Others, unsurprisingly, were deeply jealous, waiting, the more spiteful praying, for him to stub his toe.

Abelard was celibate. He poured all his energy into pursuing and distilling truth. And then, at 38, he decided to discover the passions of the flesh. He approached this goal with his usual logic. Already he had heard of Héloïse and seen her striding gracefully through the precinct of Notre-Dame, her two long braids swinging to her knees. In his book *Historia Calamitatum Mearum*, he later recalled: 'After carefully considering all those qualities which are wont to attract lovers, it was this young girl whom I determined to unite with myself in the bonds of love.'

At the same time, Canon Fulbert invited the famous philosopher to move into his home, where in exchange for room and board he would tutor the canon's niece. 'It was,' Abelard wrote, 'like giving a tender lamb into the care of a hungry wolf.'

There was no need for the tutor to cajole his young charge: he found his quarry ready and eager to be 'seduced'. Within days of starting their philosophy lessons, Héloïse could hardly sit in the same room and resist reaching out to touch her tutor.

Philosophy quickly lost its priority. Abelard wrote:

Our speech was more of passion, than of our books which lay open before us. My hands strayed oftener to her bosom than to the pages. To avert suspicion I sometimes struck her, but these blows were prompted by love and tender feeling rather than anger and irritation, and were sweeter than any balm could be. If love could devise something new, we entered on each joy the more eagerly for our previous inexperience, and were the less easily sated.

However base his original intentions, he was soon overwhelmed by love as well as lust. His celebrated lectures became repetitious.

'It was utterly boring for me to have to go to the school and to spend my days on study when my nights were sleepless with love-making. When inspiration did come to me, it was for writing love-songs, not the secrets of philosophy.'

Often his verses named Héloïse. Rumours swept Paris, and bawdy songs circulated in the street. His students felt bereaved by the distraction of his mind.

'No one could not notice, I fancy, except the man whose honour was most involved – Héloïse's uncle,' wrote Abelard. 'Several people tried to draw his attention to it, but he would not believe them, because of his boundless love for his niece and my well-known reputation for chastity in my previous life.'

Early one morning, Héloïse rode off to the convent at Argenteuil where she had been educated in her orphaned girlhood, wanting now to reflect on her own blasphemy. For Abelard was more than her lover. He was her god. Each time she offered him her naked body, she was giving herself in ecstasy to a god. She left the convent that evening to ride back to the precinct of Notre-Dame and her god. Canon Fulbert met her at the door, anxious because Abelard had for hours been seeking her.

'You know it is unheard of,' her uncle told her, 'for such a great man to give his time to a child like you. You must not vex him.' He trusted them totally.

And then, after fifteen months of enraptured 'fornication' – Héloïse preferred 'the ugly but expressive word' – she became pregnant. Not long afterwards, when they were in her bedroom, too engrossed in their frenzy to hear the foot on the stairs, Canon Fulbert opened the door to a sight far beyond any degradation he was capable of imagining. He never recovered from the trauma.

Abelard, perhaps more than Héloïse, was deeply ashamed of abusing the old man's trust. Secretly he removed Héloïse from her uncle's house while Fulbert was away. He took her to his Breton family home, Le Pallet, where his sister Denise lived with her husband and children. Héloïse gave birth to a boy. She called him Astrolabe. He was brought up by her sister-in-law.

Canon Fulbert returned to his home almost out of his mind with grief and mortification. 'I begged his forgiveness,' Abelard wrote. 'I protested that I had done nothing unusual in the eyes of anyone who had known the power of love. I offered him satisfaction in a form he could never have hoped for: I would marry the girl I had wronged. But the marriage must be kept secret.'

Abelard was not sworn to celibacy – he was neither priest nor monk – but as a canon of Notre-Dame, he would lose his job and his privileged position if he married. Thus he wanted to restore Canon Fulbert's outraged honour without wrecking his own career.

Yet Héloïse was adamantly against the marriage. She knew her uncle would be bound to publicise it, and she argued that it would jeopardise Abelard's destiny to change the intellectual history of the world. She wrote to him:

> I need not say any more about the basic impossibility of combining marriage and scholarship but think of the details of a good burgher's marriage. The spinning wheel charmingly combined with books and copy-books, style and pen with the spindle. You are immersed in your theological or philosophical ideas, and at that moment the infants begin to squall: the wet nurses try to quiet them with their monotonous sing-song. Can then your concentration remain uninterrupted?

She argued from a classical viewpoint rather than a Christian one. Entwined in all her reasoning was a deep distaste for women giving up their independence for a profitable marriage:

> God is my witness that if Augustus, Emperor of the whole world, thought fit to honour me with marriage and conferred all the earth on me to possess for ever, it would be dearer and more honourable to me to be called not his Empress but your whore.
>
> A woman should realise that if she desires her husband more for his possessions than for himself, she is offering herself for sale. Certainly any woman who comes to marry through desires of this kind deserves wages, not gratitude, for clearly her mind is on the man's property, and she would be ready to prostitute herself to a richer man, if she could.

Always determined to have his own way, Abelard ignored her arguments for preferring love to wedlock and freedom to chains. They were secretly married in St Aignan's, in the presence of Fulbert. The old man appeared to be pacified.

But, old and broken, he soon began dementedly to assault the adored niece, whom he loved at who knows how many levels. For her protection, Abelard accompanied her to Le Pallet again to stay with Denise and her family. From there he prepared to take her to the convent at Argenteuil. To disguise her on the journey, Denise tried to dress her in a nun's habit. Héloïse tore it off in horror. Kindly Denise found other clothes to conceal her.

Abelard left her at the convent, but before he rode away they went into the chapel, the only place where they could be alone. There he committed upon her the ultimate blasphemy of the Virgin and Child whose statue was above them. Then he rode back to Paris and returned to his room high up in his lodgings near Notre-Dame.

Gold has entrapped many till then loyal servants, not least when the man needs money for the whore of his heart. With gold, Fulbert wore down the resistance of Abelard's servant. Before he set off to the whore, clutching the bribe, he left the door to Abelard's lodging house ajar.

Asleep in his inner room, the first thing Abelard saw when he was wakened was the benign pink face of Canon Fulbert leaning over him, his small eyes triumphant. The two thugs he had hired did their work quickly, one holding down the trapped man while the other castrated him, severing his penis as well as his testicles while Canon Fulbert leered. Then the assailants fled down the stairs. Outside, Fulbert slipped into the shadows to return to his own house. Abelard, barely conscious, lay curled on his bed, moaning.

Passing Abelard's house, several of his students noticed the door was ajar and saw two men running away towards the river. Three students gave chase while the other two raced up the stairs to Abelard's room. In minutes one of them was tearing back down, shouting the alarm, while the other, sobbing, tried with his palms to staunch the gushing blood.

One assailant jumped into the Seine. The second was caught by the pursuing students who did to him what he had done to Abelard, blinding the man as well. Then they tracked down the servant who had betrayed his master for gold, and performed the same savage vengeance on him, scattering his gold coins about him.

'Next morning,' Abelard would write later, 'the whole city gathered before my house with lamentations, cries and groans.' His students guarded his door against all but the doctor,

> . . . and tormented me with their unbearable weeping and wailing until I suffered more from their sympathy than from the pain of my wound. How just that a judgement of God had struck me in the parts of the body with which I had sinned; how just a reprisal had been taken by the very man I had myself betrayed.
>
> I thought how my rivals would exult over my fitting punishment, how this bitter blow would bring lasting grief and misery to my friends and parents, and how fast the news of this unheard-of disgrace would spread over the whole world. How could I show my face in public, a monstrous spectacle to all I met?

He remembered that according to the cruel letter of Church law: 'No man whose testicles have been crushed or whose organ has been severed shall become a member of the assembly of the Lord.

'I admit that it was shame and confusion in my remorse and misery rather than any devout wish for conversion which brought me to seek shelter in a monastery cloister.' He withdrew to the Abbey of St Denis where he was nursed back to health as a sexually emasculated man.

'Scarcely had I recovered from my wound when the clerks came thronging round to pester the abbot and myself with repeated demands that, freed from the temptations of the flesh, I should prove myself a true philosopher not of the world but of God.'

And Héloïse, who still worshipped Abelard as her god, whose hormones raced through her in a tumult of desire for the sexual ecstasy she had relished with him?

'There were many people, I remember,' he wrote, 'who in pity for her youth tried to dissuade her from submitting to the yoke of monastic rule as a penance too hard to bear, but all in vain.'

Of course. For Abelard, unable to endure his fear that Héloïse might eventually desire an unemasculated man, had insisted she embrace the chastity forced upon himself. Weeping and sobbing bitterly, the not yet twenty-year-old girl hurried to the altar, quickly took up the veil blessed by the bishop, and publicly bound herself to the religious life.

At the Abbey of St Denis, Abelard soon discovered that the monks were wildly licentious. And they discovered they had misjudged him because of his lurid life with Héloïse. In fact, apart from that obsession, which split his life in two, he had never been dissolute. Moreover, the monks soon learned first hand what a disputatious man he was.

When his mutilation had healed over, he went on his way, though more than once he was dragged back to St Denis by the monks who were unwilling to relinquish his philosophical celebrity. They couldn't live with him and they couldn't live without him.

Héloïse did her utmost to suppress her often frantic physical desires and the constant stream of memories that haunted her, striving daily to embrace the faith that she served for Abelard's sake. Yet even as she prayed aloud to God, it was Abelard whom she envisaged. This dual worship seems not to have impaired the young woman's organisational capacity, and she soon was abbess of the convent, deeply admired and loved by the many women who came to her for help.

By chance she saw a long letter written by Abelard to comfort a friend in trouble, describing his own calamitous life and his struggle to convince himself that the desire of the flesh is nothing to the desire of the mind for knowledge. Centuries later, this autobiographical memoir, called *Historia Calamitatum Mearum*, would form the basis for Pope's *Epistle of Eloisa to Abelard*.

At the time it called forth a passionately argued letter from Héloïse, the first communication between them in ten years. She asked why he had not written to console her, as it was her tragedy as well as his. Thenceforth they corresponded regularly, Abelard often rehearsing to her his own philosophical development. In 1130, when Héloïse was 29, they published a collection of their love letters and religious correspondence.

Applying his logic to faith, Abelard had to move from one abbey to another, constantly pursued by the Church authorities (and his devoted young followers). Twice he was condemned to death for heresy. His rational approach to the mystery of the Trinity gave particular offence to the Church.

Equally his drastic analysis of sin challenged that of other philosophers, Jewish or Christian. He held that human actions do not make a man better or worse in the sight of God, for deeds in themselves are neither good nor bad. What counts with God is a man's intention: does his mind consent to the act? Abelard regarded his earlier actions with Héloïse as *ethical* flaws. It was a sin only when they intentionally committed the ultimate blasphemy beneath the statue of the Virgin and Child.

The final move of this peripatetic man was to an isolated spot not far from his birthplace in Brittany. With their own hands he and several devoted pupils built a simple church called the Paraclete. Abelard wrote down his doctrines while living as a strict Cluniac monk. In no time philosophers and theologians were flocking there.

Shortly before his death, when Héloïse was 41, he gave the Paraclete to her. She used it to found an order of her own. She buried him next to the Paraclete, where she could commune with her dead lover beside his grave, still tormented by erotic desire, unable to renounce for God the memory of unholy joy.

On her death, Abelard's body was moved to the famous cemetery of Père-Lachaise in Paris, where he and Héloïse lie buried together.

6

Anne Boleyn

1506?–36

Amused by King Henry VIII's infatuation with Anne Boleyn, the Venetian Ambassador remarked sardonically that she was 'not one of the handsomest women in the world'. All this meant that instead of the pale, blonde, blue-eyed prettiness fashionable at the time, Anne had thick dark hair, olive skin and nearly black eyes which she used to entice. She made gentleness and amiability seem boring.

Her father, Sir Thomas Boleyn, was an accomplished courtier who groomed – in other words, used – his children to advance himself and his family. When his daughter Mary became the King's mistress, her father was given a viscountcy. During Anne's rise to power, he received two earldoms. (Moralists will be pleased to learn that when she fell from power, her father's career was permanently ruined.)

Anne's date of birth is as vague as that of many a celebrity today. Her father's years as Ambassador to France placed his young daughters in the French Court where they learned to speak French fluently and dress in the French manner. When Mary returned to England with her father, she became Henry's mistress. Anne stayed at the French Court for a further six years and was trained in poetry, music and dancing. She had her own virginals and enjoyed a fine reputation for composing and performing – talents fit for a queen.

In 1521, she returned to England and joined the Court of Queen Catherine, Henry's first wife. Anne was headstrong, hot-tempered and dazzling. When she began an affair with Henry Percy, heir to the Earl of Northumberland, she was quickly noticed by the King who presented himself as a suitor, showering favours on her father.

Anne gave the ebullient King a hard time. For a start, she did not find him particularly attractive. When he had first ascended the throne, he was famously handsome, but by 1527 when he was 36, his corpulence was offputting to Anne. Above all, he had a wife. Anne had no intention of emulating her sister and settling for a role as a royal mistress, discarded without a pension. As Henry was totally bewitched by her, she could play for higher stakes.

In that same year, the King began negotiations for his marriage to be nullified, no matter that Queen Catherine had borne him five children (of whom only Mary lived). Obsessed with having a male heir, obsessed with Anne Boleyn, Henry saw her as the answer. Although he hated writing letters, there are seventeen passionate love letters to her preserved in the Vatican Library, which were used against Henry in the divorce action. He expressed his wish to be 'specially an evening, in my sweetheart's arms, whose pretty dugs I am shortly to kiss'.

Never as attracted to Henry as he was to her, Anne was consistently calculating. She permitted him some intimacies, but drew the line at intercourse. This had nothing to do with any rectitude on her part – Anne was never conspicuous for rectitude – but because she wanted to keep this domineering man in a state of hot desire. The French Ambasssador Du Bellay observed that the King's infatuation with her was such that only God could abate his madness.

The drawn-out legal debates on the marriage of Henry and Catherine of Aragon were no doubt frustrating for Anne. Her famous temper displayed itself in furious arguments with Henry in front of the Court. Late in 1532, as divorce or annulment drew near, Henry's six-year pursuit was rewarded: Anne yielded. He showed his appreciation of his new mistress by making her Marchioness of Pembroke in her own right. By December she was pregnant. 'A woman who is the scandal of Christendom', Catherine called her rival.

To avoid any question of his son's legitimacy – Henry was sure it was a boy – the King married Anne in a secret ceremony in January

1533. Four months later, Thomas Cranmer, appointed Archbishop of Canterbury by the King, proclaimed that the marriage of his patron and Catherine was invalid – and that the King's marriage to Anne was legal. Plans for her coronation at once began.

In preparation, she was brought by boat from the royal palace in Greenwich to the Tower of London, dressed in cloth of gold. Barges following her stretched for four miles down the Thames. On Whit Sunday her procession left the Tower for Westminster Abbey where Archbishop Cranmer crowned and anointed her Queen. Shortly afterwards, Henry was excommunicated by the Pope and England broke with Rome.

Soon elaborate preparations were under way for the baby's birth. The proclamation had already been written with the word 'prince' referring to the child. Edward and Henry were the favourite choices for his name. On 26 August Anne retired to her chamber and on 7 September, Princess Elizabeth was born. From that moment Anne's influence began to wane. Nothing could have been further from the King's mind than that this daughter would one day rule England.

To add to Henry's staggering disappointment, another misfortune had occurred: he had fallen out of love with Anne. Her father did not need to tell her that it was imperative she produce a boy; she already knew her life might depend on it. Her next two pregnancies miscarried. In her fear and despair, Anne grew hysterically shrewish. Small wonder that her husband became smitten with one of his wife's ladies-in-waiting, Jane Seymour. Gentle, adoring, tender, Jane was everything that Anne was not.

Yet the Queen still held the advantage: by January 1536 she was far advanced in pregnancy. Then Anne came on Henry making love to her lady-in-waiting. Her rage was ferocious. Hurling denunciations at them, she grew so frenzied that she brought on a premature labour. The stillborn child was a boy. In the words of the historian Sir John Neale: 'she had miscarried of her saviour.'

Anne had never been popular with the Court, which was now all too ready to draw her alleged adulteries to the attention of the King. Her close friend for several years, the musician Mark Smeaton was arrested and tortured until he made 'revelations' about the Queen. Three others were also charged with adultery and taken to the Tower.

Finally, Anne's own brother, George Boleyn – Lord Rochford – was arrested and charged with adultery with the Queen.

On May Day, a tournament was held outside the palace at Greenwich, Anne with her ladies presiding. Abruptly the King cantered away, leaving the Queen behind. The next day she was arrested and informed of the charges against her: adultery, incest, and plotting to kill the King. She made the same journey by barge to the Tower that she had made three years earlier to prepare for her coronation. She was lodged in the same rooms as before.

Four of the men charged with adultery with the Queen were put on trial in Westminster Hall on 12 May. Found guilty, they were sentenced to be hanged at Tyburn, cut down while still living and then disembowelled and quartered.

Three days later, in front of some two thousand people, the Queen and her brother were tried in the Great Hall of the Tower. Their own uncle, the Duke of Norfolk, presided over the judges. Lord Rochford's wife testified against him. Anne behaved with dignity, denying all charges. The verdict was read to the accused by their uncle. Condemned for high treason, they were to be burnt at the stake – the punishment for incest – or beheaded, at the discretion of the King.

Always capricious, Henry showed some mercy. On 17 May, Lord Rochford was beheaded at the Tower, and the other four men had their sentences commuted from the grotesque torture at Tyburn to simple beheading at the Tower. Waiting her turn, the Queen wrote two poignant poems, 'Defiled is my name' and 'O Deathe, rock me asleepe'.

Then her hysteria began: one minute she was wracked with sobs, the next shrieking with laughter. The King ordered that an expert 'headsman', who used a sword instead of an axe, be brought from Calais. The Lieutenant of the Tower assured the Queen she would feel no pain. 'I heard say the executioner is very good, and I have a little neck,' she replied, putting her hands around it as she laughed wildly.

They came for her on the morning of 19 May and took her to Tower Green. She was allowed the dignity of being executed privately. Dressed in a red petticoat and a gown of grey damask trimmed in fur, she wore a cape of ermine. Her rich dark hair was caught up under a white linen coif, over which she wore her usual headdress.

From the scaffold she spoke a few words of farewell:

> ... by the law I am judged to die, and therefore I will speak nothing against it ... I pray God save the King and send him long to reign over you, for a gentler and more merciful prince was there never; and to me he was ever a good, a gentle and sovereign lord ...

She knelt before the block and her ladies removed the headdress and blindfolded her. As she leant forward, she repeated several times: 'Lord Jesu receive my soul.' The swordsman decapitated her with one neat stroke. The guns of the Tower were fired to mark the act; hearing them, the King, who was hunting in Richmond Park, reined in beneath an oak tree for a moment. He would never speak her name again.

Anne's head and body were placed in a chest made for arrows and carried the short distance to the chapel of St Peter and Vincula, where she was buried in an unmarked grave beside her brother's. The following morning the King married Jane Seymour. The celebrations lasted for eleven days.

7

Catherine the Great

1729–96

Tsar Peter the Great died in 1725. He was a hard act to follow. Certainly his grandson, Peter III, was unpromising, yet the intricacies of blood relations would make him the Tsar of Russia in 1762. His marriage to Catherine, a German Princess, turned out to be the best thing he could have done for Russia and the worst thing for himself. Deeply ambitious to rule the Russian Empire, Catherine converted to the Orthodox faith. She spoke excellent Russian while the heir to the tsardom hated everything about Russia. Frederick the Great, King of Prussia, was his hero.

On her wedding night in 1745, while the sixteen-year-old Catherine lay in bed awaiting her twenty-year-old bridegroom, he played with his toy soldiers lined up in regiments on the floor. The marriage, believed to be unconsummated, was to last until Catherine was 33.

The Empress Elisabeth, pre-nuptial daughter of Peter the Great, continued to rule; meanwhile Catherine was stuck with an ineffectual husband who, having caught smallpox after they met, grew more repugnant to her daily. There were, however, ample sophisticated and handsome young men in the Court who were eager to offer their services. Several fell in love with Catherine. She was immensely attractive, intelligent and abounding in sex appeal, the last made more so by her flirtatiousness. A Polish member of the Court, at one time her lover, described her thus:

She had black hair, a radiant complexion and a high colour, large prominent and expressive blue eyes, long dark eyelashes, a pointed nose, a kissable mouth . . . slender figure, tall rather than small; she moved quickly yet with great nobility and had an agreeable voice and a gay good-tempered laugh. (In fact, her hair was auburn.)

Watched at all times, she was in a dilemma. She had to be faithful and she had to produce the next heir: as years of this sexless marriage passed, the Empress Elisabeth's sole imperative became for Catherine to produce an heir. Probably Catherine's first lover was Serge Saltykov, the handsome young scion of old Muscovite nobility. The moment Catherine gave birth in 1754 to a boy named Paul Petrovich, the Empress Elisabeth swept up the infant heir and carried him away. The new mother was left unattended in her labour linen. Saltykov was removed from the Court.

An ongoing guessing game was whether the lamentable Peter or Saltykov was the father of the future Emperor Paul I. It was not a frivolous question, for the Romanov dynasty down to the last Tsar were descended from Paul.

Catherine soon recovered from the birth and once more attended the lavish balls of Court life. At one of these she met a 23-year-old Pole who was secretary to the new English envoy. This was a true love affair. Yet Catherine was not solely engrossed in passion: coolly she prepared to usurp the throne after the Empress Elisabeth died.

When the Pole had to leave Russia – Catherine, always generous to former lovers, later make him King of Poland – she turned her attention to one of the gargantuan Orlov brothers, Grigory, a guardsman. She knew she would need the guards when the time was right for a coup. Her hopeless husband continued to Court hostility and contempt by his drunken cavorting with his German cronies outside the bedroom of the dying Empress Elisabeth. Catherine, on the other hand, attended the sick woman with a great show of affection, concealing her pregnancy by Orlov under billowing clothes.

The death of the Empress Elisabeth in January 1762 and the accession of Peter III was a gloomy day. Though flighty and cruel,

Elisabeth had helped restore Russia as a great European power. At her funeral, the absurd Tsar Peter III relieved his boredom by repeatedly lingering behind the hearse until it had advanced thirty feet and then racing to overtake it, dragging behind him elderly courtiers who carried his train. Accounts of his disrespect quickly spread and hardly endeared him to the Russian people. Soon his love of all things Prussian led to his making peace with the Russians' foe Frederick the Great, who had been on the point of surrendering.

At home he announced his intention to divorce Catherine and marry his plain mistress; in April Catherine gave birth to Orlov's son. So secretive had she been that only a hard core of guardsmen knew she and Grigory Orlov were lovers. Orlov quietly gathered more guardsmen to Catherine's cause. Had they not been discreet, she and they would have gone to the scaffold.

The coup began on 27 June. During the night, one of the Orlov brothers set off with two carriages to Catherine's palace and burst into her bedroom to tell her to dress. She borrowed a uniform from one of the guards and rode astride her stallion to the Winter Palace, her long hair and delicate face thrilling the soldiers who protected her. Gathered in the square were regiments from the 10,000 guardsmen who had made the revolt possible. Swelling crowds shouted jubilantly.

Since Peter III still controlled the army, the plotters knew he must be seized quickly. As usual he was drunk, and he gave himself up as if he had always known things would end like this. Having signed the abdication paper, he burst into tears because he was not allowed to take his ugly stupid mistress with him and had to settle instead for his fiddle, his negro Narcissus and his dog Mopsy. Frederick the Great, for whom Peter had sacrificed his Empire, said scornfully that the Emperor 'let himself be driven from the throne as a child is sent to bed'.

The Orlovs envisaged Grigory marrying the new Empress. But Catherine still had a husband. Around 5 July Peter III was strangled. One of the Orlovs was involved, though the details remain a mystery. The corpse lay in state for two days, its bruised throat covered by a cravat. A hat was pulled low over the face to conceal the black discoloration caused by strangling. Catherine ordered a traditional coronation in Moscow to take place as soon as possible.

She was crowned in the Assumption Cathedral at the heart of the Kremlin, where she chose to place the crown on her own head to demonstrate that her legitimacy derived from herself, and the congregation fell to its knees. She returned to her palace in a carriage of gold. Among the unmounted horse guards protecting her was one called Grigory Potemkin. The Empress could not know that Second Lieutenant Potemkin intended to be the greatest force in her life.

Not long after the coronation, her lover Grigory Orlov told her of the young nobleman, the most amusing man in the guards, whose mimicry was impeccable. Catherine suggested a meeting. When Potemkin was presented, the Tsarina asked for a display of his mimicry. To the acute embarrassment of courtiers, out of Second Lieutenant Potemkin's mouth came the voice of the Empress with her slight German accent. In the silence that followed this impertinence, most present assumed that was the end of his career. Instead, Catherine burst out laughing, whereupon the entire Court followed suit.

Potemkin was born in 1739 near Smolensk of a noble but impoverished Polish family. His total self-confidence was to prove justified, but for now he was on the lower rungs of his ladder. Nonetheless he had ample opportunity at Court to study the Tsarina from afar, and he made no attempt to conceal from Grigory Orlov or anyone else that he was in love with her.

In 1767, Catherine summoned an assembly to draft a new code of laws for Russia. They should be framed to secure the safety of every citizen as much as possible. Torture should be abolished.

These ideals were incompatible with the government of Russia. All owners of serfs made plain they would rebel if serfs were given any rights. One of Catherine's strengths as a ruler was knowing how far she could push things. The proposed code never came into effect, though the liberal rhetoric of the Enlightenment remained a guiding influence on the Empress. Torture was now used far less in Petersburg, though no doubt it continued to be practised elsewhere in Russia. Generally it consisted of flogging by knouts rather than the drawn-out exquisite torture of the Inquisition.

As well as being a great ruler, the Tsarina was a dedicated scholar-collector. She brought Diderot to Russia for five months to advise her on her purchases. French and Russian were spoken at her Court whose European grandeur became incomparable.

Meanwhile, her armies were engaged in the expansion of Russian territory as a result of long and successful wars. The first partition of Poland and the Turkish war vastly increased the Empire. Throughout, Grigory Potemkin showed superb leadership, knowing when and where to take risks.

He returned to the Court in Petersburg in 1774 and was as fearless there as on the battlefield, unconcerned about the machinations of the Orlovs. But Catherine still had to take care. She loved Grigory Orlov and might well have married him had she not been aware that letting the Orlovs gain too much power could endanger her son Paul's succession to the throne. There were factions within factions conspiring, and she bribed lavishly those she judged most useful. As a female usurper who had murdered a Tsar, her position remained perilous. Certainly the foreign ambassadors thought her rule would be cut short, and so it might have been without Potemkin.

He had already become one of her advisers when he was not administering the southern territories captured from the Turks. Summoning him in 1773, Catherine told him he was 'already close to her heart' and promoted him to Lieutenant-General. By the next year she was in love with him and regretting she had not begun the relationship earlier. Already she had settled a fortune on Grigory Orlov in compensation for his dismissal as her lover, and he kept his place at Court.

1774 had scarcely begun when her love affair with Potemkin, wildly passionate from the start, became total commitment on both sides. Each was overjoyed by every aspect of the other. She called him 'one of the greatest, wittiest and most original eccentrics of this iron century'.

He now had achieved what he had long believed was his destiny: he not only influenced how his beloved ruled, he shared all political decisions as her intellectual equal. Potemkin was 34, a colossal man, still lithe, his thick brown hair unbrushed, with much of the wild Cossack about him. He had driving intellect, manic energy, sensitivity and almost priapic sexuality. Catherine was ten years older and in her prime.

He was given apartments in all the imperial palaces, separated from the Tsarina's bedroom by a private staircase, arriving unannounced when he felt like it, barefoot, naked and hirsute beneath a half-open dressing gown. Francophile courtiers and the ambassadors were horrified by his uncouth appearance, yet when the mood came upon him his military uniform or courtier's dress was immaculate.

They sent one another endless notes. In some he used code to describe the way he intended making love to her, but political strategy was never far distant: Catherine wrote how 'when you caress me, my caress always hurries to answer you', and a few sentences later, without transition, she turned to detailed statecraft.

The Empress humbled herself before Potemkin. He never wearied of demonstrations of her love, and in his jealousy he berated her for past lovers. At the same time, this tumultuous couple were dealing with uprisings and a plot to assassinate Catherine. They displayed the unending skill and force needed to administer Russia's sprawling Empire.

During a summer evening in 1774, Catherine was taken by boat to the unfashionable side of the great Neva River. She was wearing her long regimental guards uniform, which she knew was bewitching, the cape trimmed with gold lace. Waiting inside a church lit by many candles was Potemkin in his uniform of a general-en-chef. There were two witnesses to the marriage. When the one reading from the Gospel came to the words 'wife be afraid of her husband', he hesitated. The Empress nodded and he continued. A priest conducted the lengthy Orthodox ceremony, and at its end all were sworn to secrecy. Potemkin had been behaving as the Consort of the Empress. Now he was legally her husband.

During the second year of their consuming love, linked daily with the demands of drafting legislation and administration, Potemkin began to feel the tension between his political and social position. He became ill-tempered, sometimes impossible. Catherine tried with honeyed words to soothe him, but in time her patience turned to anger.

Potemkin was falling out of love with her. This hurt her deeply, although the love between them was losing nothing but its explosive sexuality. As he grew more restless, she took a new interest in her young secretary Peter Zavadovsky. Perhaps the fact that his equable temperament was the opposite to Potemkin's sparked her sexual attraction to the young man. Embarrassed by her wanton reputation, Catherine claimed that her love affairs were serial, but there was sometimes an overlap. She chose this moment to acclaim Potemkin as Most Serene Highness, and they both awaited the opportunity for him to become King in a country outside Russia.

Zavadovsky was her first lover while 'Serenissimus' was still master of the household. From then on, each of Catherine's lovers found themselves in a triangular relationship with Potemkin, seeking his approval. At times when the Empress had wearied of a young man, Potemkin would act as pimp, coming up with lovers in their twenties. Unlike most ageing women, the Empress could – and did – choose whoever took her fancy.

Potemkin's lifetime promiscuity had slowed down during the year and a half of sexual rapture with Catherine. Now he resumed it, demonstrating the same taste for the very young as Catherine was showing. One by one each of his nieces had affairs with him. Several remained devoted to him for life. His debauched pastimes took its toll on his looks, yet he remained irresistible to women.

Potemkin and the Tsarina never ceased loving one another dearly, and delighted in each other's company. Their astounding energy continued in public and private life, and under their joint direction – with Potemkin leading the Russian Army – a war with Sweden and a second war with the Turks vastly increased the Empire. For Potemkin was both fearless conqueror and able coloniser.

In 1791, when he was 52, he was struck down by illness. More and more letters were couriered between the Winter Palace and the General-en-Chef's headquarters in the Turkish campaign, for Catherine and Potemkin realised twenty years of interdependency were coming to an end. 'Goodbye, my friend,' she wrote, 'I kiss you.'

Despite a raging fever, Potemkin rode south to negotiate peace with the Turks. As he and his entourage – doctors, Cossacks and one of his nieces – were crossing the steppes towards the Bessarabian hills, Serenissimo collapsed. He asked to be laid on the ground to die in the open air in the arms of his niece.

Devastated, Catherine ordered the Court into mourning. But her son Grand Duke Paul exalted that the man who had kept him from his rightful place for twenty years was dead. The Tsarina's wish to disinherit her 'unstable' son and pass the crown directly to her grandson Alexander lost its momentum without Potemkin's will to stiffen her resolve.

Her current lover, the 24-year-old Prince Platon Zurov, had a sense of liberation at the removal of the colossus to whom he felt desperately inferior, but when Catherine gave him several of Potemkin's political posts, Zurov could handle none of them. His role was a sexual one, which he performed well.

For a further five years the Empress continued to govern effectively, though her will for innovation was gone. When she was 67 and still sexually comforted by Zurov, she was struck down by a massive stroke. Emissaries galloped to the palace of Grand Duke Paul who at first thought they had come to arrest him. On learning his mother was lying helpless, he hurried to Petersburg to destroy papers suggesting he be passed over for the crown. Catherine died the next day.

8

King George IV

1762–1830

Like all the Hanoverians, the Prince of Wales was in open revolt against his father, King George III. As a youth, 'Prinny' was slim and exceptionally handsome. He soon came under the influence of wilder members of the Whig Party, notably the rumbustious Charles James Fox. As the Whigs wanted parliamentary supremacy, and Fox was famously unimpressed by conventional morality, small wonder that George III deplored his son's friendship with the politician.

Clever, witty, shrewd, Prinny was one of the most gifted of royal princes. But he was self-obsessed. At eighteen he took as his mistress the famous Drury Lane actress Mrs Robinson, known as 'Perdita'. He always preferred intelligent women, and Perdita was also an accomplished playwright and poet who could fight her own corner. With the masculine tendency to promise *anything* in the heat of passion (or in anticipation of it), Prinny gave her a bond for £20,000 which he then declined to pay – whereupon Perdita threatened to publish their letters. Poor old George III had to pay her £5,000 to get the letters back.

However promiscuous his nature would remain, Prinny found the love of his life at 21 when, standing on the steps of the Opera, he saw Mrs Maria Fitzherbert. On first sight he became besotted with the enchanting widow who was six years his senior. The chase began. Mrs Fitzherbert was no easy conquest.

Raised in a well-off genteel family, Mrs Fitzherbert had seen both her marriages end in premature widowhood, which further increased her wealth. She was a popular figure in London society. Above all, she was a devout Roman Catholic. Unlike most married women in Regency high society, her last desire was to be anyone's mistress, even a royal one.

Prinny gave her no peace. He wrote to Whig hostesses informing them that if they wanted him to attend their dinners, Mrs Fitzherbert must be invited and seated beside him. As well as being highly attractive, she had sweetness, and the Prince, despite having various mistresses, knew he could not live without her.

In 1884 she was just preparing for bed in her house in Park Street when a tremendous rumpus was heard at her front door. Her maid let in four gentlemen who told Mrs Fitzherbert that the Prince had attempted to take his own life. 'Unless you go to him, nothing will save him.'

Maria threw on her cloak but insisted that they first collect her close friend the Duchess of Devonshire. When they all reached Carlton House, they found Prinny bleeding and weak – though he still had enough strength to coerce the reluctant Maria into agreeing to marry him lest he harm himself further. Producing a borrowed ring, he slipped it on her finger, promising to tell his father as soon as possible.

Knowing that she could never be Prinny's wife for two reasons – her religion and the fact that the King's required approval would, she knew, be unforthcoming – Maria and the Duchess of Devonshire had a document drawn up saying that her agreement was obtained by extortion and that she declared it null and void. Then she fled to Paris.

The Prince was inconsolable. Soon the whole country knew how utterly wretched he was. The King forbade him to leave England and seek Maria in France, so instead he harassed her parents until they dreaded the sound of the royal carriage approaching. For eighteen months he bombarded her family with letters for her. The last one – 48 pages long – wore her down. She returned to London.

On 15 December 1785, having bribed the Reverend Robert Burke with £500 to perform the ceremony, the Prince went through a form of marriage with Mrs Fitzherbert in her house, he now 23, Maria 29. Their honeymoon was taken at her villa in Richmond. They kept separate houses, but that in no way discouraged gossip, for when they did appear it was in each other's company. Prinny soon built a house for his wife in Pall Mall, so that she would be nearer his own home at Carlton House. The royal dukes welcomed her, and needless to say society followed suit.

There were hiccups, however. Although Maria settled many of Prinny's bills, his debts continued to soar. For as well as being profligate in his dissolute personal life, he was a man of culture, patronising architecture and the arts. He built the Royal Pavilion at Brighton for Maria, and together they directed its exquisite decoration.

Two years after his wedding, his debts were so stupendous that the matter was brought before the House of Commons. The subject of his marriage to Mrs Fitzherbert was also raised. Prinny had never told his Whig friends – nor almost anyone else, including his ongoing series of mistresses – that he was married. Charles James Fox stood up in the House of Commons and denied that such a marriage had occurred.

Naturally Maria, supposing that the Prince had told Fox to make this statement, took it badly. The couple had agreed that if asked they would remain silent. She told the Prince she would have nothing more to do with him. Once again Prinny went into hysterics. In the end they got back together and their marriage continued happily.

Then disaster struck. Prinny's new debts were so vast that the King ordered that they should be paid only if the Prince wed a rich princess. At this point one of the Prince's married mistresses, Frances Lady Jersey, a well-born and beguiling manipulator who had already made a number of advantageous liaisons, saw her opportunity to wrest the Prince away from Maria later on. Of the choice of possible brides, she urged him to choose a German princess, Caroline of Brunswick, a first cousin whom he had never clapped eyes on. Knowing that Caroline was hardly Prinny's type, Lady Jersey calculated that she could thus gain control over him.

The Prince denied to his father that he had ever married Mrs Fitzherbert. And he told his wife that they must part. Maria moved out of the house he had built for her in Pall Mall, and into one just off Park Lane. He gave her an annuity of £3,000 for life.

On 2 April 1795, Princess Caroline arrived at Gravesend and that afternoon met the Prince of Wales at St James's Palace. When he saw this plain, vulgar, dumpy woman and – worse – smelled her, he cried to an attendant, 'Harris, I am not well; pray get me a glass of brandy!'

Six days later the 32-year-old Prince and his 26-year-old cousin entered aptly named wedlock in the Chapel Royal at St James's Palace. The Archbishop of Canterbury performed the ceremony. The Prince of Wales was extremely drunk on arrival and made plain his reluctance towards this marriage, refusing to look at the bride and instead gazing like a rat in a trap, at Lady Jersey.

Fortified by drink, he did his duty. Nine months to the day later, Princess Charlotte was born, securing the throne for George's line. But those nine months of wedded misery were frightful. The mutual detestation of husband and wife caused continuous noisy and embarrassing scenes. Matters were not improved when he insisted that Lady Jersey be one of Caroline's ladies-in-waiting. Nor did it go down well when he helped himself to some of his wife's wedding jewels and gave them to Lady Jersey, who took bitchy delight in flaunting them in front of Caroline.

Days after Charlotte's birth, her parents separated. Cold-heartedly, the Prince let his wife live by herself in Blackheath, the object of much sympathy. The child, lively and warm-hearted, saw her father rarely and her mother for two hours a week. The Prince made out a new will, leaving all his possessions to Mrs Fitzherbert and a shilling to the Princess of Wales. Two years later, tired of Lady Jersey, he began to woo Mrs Fitzherbert again. She resisted his blandishments.

With his taste for melodrama, in the dead of night he summoned his brother, the Duke of Cumberland, and dispatched him with a letter for Maria, threatening suicide if she did not rejoin him, and threatening her mother and uncle as well.

Maria would have none of it, and asked the Pope what she should do. When he ruled in 1800 that she must regard herself as the only true wife of the Prince, she agreed to be reconciled with Prinny.

Clearly, when it was in his interest, Prinny evinced his undoubted charm and wit.

Once again they went out together in society in London and Brighton, a happy couple for ten years. Then in 1810, King George III went completely mad. The Prince of Wales became agitated and distressed as the likelihood of Regency approached. Once it was declared, he again turned his back on Mrs Fitzherbert.

The final affront was when she attended a grand banquet given by the Prince Regent at Carlton House, only to discover no place had been assigned to her at the royal table. She withdrew into private life with an increased annuity of £6,000, not altogether sorry to leave behind the plotting and backbiting of the Court. In private, she and Prinny remained devoted friends.

During the Regency, Princess Caroline went abroad and lived her own loose life. George's love of women and his extravagant patronage of the arts continued, the latter giving the name Regency to the culture and fashion of the period. His principal mistress was Isabella, Lady Hertford. Her husband took her to Ireland to remove her from George's pursuit. To no avail. She was influential in the Prince Regent's turn from the radical Whigs to the Tories.

In 1817, the young Princess Charlotte's happy marriage to Prince Leopold of Saxe-Coburg, was cut short by a botched child-birth. The Prince Regent's brother, the Duke of Clarence, became his heir. In 1820, the insane King at last died and the Prince Regent became King George IV. At once he increased Mrs Fitzherbert's annuity to £10,000.

His next act was to try to rid himself of his legal wife before his coronation. For years the Princess of Wales had been openly disporting herself on the Continent with men who appeared to have no serious problem with her hygiene. For some time she resided in Italy with an Ialian lover who had been one of her servants. The King offered her an annuity of £50,000 to renounce her title of Queen and live abroad.

But Caroline was rather taken with the idea of being a reigning Queen. She made a triumphal entry into London where she won the people's sympathy because of her husband's callous treatment of her. The government then charged her with adultery.

The resultant divorce case before the House of Lords was messier than most. The double standards of the day meant that the Queen was charged with exorbitant adultery though her conduct had not differed greatly from the King's. Her unseemly behaviour was easy enough to prove, but because of her mistreatment by her husband and a superb defence by the great lawyer Brougham, there was such a surge in her favour that the government had to abandon the divorce action. Caroline now assumed the rank, if not the role, of Queen Consort.

The coronation was somewhat different from that of our own dear Queen. The King was adamant that his legal wife would not be formally crowned and anointed at his side. Queen Caroline was equally determined to be there. The King had chosen as ushers his favourite pugilists (even though prize-fighting was at the time illegal). When the Queen arrived at Westminster Abbey, she found the doors barred. Her retinue rushed the north door, but the pugilists guarding it against her held their ground.

Eighteen days later the Queen was out of her husband's way for good, dead from a mysterious gastric ailment. That she had been poisoned was, unsurprisingly, not ruled out.

Throughout his reign as King, George IV's *maîtresse en titre* was the much-bedded Marchioness of Conyngham. She was voluptuous, greedy and shrewd, and she knew how to brighten his mood, as his lavish expenditure on her clothes and jewels testified.

On his deathbed in 1830, the King called for Mrs Fitzherbert. Putting his hand up to his breast he exclaimed, 'Good God, what do I feel? This must be death!' It was. He died a few minutes afterwards with a locket containing a miniature of Maria around his neck, where it remained when he was buried.

Maria Fitzherbert died seven years later in Brighton and was buried in the Catholic Church of St John the Baptist. Her memorial shows her kneeling with three rings on her finger.

9

Lord Byron

1788–1824

'Mad – bad – and dangerous to know,' Lady Caroline Lamb recorded in her journal on the evening in 1812 when she first saw Byron. The same could have been written about her, as the notorious Romantic poet found when he tried to disentangle himself from their love affair.

His childhood had been pretty wretched. His father, 'Mad Jack' Byron, squandered the fortune of his Scottish heiress wife and then deserted her. Excessively vain, hysterical, with a vicious temper, she destroyed whatever self-confidence her son, who was born crippled, may have had. Later Mary Shelley would write: 'No action of Lord Byron's life – scarce a line he has written – but was influenced by his personal defect.'

On unexpectedly inheriting his great-uncle's title, George Gordon Lord Byron's education and shabby surroundings changed. He was still at Harrow when he discovered that the club foot he so hated in no way lessened his hypnotic effect on women. He created his own cult of personality – the 'Byronic hero', defiant, debonair, brooding. At Cambridge he read, swam and boxed, ran up debts, enjoyed sodomy, and led a decidedly dissipated life. His first collection of poems, published when he was nineteen, was panned by the critics.

Histrionic, Byron lived in action. In 1809 he took his seat in the House of Lords and then travelled for two years in Europe and Asia

Minor, swam the Hellespont, indulged indiscriminately in bisexual love, wrote continually, and became fired with the desire, which would lead to his early death, that Greece should be freed from the Turks. On returning to England, his first speech in the Lords was a passionate defence of workers who had wrecked newly installed machinery that threatened their future. Success came with the publication of *Childe Harold's Pilgrimage* in 1812. He was lionised by aristocratic and literary London.

In 1813, Byron and Augusta Leigh met for the second time. The first meeting had taken place when he was fifteen and she was twenty. Both were fathered by 'Mad Jack' Byron. Augusta's mother deserted her husband, the Marquess of Carmarthen, to elope with Mad Jack. She died a year after Augusta was born, and the child was subsequently shunted between grand houses. She married into that world, taking as her husband George Leigh, a cousin and charming wastrel. They had three children.

Now Augusta and her half-brother came together again. She had gone to Byron to ask him for money to help settle her husband's debts. This time the sexual attraction between them was electric. They were crazy about each other. Augusta was generous, playful, impulsive, blind to consequences.

Byron saw incest as the highest form of self-expression. Narcissism increased the attraction between blood relations, each reflected in the other. He was exhilarated by knowing he was committing a deadly sin. He pleaded with his sister to accompany him to Sicily, but she refused because she was pregnant with her fourth child. Instead, they went to his ancestral home in Nottinghamshire, the dilapidated Newstead Abbey, for a blissful fortnight creating a fantasy of childhood. In 1814, Augusta gave birth to a daughter, Medora. Rumours flew. Was George Leigh the father? Almost certainly Medora was Byron's child.

Unlike any of his myriad hectic affairs, his sexual passion for his half-sister was coupled with devotion. She was the love that dominated his entire life. In an effort to control their lust, he rashly courted Anne Isabella Milbanke, the rich niece of his confidante Lady Melbourne, known as Annabella. She was everything that Augusta was not: pretentious, prim, chilly, humourless. And she thought she could reform Byron. When disastrously, he proposed to Annabella, his sister insisted he go through with it: it would give them both a cloak of moral respectability.

The marriage was hell. From day one he made plain that he wanted only to be with his sister. But Annabella had thrown herself into the role of redeemer and would not let him out of her sight. There were daily outbursts of rage from him at his self-willed immolation, and tears from her. They went on a fortnight's visit to Augusta in her marital home in Newmarket. There he mocked his bride for the difference between her kisses and his sister's, and taunted her about how her underwear compared to Augusta's.

No sooner did the impossible couple return to London and settle in a house off Piccadilly than Augusta came to stay with them. Upstairs in her bedroom, Annabella had to listen to sister and brother's giggles as they romped in the room beneath her.

Towards the end of a year of this hopeless marriage, Byron was summoned to gaze upon his newborn daughter, Ada. He gave a terrible cry, 'Oh! What an instrument of torture I have acquired in you!' With Ada in her arms, Annabella swept out and returned to her family home in Leicestershire. She told her mother how she had been treated, and lawyers were summoned.

London society was already agog with rumours that Medora Leigh was Byron's daughter. There was even talk of sodomy in Byron's marital bed. Close to a breakdown, Augusta, too fled London. Charges of incest forced Byron, already debt-ridden, into a financial settlement with his wife. Ostracised by society in what Macaulay called 'one of its periodic fits of morality', deeply embittered, in April 1816 the poet went into self-imposed exile on the Continent, never to return. 'The only virtue they honour in England is hypocrisy,' he wrote to a friend. Brother and sister would not see each other again. The last lines he wrote before leaving England were to Augusta:

> When fortune changed – and love fled far,
> And hatred's shafts flew thick and fast,
> Thou wert the solitary star
> Which rose and set not to the last.

In exile he had a flowering of creativity, writing as much drama as poetry. Joining the Shelleys' party in Geneva, he embarked on a long affair with Claire Clairmont with whom he fathered another daughter, Allegra. With Newstead Abbey at last sold, he now had money, and when they all moved to Venice, his life was riotous. Proudly and childishly he boasted of having a different woman on two hundred consecutive evenings. Throughout all these grapplings, the only woman he loved was Augusta.

In 1823, deeply shaken by Shelley's death from drowning, his thoughts turned to a cause. Increasingly he felt that action was more important than poetry. He determined to take charge of the Greeks' fight for freedom against Turkish rule. He wrote to Lady Blessington: 'I have a presentiment I shall die in Greece.'

And still he railed against England, writing to his publisher John Murray, 'I am sure my bones would not rest in an English grave, or my clay mix with earth of that country. I believe the thought would drive me mad on my deathbed, could I suppose that any of my friends would be base enough to convey my carcass back to your soil.'

With good wishes from Goethe, Byron armed a brig, the *Hercules*, and set off to fight for Greek liberation. After various mishaps and escapes, the *Hercules* arrived at the mud-sodden port of Missolonghi in western Greece in January 1824, where he formed the 'Byron Brigade'. He gave money generously to the insurgents and was a huge inspiration to them. But before he could see any serious military action, he contracted swamp fever in Missolonghi and died in April. He was 36.

The Greeks wanted to bury him in Athens, but only his heart stayed in the country. Memorial services were held all over the land. When his body was returned to England, it was refused by the deans of both Westminster and St Paul's. An old friend, the statesman John Hobhouse, arranged for it to lie in state for a few days in London. It was interred in the family vault near Newstead Abbey.

Augusta's attraction to her own blood did not die with Byron. When her daughter Medora was fourteen, Augusta colluded in drugging the girl who was then raped by an uncle, Henry Travanion, who went on to have an affair with Augusta.

And Annabella? Once Byron had left the country, she worked ceaselessly to blacken his reputation further. Once he was dead, she threw her energies into alternately wooing and bullying his sister, using every technique to wear down Augusta into publicly taking her side. Purely out of spite, Annabella told Medora – who, poor girl, was entirely unprepared for the revelation – that she was the daughter, not only the niece, of Lord Byron.

A month after Byron's death, his publisher, John Murray II, and five associates stared at the two bound volumes lying before them: they contained Byron's unpublished diaries. After heated debate about whether they should burn the books to spare Byron's reputation and his family's feelings, they consigned the two volumes, page by page, to the roaring fire in the grate. Do not ask me why they did not simply put an embargo for one hundred years on this precious material.

Altogether a sorry business.

10

Lady Jane Digby

1807–81

Her childhood was bliss. Born in Dorset into the aristocratic Digby family, Jane was treasured by her parents and the whole of her attractive extended family; she adored her naval-hero father and her pretty mother. She took for granted all the privileges attached to rich aristocracy in that day. Already her charm, intelligence and beauty bewitched male and female, young and old. (Not for nothing was she the heroine of her descendent Pamela Churchill Harriman. See Chapter 23.)

At seventeen she married Lord Ellenborough. A widower twice her age, he was an experienced womaniser; on the first night of their honeymoon, he found his bride a naturally talented student. Driven by hormones and without a trace of self-consciousness, from the outset she experienced the ecstatic joys of sexuality.

But political ambition took her husband away to frequent debates and meetings. Jane thought his neglect indicated loss of interest in her. Her disappointment was soon allayed. Indifferent to the mores that decreed promiscuity to be permissible in a man but unacceptable in a woman, she was soon sexually involved with a cousin, George Anson. 'Oh it is heaven to love thee and rapture to be near thee,' she wrote to him. This liaison became known to the amoral world of London's international set, to the dismay of her conservative family.

As in other upper-class homes, Jane's childhood nanny remained with the family after the children had grown up, and her former governess, the aptly named Miss Steele, kept in touch. 'Steely' now lectured her former charge on the importance of reputation. She even took the matter to Lord Ellenborough, who was amused that this former employee, however gently born, should be discussing his wife with him.

Jane threw herself into her love affair with George Anson as if it would be the only one in her life, and she preferred to remain faithful while it was in full flow. At moments, however, her hormones got the better of her – as when on a visit to her family's home she seduced the newly arrived young librarian. 'She is not yet twenty and one of the most lovely women I ever saw, quite fair, blue eyes that would move a saint, and lips that would tempt one to forswear heaven to touch them,' he confided to his diary.

It was completely normal for men to take one look at Jane and be smitten, but the sober scholar held no hope of reciprocation. And then . . . 'Lady E lingered behind the rest of the party and at midnight I escorted her to her room,' he wrote. 'I will not add what passed. Gracious God! Was there ever such good fortune?' Poor man: his good fortune was short-lived. The following day Lady E ignored him.

Generally, however, she was not a hard-hearted beauty: mischievous, yes, but usually tactful in deflecting her admirers. Throughout her life, people spoke of her sweet nature.

When George Anson decided his affair with his cousin was becoming risky for his army career, he pulled out as kindly as he could. For George was not brutal: he was a warm, exceptionally attractive man who liked a good time. Too late he realised Jane wanted long-term commitment, unlike those worldly women whom he normally fancied.

Then she rejoiced: during one of her husband's prolonged absences, George came back for a few weeks. This time when they parted, he made clear it was for ever. Not long afterwards Jane realised she was pregnant and knew the father of her child could only be George Anson.

She got away with it. When her husband was home, they resumed normal marital relations, and it did not occur to him to calculate the date of the beginning of his wife's pregnancy. He was thrilled when a son was born. Despite her warm nature, Jane failed to bond with the child.

While attending a ball given by the Austrian Ambassador, she was glimpsed by Prince Felix Schwarzenberg, the newly arrived Austrian diplomat whose family was among the grandest in Europe. One look was enough: he set out to seduce her. Still smarting from George Anson's desertion, Jane was glad to have society think she had cast him aside for the Prince. After a few months of being escorted by the adoring Schwarzenberg, she found herself passionately in love with him.

Unfortunately, this passion made sexual intercourse with her husband repugnant to her. She told him she could no longer share his bed. Thus when she became pregnant, it was obvious that the father was Felix Schwarzenberg. By now back in Austria, the Prince greeted her news with less enthusiasm than she had anticipated. In vain Jane's family pleaded with her to give him up. When their daughter, Didi, was born, Jane's maternal feelings were again limited. Her rapture with Felix was all-absorbing. She moved to Basle with Didi to be near the Prince's latest posting. His family and friends were doing their best to sew discord which would break up his liaison with the now notorious Englishwoman.

Meanwhile her husband experienced heartbreak: Arthur, his son and heir (in truth, George Anson's son), died just before his second birthday. Always considerate towards his wife, Lord Ellenborough wrote her a kind letter breaking the news. Enclosed was a lock of Arthur's soft, golden hair. Paradoxically, Jane would keep it with her throughout her life.

There were seldom more than two divorces a year in Britain at that time. Eager now to father another son and heir, Lord Ellenborough sued for divorce. *The Times*, which then ran advertisements on its front page, dispensed with them for a day and devoted the entire page to the Ellenborough Court action. Witnesses provided the public with sly accounts of Jane's long visits to Felix's home when he was in London, and staff at the Brighton hotel where they had shared a room proved eager to describe the state of the bedclothes and so on. Everyone knew that Ellenborough had committed his own share of adulteries, but when the divorce was granted, he was not ostracised by society. Jane, on the other hand, was not welcome in the country.

Soon after she settled in a large apartment in Paris, she gave birth to her second child by Felix, a boy who died ten days later. Although Felix sent a letter of condolence, and wrote her regular letters professing his love for her, he saw her less and less. His nickname, Cad, became synonymous for callous behaviour.

The English contingent in Paris declined to attend balls given by Lady Ellenborough, and the louche unmarried continentals who attended were very different from the high society that had previously clamoured for her presence. Balzac wrote a novel openly portraying Jane, describing 'her fatal notoriety' and 'the beauty of her person, her charms, her manners, her intelligence, an indescribable brilliancy which dazzled before fascinating.' As for the excitements of sharing a bed with Lady Ellenborough, 'When she loved, she loved with frenzy; no other woman of any country could compare with her, she was as good as an entire seraglio.'

Believing that Munich would be Felix Schwarzenberg's next posting, she moved there, only to find he was sent to Berlin. Still, Jane made the most of her time in Munich: she quickly was spotted by King Ludwig I, whose family had ruled Bavaria for a thousand years. Enchanted by her open adoration of the elusive Felix, the King became her closest confidant, though it remained socially impossible to receive her at Court. He had many mistresses, but history seems only 95 per cent confident that this kindly man's intimate friendship with Jane extended to the bedroom.

At the same time, the eminent Baron Carl Venningen had fallen in love with her and wanted to marry her. Charles, as she called him, was a tall, red-haired and good-looking German aristocrat who took life seriously. No matter that he was a Catholic, Jane's family urged her to wed him for the status he could provide, which would restore her to social acceptability among her peers. Jane told him of her love for Felix, but Charles continued his dogged pursuit.

King Ludwig advised her that it was possible to be contentedly married without the intense and delicious love they both had experienced outside marriage. He intervened to make it possible for

Jane to have a Catholic marriage to Charles. Felix wrote a cold letter giving his approval. Jane vowed to herself that she would make Charles 'a good wife'. Her father attended both the Protestant and Catholic marriage services to show his approval (and perhaps to deter her from running out at the last moment). Overnight Jane became acceptable at Court.

Alas for the happily married Charles, at a masked ball during Oktoberfest, a Greek came into Jane's life – Count Spirodon Theotoky. His temperament was the very opposite to that of the uxorious, stolid Charles. Four years younger than Jane, at 24 Theotoky's sole aim was to enjoy himself. He had never met anyone like Jane, and he wooed her with all the dash that had been shown by Felix Schwarzenberg. That he had little money presented no difficulty: Jane was now an independently rich woman. After her divorce, Lord Ellenborough had settled money on her. And her father, though angered by the obloquy his only daughter had brought on the family, had done the same. Freshly smitten, Jane eloped with Theotoky.

Charles overtook them on the road to freedom, pulled Theotoky from the carriage and challenged him to a duel with pistols. The Greek had no training in duels and shot wide. Charles's shot found his mark, and Theotoky fell to the ground, blood spurting from his chest. Surprisingly, he did not die. Jane nursed him back to health.

Her mother and Steely came to Germany in an attempt to persuade her to return to Charles. They found her so happy that they saved their breath. Also, they both liked the Greek. By this time Jane was pregnant with his child.

However shattered Charles was, he reluctantly consented to a divorce. 'I have *never* loved anyone, heart and soul, with my whole being, as I loved you,' he wrote to his wife. 'Farewell, my darling, farewell my life, farewell my Jeane.'

When Jane's son was born, she had her first experience of maternal love. The child was named Leonidas. Six blissful years of marriage to Theotoky followed. Jane's family accepted the marriage, and on visits to England he was always introduced as Count. On her Greek island with the husband she loved passionately, she believed she now had everything.

Then she learned that her husband was madly in love with another woman. She pulled up stakes and left him. In Italy she was met by her mother and Steely. The three women took a large Italian villa where Jane had the consolation of six-year-old Leonidas. Precocious and lively, one day he went to the top of the house to slide down the banisters and surprise his mother where she stood in the central hall saying goodbye to guests. The child overbalanced and fell to the marble floor, dead at her feet.

From then on she was a wanderer. Theotoky now loved his mistress as previously he had loved Jane. She was forced to make a large financial settlement on him in order to obtain a divorce. She knew that Charles would have her back, but she had no wish to return to that stolid life in Germany.

In 1849 when she was 42, looking many years younger, she took a house in Rome and was soon besieged by three suitors. An artillery officer gave her a diamond necklace and offered marriage. She learned he was a thief and he went to prison. The other two proposed a duel to fight it out, assuming the survivor would marry Jane. They fought with swords, and the young diplomat ran the captain through. When the diplomat then demanded Jane's hand, she refused him and he killed himself.

Jane returned to Athens where she rented a house and entertained lavishly, but her heart was empty. King Otto of Greece took a special interest in her, to the jealous chagrin of the Queen, and he introduced her to an Albanian chieftain who had earlier been his sworn enemy. Half soldier, half bandit, General Hadji-Petros was wildly glamorous. Soon Jane left Athens to live openly as his consort in caves, camps and deserted castles. She cooked for him, and more importantly, looked after his eight-year-old daughter who filled some of the void left by Leonidas. Always an accomplished rider and expert shot, she rode beside the General. Her loyal French maid, Eugenie, managed to look after her clothes despite the circumstances.

In Athens her new house, almost completed, was the talk of the town. The bedroom designed for Hadji-Petros was said to be like a throne room. There was a garrison for his troops. But a difficulty arose: Jane discovered her maid Eugenie was having an affair with the General. On every count this perfidy was deeply insulting to Jane. Deciding it was harder to find a good maid than lover, she threw out the General and retained the sulking Eugenie. Already packed to go to Syria, she embarked for Beirut with her resentful maid in tow. Reckoning that men were more trouble than they were worth as she approached her fiftieth birthday, she declared she would henceforth live without them.

Yet her diary reveals that she still brooded about Hadji-Patros: 'Why was he so infamous with Eugenie? Eugenie! who he never could love. While I? . . .'

Jane was in no hurry to return to Athens. She always travelled with her sketchbook, and, with her companionable little group, she sailed to Jaffa where she sketched for days. On riding away from Jericho, they met a group of Bedouin Arabs travelling in the same direction. Their handsome leader, Saleh, made no attempt to hide his frank appraisal of Jane. She was the only woman invited to his tent where the diners sat on rugs and ate freshly killed lamb with couscous, helping themselves with their hands. Just before sunset, Saleh gave a spectacular performance with horse and lance accompanied by his wild battle-cry, galloping straight at the group before pulling up sharply and plunging his lance into the ground at Jane's feet. Within days, infatuated with him, she was in his bed.

When their groups parted and he rode off, Jane's most momentous love affair presented itself out of the blue. She and her comrades came to low black Bedouin tents where they were to meet Sheikh Medjuel el Mezrab. The Mezrab tribe controlled the desert around Damascus and escorted travellers through the ever-present dangers of attack. Payment for this hazardous service was an important source of income. The Sheikh was in his late twenties and wore the scarlet robe and gold insignia of a desert Prince. Extremely cultured, he spoke a number of languages and, unusually for a Bedouin, could read and write Arabic.

He was a magnificent horseman. He and Jane rode together, talking in a relaxed comradeship about their different journeys and ways of life, his two wives and young son, and her attraction to Saleh, which still blinded her to what lay ahead. Medjuel arranged that she first see Damascus in its full beauty, and her diary and sketchbook reveal her love of the desert life, its colours, sleeping under the stars, the night-time silence.

The Damascus hotel was without baths, and she washed near by in a women's communal public bath-house. On Medjuel's advice, she bought the free-flowing Arab dress for herself and Eugenie to make them less conspicuous. Medjuel taught her how to fold a *keffiyeh* to cover her head.

The British consul, horrified by the thought of an Englishwoman and her maid travelling with Arabs, tried his utmost to stop Lady Ellenborough, as he called her, going on to Palmyra. She ignored his advice and was soon learning – as was the heroic Eugenie – how to mount a camel, and Medjuel showed Jane how to position herself to sleep on a camel. In camp the men prayed on mats, performing the washing ritual with sand. As it was Ramadan, they fasted from sunrise to sunset, their evening meal caught by Medjuel's hawk.

Suddenly the camp was overrun by shrieking raiders brandishing lances. Medjuel drew his sabre and pistol from his sash, positioned himself before Jane's tent and calmly shouted orders to his men. While Eugenie screamed: 'Oh, we shall be sold as slaves!' Medjuel wielded his weapons effectively and the raiders withdrew. Deeply thrilled, Jane decided to sell her Athens house and start a new life in Damascus.

Meanwhile, they at last emerged from the pass to Palmyra, the oasis city built by King Solomon, in ruins since the defeat of Queen Zenobia in the third century – three miles of massive uninhabited temples, triumphal arches and colonnaded streets, more moving in their emptiness than any place Jane had yet seen.

At the journey's end, Medjuel sent her back to Damascus with another escort. Half a year passed before they met again in Damascus. She told him she wanted to make another desert journey, but Medjuel was committed to accompany his tribe to their winter grazing. Would she be willing, he asked in his soft-spoken voice, to marry a Bedouin?

Unusually, Jane had not realised that he, more than twenty years her junior, was bewitched by her. He had never kissed her or spoken any words of love, and she saw him as her friend rather than a lover. She replied that if she loved him she would certainly consider marrying a Bedouin, but her religion did not permit more than one wife (at a time, she might have added).

Soon afterwards another well-known Bedouin, Sheikh el Barak, invited her on a four-month desert trip while he bought camels. He, too, was a striking and confident man of the desert, though not cultivated like Medjuel. She went, having sensibly died her hair black. They were captured by raiders – Jane masquerading under her veils as Barak's wife, for Christians did not qualify for the Bedouin code of honour. 'Not one prepossessing face among them,' she scribbled hastily in her diary. 'How different from the Jordan set.' Only after days of negotiation over camels were they released. In truth, she enjoyed the whole experience, only wishing that she were with someone she loved and who loved her.

A few nights later, Jane was in Barak's bed. She did not particularly desire him sexually, but in their difficult situation she was not prepared to make a big issue of it. Her brief cryptic note in her diary suggests that she (as usual) enjoyed the experience for itself, 'I went to his fire after dinner on his pressing me. Oh the night, and the times . . .'

When finally their party was approaching Damascus, a lone horseman was seen coming to meet them, leading a riderless horse. Jane switched horses and rode into the city beside Medjuel. While they were riding together the next day, as she recorded in her diary, she 'Received 1st kiss.'

Without a moment's hesitation, she decided to close up her affairs in Athens and build a house in Damascus for her new life in Syria. She wrote to her mother that she was considering marriage to a Bedouin, but she did not have the nerve to tell her one-time governess Steely. The English consul made no attempt to conceal his angry disapproval.

On their long and ardent wedding night, Medjuel discovered his bride was as youthful 'as a girl', and Jane discovered that this Bedouin had a talent for love-making. During the honeymoon, much of her diary was written in code.

'All days *d'or* and *de joie*, passed in delightful intercourse with this simple, upright and affectionate character.' At the end of twenty days of this she wrote, 'I leave Damascus for the loved desert with my adored, and adoring, Medjuel. His *slave*. Oh that I had 20 years less to excuse this last folly.'

Jane knew that her own background meant nothing to the Bedouins. They regarded theirs as the only pure blood. During centuries of harsh living, only the strongest survived, no doubt accounting for their lean and handsome features. She was under Medjuel's protection, but she quickly realised she would have to earn the approval of his people.

The fly in the ointment was his girl-wife Mascha. He had no regrets in divorcing his other young wife because he did not like her smell. But he was still attracted to Mascha. Now she was demanding that he sleep with her. Jane, who had never previously taken another woman's husband, felt guilt about insisting that Mascha must go, but insist she did. Jane intended to live with Medjuel for the rest of her life, and she dreaded the day that her own body would grow less desirable to him. The thought of Mascha's youth haunted her.

She enjoyed learning to milk a camel and doing the menial work that other Bedouin wives took as a matter of course. These tasks were her offering to Medjuel. And she accepted that raiding was endemic to the Bedouins as the primary source of wealth. Even poor families would sacrifice their only sheep to entertain a stranger: it was the code.

Jane gave Medjuel an enormous tent for his travelling. It easily accommodated sixty people for a celebration or a conference, and it housed a bedroom for her. When he travelled without her, she eased the pangs of missing him by designing and overseeing a large house in Damascus. This was decorated in the manner of the English upper classes: the gauze curtains of her massive bed fell from a coronet. There were stables and a garden large enough for a menagerie of animals to wander among fountains and exotic trees, which included an English pear tree. When Medjuel was there, his tribe could camp in the garden. Western travellers vied for invitations to this marvellous house.

The Prince of Wales made an informal visit – 'mere curiosity I suppose,' she noted in her diary. He wrote in his own diary about this person who was the most famous European in Syria, observing that she 'was once very handsome, & is still very good looking tho' more than 50'.

On visits to her family in England, Jane dressed in the most fashionable clothes from Paris. Only Steely, the former governess, still lectured her on marrying 'black heathen'. When Jane returned to her 'black heathen', Medjuel's tenderness and ardour dispelled her fears that in her long absence he might have returned to Mascha – or to another young woman.

Bedouins were great gossips: again and again someone told Jane that while Medjuel was absent from Damascus, he had taken a younger wife. Yet when Medjuel returned from the desert and Jane rode out to meet him, she learned that the rumour was untrue. When he realised her doubts about whether he still desired her, he threw off his clothes and took her to bed, where they remained all day.

Sometimes when he was away, Jane herself acted as guide through the desert to Europeans, relying on her Arab clothes and her reputation as Medjuel's wife to protect her party from attack. While Medjuel was absent in the desert, news reached him that an outburst of racial and religious violence in the villages near Damascus had led to Muslims butchering Christians, wiping out hundreds of families. Soon the insurrection swept through Damascus where Muslims outnumbered Christians three to one. From her flat roof Jane looked down on women being raped in the streets. Girls were carried off. Men and boys were savagely circumcised before being put to death.

Medjuel dashed back to protect his wife who in her enveloping robes and veil walked through the Christian quarter helping the wounded. He insisted she return to their house, stationing armed Bedouins around it while he led those Arabs who were trying to stop the slaughter. After a week, the city still lay beneath a black pall of smoke from burnt-out buildings. 'In all the many wanderings of my adventurous and *adventureful* life,' Jane wrote, 'I never was in such a *mess* as this and the distress of those around is heart rending.'

Yet no danger could remove her from Medjuel and their alternating lives, half in the desert, half in Damascus. Despite her bouts of acute anxiety about younger wives, these 23 years with him were the most fulfilling of her life.

Only in her seventies did her strong lithe body begin to age. At her funeral, as chief mourner Medjuel sat in a black carriage behind the hearse. Halfway to the cemetery, hating the confinement, he jumped out and ran in the opposite direction. The interment service was already under way when he galloped back on Jane's beautiful mare and together – her adored husband and her favourite horse – they watched her committed to the dust.

On her grey granite tombstone was carved: 'Jane Elizabeth Digby, daughter of Admiral Sir Henry Digby GCB. Born April 3rd 1807. Died August 11th 1881.' Across the foot of her gravestone, Medjuel placed a block of pink desert limestone from Palmyra, where they had spent the happiest days of her life. He carved her name in his own hand, in Bedouin Arabic characters: 'Madame Digby el Mezrab'.

He never remarried.

11

John Ruskin

1819–1900

The dictator of English artistic opinion in the second half of the nineteenth century was John Ruskin. An exceptionally beautiful man and a dazzling prose stylist, he was fearless in his public derision of accepted wisdom in art and morality (finding the two inseparable). 'Life without industry is guilt, and industry without art is brutality.' He supported his ever more revolutionary views with intellectual argument. Biting the hand that fed him, he was more extravagant than Marx in his denunciation of greed as the guiding principle of English life.

His first youthful passion had been the study of nature in painting – ironic, really, for his complete ignorance of a normal aspect of the nature of women would later cripple him as a man. Born into the upper middle class, the only child of a sherry merchant and a domineering mother, he grew up in Surrey. His parents adored one another and doted on John. He was educated at home, thus missing most boys' adolescent sexual experiments and exchanges of information about girls.

Their son's gifts led his parents to hope for a brilliant marriage for him. He was sixteen when his father's Spanish partner, Peter Domecq, came with his family to stay with the Ruskins. Mr and Mrs Ruskin would have welcomed a union with one of the Domecq daughters, and John fell madly in love with the second eldest, Adèle

Clotilde. (Her family called her Clotilde, but John called her Adèle because when he wrote love poems to her he could find no rhymes for Clotilde.) Her total indifference made him physically ill for three years. He had barely entered Oxford when he had to leave because of his heartbroken pining for Adèle. Two years later he learned she was engaged to be married and almost went out of his mind.

John's paternal grandfather had lived in Perth until he cut his throat in 1817. The Ruskins were good friends of the Gray family who had a substantial house near by and held considerable position in Perth. The friendship would continue throughout their lives. Mr Ruskin had no wish to be in Perth after the tragedy, and on the Grays' trips to London they always stayed with the Ruskins at Denmark Hill. On one such visit, John became sufficiently interested in Euphemia Gray to write for her his only fairy story, *The King of the Golden River*.

With her thick auburn hair, her flair for clothes, her beautiful dancing, clear-toned voice and what her headmistress called 'her artless affectionate disposition and her wish for improvement' (along with a light Scottish accent, which defied her private school's attempts to erase it), Effie was popular with both sexes. On the next visit, John fell in love with her.

Despite their families' close friendship, Mr and Mrs Ruskin were dismayed by the prospect of an engagement: they had expected a grander marriage for their beloved son. With offensive frankness, they cut short the visit from Effie and her father.

Six months later Effie was back, the Ruskins deeming it safe because by now another young lady had come into John's life. 'She is elegant and high bred and in a higher rank of life than our own,' Mrs Ruskin informed Effie on the evening of her arrival. In fact this paragon had already turned John down. Effie sized up the situation, writing to her mother that John 'adores his parents and will sacrifice himself for them, as I see, too easily.'

Soon Mr and Mrs Ruskin observed that John had fallen in love with Effie all over again and that she was flirting with him despite knowing how they felt. This time the parents trod carefully, fearful that their son would have another nervous breakdown if they continued overtly to reject Effie.

Was she in love with him? Certainly she was impressed by his growing reputation. He was the first to acclaim the painter J M W Turner, until then scorned, as a genius of Romanticism. John invited his aristocratic friends and acquaintances to the Ruskin home in Denmark Hill to see his collection of Turner's work and to meet Effie. All these things influenced her feelings for him. When the time came for her to move on to her other summer visits, she asked her father if she could come home to Perth instead.

John returned to Oxford, but he soon was so ill that his parents took him away again for a cure under the same doctor who had treated his acute suffering during his passion for Adèle. They finally capitulated and gave their permission for their son to marry Effie. When he went to Perth that autumn, he found her cold: she was proud and had been offended by his long silence. Nonetheless, by November she and John were engaged. She was eighteen, he 28.

The engagement lasted six months, during which time they did not meet. John's daily letters grew increasingly passionate. His mother wrote to him, 'As you say you love her more the oftener you write to her, may you not be in some degree surrounding her with imaginary charms – take care of this.'

Their plan was to have a short honeymoon in the Lake District and then embark on a three-month tour abroad with John's parents. He longed to show her the places he loved so well, Venice most of all, but was afraid to go with her alone lest 'the double excitement of possession and marriage travelling' be too much for her and make her ill. Effie's physical health had long been fragile.

On 10 April 1848, the marriage was performed according to Scottish custom in the Grays' drawing-room by the minister of the local church. The young couple spent their first night at Blair Athol. After so many months of anticipation, both were deliciously keyed-up as John undressed his bride. Abruptly he recoiled in horror.

In all the galleries he had visited, female nudes were discreetly veiled or depicted with the bare pudenda of pre-pubescent girls. The discovery of Effie's pubic hair revolted him, its auburn luxuriance increasing the shock. He thought she was uniquely deformed, and the trauma made him impotent – then and for ever.

Seven years later when Effie procured an annulment – almost unheard of in that day – two doctors examined her and pronounced her a virgin, despite her having shared a bed with John throughout.

Yet in their two long visits to Venice, it was evident that in many respects they were well matched. Their large rooms were in what is now the Danieli Hotel, facing the lagoon and five minutes' walk from the Doge's Palace. John made plain that his wife must be self-sufficient while he was engrossed in his daily studies and drawings of architecture and sculpture for his famous three-volume *The Stones of Venice*, happily spending an entire day sketching a capital of the Doge's Palace. They had invited Charlotte Ker, a neighbour in Perth, to come with them, and Effie's letters home were filled with spirited, vivid descriptions of her social life with Charlotte.

John's reputation and Effie's charm gave them entrée to the Italian nobility, and soon she was chattering away in Italian. Next she learned German. 'To get into Austrian society, it is indispensable,' she wrote to her mother. (When she did eventually get into Austrian society, she found that only French was spoken.)

But Effie was not a crude social-climber: she enjoyed herself wherever she went. Part of her attractiveness lay in her unself-consciousness. Papa Ruskin tut-tutted when he heard she walked bareheaded in San Marco Square. So well known was Effie through-out fashionable Venice that inevitably he was told that she often rowed a gondola herself on the Grand Canal, and he tut-tutted again.

An Austrian officer became her most devoted friend, and had she been ready to love someone other than John, it would probably have been this young Austrian. When she and her husband went together to military balls, John usually left at twelve, Effie and Charlotte dancing until two or three when the favoured Austrian would see them home. This social offence drew criticism, but neither Ruskin cared. John was proud of Effie's success and her speed in finding her way around these new worlds.

On their return to London, her grand social life continued. Of one luncheon she wrote merrily to her mother, 'Everyone was distinguished except myself.' Her noble hosts were delighted to have her without her celebrated husband, as John's hostility to social life made him dull in company.

Mr Ruskin commissioned two portraits of his daughter-in-law, which were hung in that year's Royal Academy exhibition, along with other paintings by a new Romantic movement known as the Pre-Raphaelite Brotherhood. After the exhibition, John undertook his championship of the Pre-Raphaelites, who until then had been venomously attacked by the critics. Thus he met J E Millais, a 24-year-old member of the Brotherhood who was enormously impressed by John's impassioned writing.

In 1853 all three went together to Scotland for a holiday. When back in London, Effie wrote to her mother, 'These last few days I have been sitting to Millais from immediately after breakfast to dinner, through all the afternoon till dark.' At the same time Millais was engaged on a portrait of John. The beautiful unfinished picture would mark a turning point in all their lives.

Effie, regarded by herself and others as too open ever to be secretive, without a word of warning to John returned to her parents. Three months later she scandalised society by seeking a divorce on the grounds of her husband's impotence. In that day the husband could easily block the procedure, and John could thus have put an end to a case that was deeply mortifying for him. Instead, he decided to defend it. He denied the impotency with which Effie charged him. In a statement he said:

> It may be thought strange that I *could* abstain from a woman who to most people was so attractive. But though her face was beautiful, her person was not formed to excite passion. On the contrary there were certain circumstances in her person which completely checked it.

Effie's version of the honeymoon confirms this. When at last she left him, she wrote to her father outlining the various reasons he had advanced for not consummating their marriage. Only after six years did he tell her his true reason: 'He had imagined women were quite different to what he saw I was and that the reason he did not make me his Wife was because he was disgusted with my person the first evening 10th April.' In other words, her pubic hair.

The humiliation and behind-the-fans mockery of John became unbearable, and he decided not to defend the suit. Soon after the annulment, when Ruskin was 36, Effie and John Millais both 25, she married the painter. Only then did Millais complete his sensitive portrait of John Ruskin.

In her second marriage, which produced eight children, Effie found fulfilment for all her talents. Millais went on to spectacular success. In his *Life* of his father, Millais's son gave not a hint that the Mrs John Ruskin whom the painter met in the Highlands in Chapter 5 was the same person as Miss Euphemia Gray whom he married three chapters later. Ruskin's biographers made only a cursory reference to his marriage.

John himself threw all his energies into his books, in which art criticism was now dominated by his moral argument against competition and self-interest. A burst of puritanism led him to destroy erotic drawings by his adored Turner, despite the fact that these had been left to the nation as part of the Turner Bequest. Ruskin taught at the Working Men's College in Red Lion Square and started a drawing school – a kind of one-man open university. Crowds flocked to his lectures. Unfortunately some of his devotees grew uneasy at the 'peculiar opinions' he recklessly included in his lectures, his social schemes becoming increasingly wild.

His dreams about young girls – which he described – also disturbed the academia. Twice he had to resign from Oxford. Rose La Touche, an Anglo-Irish girl, was eleven when he met her, eighteen when he proposed. But he could not accept her religious evangelism, her parents were opposed, and she died mad.

As Ruskin's health deteriorated and he grew reclusive, he wrote to the dead young woman, and intended describing her in the autobiography he never completed. For the last ten years of his life, he wrote nothing and rarely spoke, preferring to dwell in his dreams.

12

King Edward VII

1841–1910

It is as well that the first-born boy of Queen Victoria and Albert the Prince Consort was essentially good-natured. Neither parent bonded with Albert Edward. He was slow to learn and quite probably dyslexic in an age when that affliction was unrecognised, whereas his elder sister Vicky was clever and quick. The royal children were taught at home, and their parents wanted them to learn in tandem, resulting in Bertie's tantrums of frustration.

The Prince of Wales was seven-and-a-half when a 30-year-old tutor, Henry Birch, entered the household, 'a young, good-looking, amiable man, who was a tutor at Eton,' Prince Albert reported. The first thing Birch did was put Bertie in classes with his younger brother, Affie. Even so, Bertie's short attention span led to outbursts of frustration with his teacher, although he liked Birch with whom he spent more time than with anyone else.

It was companionship with boys his own age that he craved. Several from nearby Eton were invited to tea, but the presence of Prince Albert proved socially restricting, the visitors' moods not improved by having to call their sullen young host 'Sir'.

To Bertie's distress, Birch departed. The new tutor, Frederick Gibbs, managed to stay the course for eight years, despite Bertie's slowness to learn and consequent unruliness.

When he was nearly fifteen, Bertie and Vicky accompanied their parents on a State visit to Paris. The lovely Empress Eugénie treated the affection-starved youth with warmth and understanding. The Emperor made every event exciting. The perfumed ladies-in-waiting, their breasts half-bared, fussed over Bertie, and he learned he had a charm that he had not known was there. Having experienced only tension with his own parents, he told the Emperor, 'I would like to be your son.'

Bertie's tutor arranged for some chosen Eton boys and more tutors to accompany the Prince on a walking holiday in the Lake District. Assigned to write an essay on 'Friends and Flatterers', Bertie shrewdly said that a friend would 'tell you of your faults', while a flatterer would 'lead you into any imaginable vice'. Prince Albert was informed that his son's essay was 'not fully worked up' but 'right-minded'. Left to his own devices, Bertie led the Eton boys in driving a flock of sheep into Lake Windermere.

With the same young companions, he was sent to Albert's beloved Bonn to study for four months. On their first evening out, Bertie kissed a pretty girl. The boys' tutors tactfully omitted to mention this lapse, yet news of it got back to London, eventually reaching the ears of the Chancellor of the Exchequer, Gladstone, who moralised to his wife about 'this squalid little debauch'.

On the eve of his eighteenth birthday, Bertie's parents gave him Marlborough House as his new home. Not quite the emancipation it at first appeared, he was to be overseen and limited to male company until an arranged marriage could be effected. His father wrote him a long birthday letter of advice concluding, 'Life is composed of duties, and in the due, punctual and cheerful performance of them, the true Christian, true soldier, and true gentleman is recognised.' Bertie took the letter to his tutor and burst into tears.

Oxford was chosen for him in the company of six handpicked Christ Church undergraduates – the first time he had companions of his own age without a supervisor nearby. And then a second wonderful thing happened: in the long Oxford break he set off for the New World as representative of the Queen. He was a wild success. Forbidden any role at home, abroad he played the sovereign with charm and gusto. His unfailing courtesy to one and all across the social spectrum – as if he were paying a visit to a high personage – would become the Prince's trademark.

Following seven weeks in Canada, he was happy to move on to the United States, the first royal to visit there since the American Revolution. Travelling under the name of his subordinate title Baron Renfrew, he was welcomed almost everywhere he went, travelling in a splendid new carriage furnished by the Pennsylvania Railroad, crowds pouring out to see him and trying to shake his hand. After each stop, the assemblage sang loudly, 'Never will I forget you.' He was one of the first celebrities to be widely photographed by the new cameras. Yet none of his triumphs altered his parents' perception of him.

Within four days of his return, he was back at Oxford before beginning a stint at Cambridge, where one of his friends was Natty Rothschild. It was a great social breakthrough for the Rothschilds. No Jews were allowed as undergraduates at Oxford, and Natty was only the second generation permitted at Cambridge. Bertie's generally equable disposition was without a trace of anti-Semitism.

His father brought the news that in the Long Vacation, Bertie could have the military experience he had longed for. Sent to Curragh Camp in Kildare, he learned to command a battalion and manoeuvre a brigade in the field, all the time discomfited by his unearned commission in the Grenadier Guards. What he had wanted was camaraderie with young officers. Now that he had it, they quickly introduced him to the pleasures of lust. On returning to his room one evening, he found Nellie Clifden waiting in his bed. She was one of the harlots passed around by the trainees at Curragh Camp. Bertie took to sexual intercourse like a duck to water. Miraculously, Nellie Clifden did not carry gonorrhoea among her charms.

Meanwhile Bertie's parents were eager to marry him off, no matter that he was still nineteen. His elder sister Vicky, married to the Crown Prince of Prussia and living in Berlin, was delegated to find a suitable German bride. The most attractive candidate, Princess Alexandra, was Danish, alas, but Vicky could find no suitable German whom she liked as much.

Before matters could advance, trouble arose. On the eve of Bertie's twentieth birthday, the most hateful member of the human species, the candid friend, told Albert about his son's dalliance with Nellie Clifden. In the excessive propriety of Victoria's reign, Prince Albert viewed Nellie Clifden as moral defeat. In an almost insane letter to his son, he wrote that the subject had caused him 'the greatest pain I have yet felt in this life'. He raved on about how the harlot would point the finger at Bertie if she became pregnant:

> She can drag you into a Court of Law to force you to own it and there, with you in the witness box, she will be able to give before a greedy multitude disgusting details of your profligacy . . . Oh horrible prospect, which this person has in her power, any day to realise! and to break your poor parents' hearts.

His upbringing was enough to make the heir to the throne a psychotic, but Bertie's relaxed temperament saw him through. He wrote his father a contrite letter. Albert then went to Cambridge on a special train to talk with his son. As the two walked through the late November afternoon discussing whether Albert and God could forgive Bertie, Albert caught a chill and was unwell before the train got him back to Windsor. Although only 42, he was prematurely aged and susceptible to illness.

By 7 December, the doctors recognised his rash as typhoid. He died on 14 December, Bertie kneeling at the foot of the bed. Only later was Victoria able to record the scene in her diary:

> Two or three long but perfectly gentle breaths . . . the hand clasping mine and . . . *all, all*, was over . . . I stood up, kissed his dear heavenly forehead and called out in a bitter and agonising cry 'Oh! my dear Darling!' and then dropped on my knees in mute, distracted despair, unable to utter a word or shed a tear!

Typhoid notwithstanding, the heartbroken widow was convinced that the shock of the Nellie Clifden episode was what had killed her 'adored Angelic Husband'. A month after Albert's death, she instructed Vicky to tell others of the 'sad truth' that the affair at Curragh was what made 'beloved Papa so ill – for there must be no illusion about that – it was so; he was struck down – and I never can see B – without a shudder!'

Vicky wrote back defending Bertie to no avail. Her mother replied, '. . . if you had seen Fritz struck down, day by day get worse and finally die, I doubt if you could bear the sight of the one who was the cause . . .'

Bertie had two immediate responsibilities – to organise the funeral arrangements, his mother having retired to Osborne House to grieve, and to pack up and leave Cambridge. Despite having come to love Cambridge, he had to be in London to perform boring ceremonial duties in Victoria's place.

His mother's hostility continued long distance. When Mary Anne Disraeli suggested that the Prince of Wales must be a great comfort to her, Victoria replied, 'Comfort! Why I caught him smoking a cigar a fortnight after his father died!'

In 1862 Prime Minister Lord Palmerston, along with others, decided that the best thing would be for the Prince of Wales to travel, 'for things would only go from bad to worse if he remained at home.' These family advisers recognised that the fault was the Queen's 'as the poor boy asks nothing better than to devote himself to comforting his Mother.'

Following months of travel in the Near East, the Prince's party lingered in Europe. At a French ball held in his honour in one of the great houses, he was particularly attracted to an unmarried young Parisian who was staying overnight. Although she showed surprise at the Prince's attentions, his perseverence led her to tell him that she would place a rose outside her door so that he could identify her room. When he saw the rose, he knocked quietly. '*Entrez.*' He did. Sitting up in bed was a maid. No matter. She was charming.

After two years of negotiation, marriage neared. The Queen and Bertie and entourage set off for an uncle's country palace near Brussels, where a meeting had been arranged with the Danish royal family, after which Victoria would continue to Albert's birthplace in Coburg. The Prince of Wales and every member of the entourage – and, most importantly, the Queen herself – were enchanted by the slight, lovely eighteen-year-old Danish princess, Alexandra, unaffected and unconscious of her beauty.

Best of all, after the Prince had gone through the formalities of asking for her hand, he and Alix fell in love. (One of them would always remain in love.) For four days they rode together, and in the evenings Alix played the piano and sang, while her mother (at Victoria's insistence) sat in the next room.

In March, Alix and her family arrived for the wedding, the greatest London spectacle of the decade. On the wedding eve, Victoria took the young couple to the newly completed mausoleum at Frogmore in the grounds of Windsor. 'I opened the shrine and took them in. Alix was much moved and so was I. I said, "*He* gives you his blessing!"'

With Victoria now living at Windsor, the honeymoon could be at Osborne, the royal residence on the Isle of Wight. Anyone seeing the newlyweds on *Fairy* crossing the Solent would have known theirs was much more than a marriage of convenience. Albert had been anxious for Bertie to marry as the only way for him to avoid fornication. Now he and Alix together discovered techniques to enhance the marriage bed, for his previous experience was limited to the famous Nellie Clifden and the French maid.

As each believed that abstinence was the only method of contraception, Alix was soon pregnant. For the present, marriage was an idyll for both. Alix had no way of knowing that Bertie in his new-found independence from his parents would soon prefer the excitement of variety to a settled passion.

They had two establishments of their own: Marlborough House near St James's Palace, and Sandringham in Norfolk. When Sandringham's redecoration was completed, Bertie invited his mother to come and tour the house. Only when she arrived did he remember the Smoking Room. But when the Queen reached it, she sailed past, for on the door was a sign with the scrawled words: 'Lavatory. Under Repair.'

Queen Victoria still refused to allow her son a role in government. When Prussia invaded disputed Danish provinces, the Foreign Secretary, Lord Russell, was anxious for the heir to the throne to see official dispatches relating to the crisis. The Queen would have none of it: she would not permit the Prince to have a 'separate and independent communication with the Government.' *She* would show him what she wanted him to see.

Despite her insistence that he remain Albert Edward, Bertie defeated her by his amiable reasonableness. Some skilful leaking from Marlborough House led American newspapers to claim: 'The name by which the Prince of Wales will ascend the throne will be King Edward the Seventh.' No denial was issued.

Because Alix was pregnant with her third child, she could not accompany her husband to the magnificent wedding of the Grand Duke Alexander in St Petersburg. It has to be said that Bertie welcomed his freedom. By the end of the second splendid ball, he had learned from the ladies in deep décolletage that he could bed virtually any woman he wanted.

Soon after his return to England, it became evident that Alix was in for a difficult childbirth. When rheumatic fever was diagnosed, only a third telegram persuaded her husband to leave the Windsor Races and return to Marlborough House. Alix gave birth without the mercy of chloroform, as the doctors thought her too weak to risk it. (No comment.)

For a time the Prince demonstrated his concern and affection. He had his desk moved into her bedroom suite so he could write letters beside her bed and gossip with her. He showed his devotion, and she knew he loved her 'the best'. But after some days of constancy, restlessness overtook him.

Who is to say how many men with such opportunities for philandering would resist them? Bertie did not even try.

Sometimes it seemed as if this man of 25 was making up for his emotionally impoverished childhood. So thrilled was he when he plunged into a fire in his children's nursery and put it out, that he asked the Captain of the Metropolitan Fire Brigade to let him know of any large fires in London so he could lend a hand. He was with the firemen at the blazing El Dorado music hall in Leicester Square. He encouraged his playboy friends to race to other scenes of fire to help.

Alix's ghastly third labour left her convalescent for a long time, and when at last she could get out of her wheelchair, she found that the rheumatic fever had crippled one leg. With her love for her husband to motivate her, she taught herself to walk with a gliding motion to conceal what became known as the 'Alexandra limp'.

As well she was becoming increasingly deaf, and this enabled the Prince to enjoy continuous social forays on his own. His taste for hunting caused uproar among farmers wherever he rode. On one occasion when pursuing a deer, he led a party of horsemen for 24 miles through Wembley and Wormwood Scrubs to the goods yard at Paddington Station, where to the horror of porters and guards the deer was dispatched by the hunters – after which the Prince left his mount with his friends and hopped on a train back to Windsor.

Members of the royal household were highly critical of the Prince's 'callous neglect' of his wife. Some of his self-centred frivolity was a result of Victoria's stubborn refusal to allow the heir apparent any role in Government. Alix, recovered and ravishingly beautiful, wearing elegant clothes that emphasised her hourglass waist, a nine-strand pearl choker around her slender throat, accompanied the Prince on a number of public occasions. But more and more her deafness led her to live at Sandringham and make long visits to Denmark. She could always rely on her husband to be at the station to meet her on her return.

With so many sexual affairs in Bertie's life, it was inevitable that some would reach the limelight. Having 'consoled' the widowed Lady Susan Vane Tempest for four years, the Prince was less than pleased to receive a letter from her closest friend telling him that 'the facts in question', which she knew had been revealed to him earlier that summer, were now within two or three months of 'the crisis'.

'I dread,' the close friend continued in a rather sinister fashion, 'some catastrophe that may awaken public attention to facts which have hitherto been confined to *my* knowledge . . . I do not think it possible to surmount all difficulties incident to the event in question under the sum of two hundred and fifty pounds at the least . . .'

In the same post was a letter that errant men dread. Lady Susan wrote, 'I cannot tell your Royal Highness how *utterly miserable* I am . . . You have shown me *so much* kindness for the last four years that I cannot understand your having twice been in London for two days without coming to see me. What have I done to offend you?' Lady Susan assured the Prince that she had done her best 'to obey the orders your Royal Highness gave me the last time I had the happiness

Left: The Prince Regent, 'Prinny' (later King George IV) by Sir Thomas Lawrence, *c.* 1814
Clever, witty, gifted, he lost track of his mistresses and his exorbitant debts.

Right: Frances, Countess of Jersey An engraving after D. Gardiner (*c.* 1870)
The well-born and most manipulative of Prinny's married mistresses.

Left: Lord Byron by Thomas Phillips
Of all his lovers, female and male, Byron's half-sister was the only one he loved.

Opposite page

Main photograph: 'Bertie', Prince of Wales (later King Edward VII), 1870
Amiable, politically informed, restless, Bertie soon learned he could bed virtually any woman he wished.

Top inset: 'Daisy', Countess of Warwick (Lafayette, 1898)
Bertie called her, 'My own darling Daisy wife.' (His real wife was the lovely Princess Alix.)

Bottom inset: Lillie Langtry, 'The Jersey Lily'
Bertie's passion for Lillie abated as she became increasingly inconvenient. Painting by Henry van der Weyde, 1885.

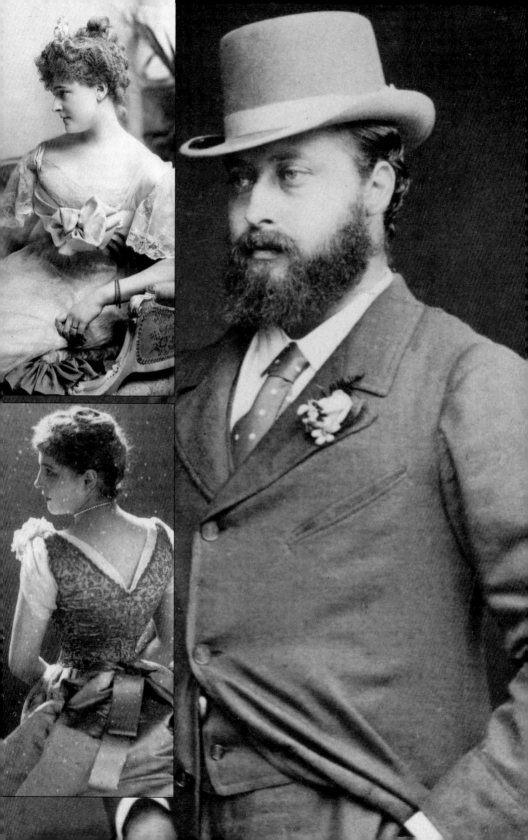

Oscar Wilde and 'Bosie', Lord Alfred Douglas (1885)
Never without courage, at his trial Wilde delivered a magnificent defence of 'the love that dare not speak its name.'

The Duke and Duchess of Windsor followed by Jimmy Donahue, *c.* **1952**
Jimmy was a New York society homosexual twenty years younger than the Duchess. He gave her the first sexual ecstasy she had known.

Right: Robert Boothby MP (later Lord Boothby), 1949
Other men increasingly saw him as a rascal. 'All those poor chumps who had got married and had to pay for their fun resented the fact that Boothby didn't,' explained AJP Taylor.

Below: Fatty Arbuckle, 1921
Hollywood's highest paid star in 1921, the comedian paid for his fun in a big way: he was charged with rape and murder.

of seeing you [the unspecified order was an abortion], but the answer was "*too late* and *too* dangerous".'

I am afraid that Bertie treated these missives in a cavalier manner. The doctor who had declined to perform the abortion was the Prince's own physician and a tremendous snob; the Prince persuaded Prime Minister Gladstone to give the doctor a knighthood. The financial matter was handed over to Bertie's loyal and discreet advisers. When the month of 'the crisis' arrived, he went off to Cavalry Brigade manoeuvres for the first time in two years. The last we hear of Lady Susan is her death three years later, though it was often remarked among the aristocracy that her child was the spitting image of the Prince.

Since the days of Henry IV, no Prince of Wales had ever been summoned before a Court of Justice. Alas, this one became entangled with Lady Mordaunt, who went mad after the birth of a boy who appeared to be blind. She told her husband that he was not responsible for the child because she had behaved very wickedly with a number of other men, including the Prince of Wales, 'often and in open day'.

Despite her evident lunacy, Sir Charles Mordaunt MP chose to take her at her word and serve a writ for divorce. During the trial it transpired that the Prince had several times visited Lady Mordaunt whom he had known since childhood, and he had written letters to her, innocuous but embarrassing. Anti-monarchists rubbed their hands in gleeful anticipation.

In the witness box, Bertie conducted himself with aplomb, answering the questions with brevity: 'I was', 'I did', 'I did also', 'I have', 'I do', 'There was', 'I believe so', 'She was', and 'It is so'. Finally, as the packed courtroom waited intently, the QC said, 'I have only one more question to trouble your Royal Highness with. Has there ever been any improper familiarity or criminal act between yourself and Lady Mordaunt?'

In a firm voice, 'There has not.'

The spectators, apart from the anti-monarchists, burst into wild applause and had to be admonished by the presiding judge.

Bertie could not get enough of travelling. Boar-hunting in India left young Prince Louis of Battenberg with a fractured collarbone;

Lord Beresford lost some teeth; Lord Suffield was injured by his own spear. Only Bertie, no less involved, and riding well despite his weight, came through unscathed. Tigers were felled in abundance, elephants shot.

While this carnage was causing criticism at home, in India the Prince outraged the white colonials because he failed to realise they were 'superior to everything else in creation'. They were convinced that he was snubbing them and spoiling the natives. Otherwise his India trip was judged a success.

As the royal party moved on to Nepal, guns at the ready, word came from London that indiscreet letters to the promiscuous Lady Aylesford had surfaced, and half the party had to return urgently to attend divorce proceedings involving them. Hoping he would not be subpoenaed to give evidence in another divorce suit, the Prince continued with his tour. On the first day in Nepal, six more tigers fell to his rifle.

Greed was a pronounced quality in the mature Prince of Wales. Just as one woman could not suffice him, the more delicious food offered to him, the happier he was. At Sandringham, his custom was to eat his usual vast breakfast in his bedroom suite while his guests ate downstairs. At 10.30 he would turn up in boots and tweeds for a late morning's shooting, interrupted long enough to drink hot soup brought in tureens.

A few hours into the hunt, a four-course lunch was served in a covered marquee. Like his mother, the Prince could eat substantial meals in a short time, and as soon as he had finished, the dishes were removed, whether anyone else in the party had finished or not. After that, bearers of baskets of iced champagne kept up with the hunters as best they could.

Shooting ended in time for an enormous tea, followed a few hours later by a ten-course dinner, usually starting with oysters, prawns, beef and lamb, over which the willowy Alix presided. By midnight the Prince was ready for another large repast. Always loath to be alone, he then sat up all night at cards, fortifying himself with brandy and cigars. At 30, the girth of the once slender Prince caused widespread comment, though it in no way inhibited his promiscuity.

Alix's sixth child died soon after birth, and sexual relations with her husband apparently ceased. Prince Albert was proved right: as soon as the marital bed lost its sex appeal for Bertie, he embraced fornication with unabating relish. His trips to Paris were frequent, providing as they did many *grandes horizontales*, including the erotic tragedienne Sarah Bernhardt. Over the years, she continued to return to his bed.

He had not seen the last of subpoenas. The Tranby Croft case, also known as the Baccarat case, concerned a subject more emotive than adultery – cheating at cards. While attending the St Leger race, the Prince was a guest at an Italianate mansion called Tranby Croft, where he organised a game of baccarat in the evenings. Another guest, Sir William Gordon-Cunning, was seen to be cheating. Once again the Prince had to appear in a witness box.

Uproar ensued. The Prince was, of course, innocent of cheating, but gambling at baccarat was banned. Asking to play it in a private house was normally considered deeply discourteous to the host. The press, particularly the religious press, had a heyday. The Queen publicly deplored her son's gambling and the company he kept.

Other members of the public thought the Prince a fine fellow. They had never taken to the Prince Consort's impeccable rectitude. Bertie, who made no pretence at virtue, was greatly loved. What nobody could say was that he was a hypocrite.

In 1877, he began his liaison with Lillie Langtry, a 23-year-old actress who had more ambition than talent. Arriving from Belfast with her dull well-to-do husband, she was instantly pursued by photographers and painters. Within weeks she beguiled Londoners from penny-postcard stands.

Needless to say, the Prince of Wales, who already knew her face, met her at a supper party. No explanation was required when he called on her the next day. Soon when Mrs Langtry rode side-saddle through Hyde Park, her black riding habit appearing to be sewn on her, the Prince of Wales rode beside her. Men and women stood on benches to gaze at 'the Jersey Lily', her soubriquet since John Millais painted her portrait under that name.

Bertie built a house for her atop a cliff near Bournemouth, a watering place for society. Its large bedroom for him included his monogrammed brushes on a bureau. Friends came and went unselfconsciously.

The Prince arranged for her to attend a presentation at Buckingham Palace with her husband: Victoria wanted to meet the most famous woman in England, and as Lillie was not divorced, there was no protocol problem. Coolly Bertie stood with his mother and Alix while his number-one mistress was presented to the Queen.

What Lillie did not realise was that despite the openness of their relationship, there were limits. At a society charity bazaar in the Albert Hall, she presided at a refreshment stall. To be served a cup of tea by her hands cost a gentleman five shillings. For an extra guinea – 21 more shillings – she would take the first sip, providing a sexual frisson for her admirer.

When the Prince and Princess of Wales arrived at the stall with their daughters, Lillie poured tea and, unasked, put her lips to his cup. The Prince set down the cup untasted. 'I should like a clean one, please,' he said curtly. Accepting another, he took a perfunctory taste, set down some coins and walked away. While enamoured of Lillie, in public he remained loyal to Alix.

Generous with her favours, Lillie became pregnant at a time which indicated that Louis, Prince of Battenberg, the Prince of Wales's cousin, was the father. Bertie was rather pleased to have an excuse to loosen his bonds with her, as she was becoming increasingly inconvenient. In addition, Sarah Bernhardt was again accessible, and he still found her enchanting. Though he continued to give moral support to Lillie in her unwanted pregnancy, the flames of passion were no more.

His roving eye took much pleasure in American women. 'They are original and bring a little fresh air into Society. They are livelier, better educated and less hampered by etiquette,' he said.

Be that as it may, Lady Brooke – 'Daisy' – was born an English aristocrat, as reckless as she was beautiful. Lord Brooke, whose main interest fortunately was fishing, took as relaxed an attitude to his wife's infidelities as he did to her eventual conversion to Socialism. She was no more than acquainted with the Prince, but on finding herself in a social embarrassment, Daisy decided to appeal to him, arranging an interview at Marlborough House.

At 28 she was slender, blooming, stunning. The Prince was approaching 50. 'He was charmingly courteous to me,' she wrote later, '. . . and suddenly I saw him looking at me in a way all women understand. I knew I had won, so I asked him to tea.'

Before long, he gave her a gold ring inscribed 'V & A', which his parents had given him as a confirmation present. According to the customs attending royalty, when the Prince was a guest at a country house, Lord and Lady Brooke were invited and given separate bedrooms so that the Prince could call on his inamorata at night. By now the press was printing gossip about them – though separating their names by a semi-colon.

When the Prince visited spas on the Riviera, Lady Brooke was at a villa nearby. He called her 'my own darling Daisy wife'. She sailed with him at Cowes; they attended the races together; he accompanied her when she shopped at elegant couturiers; she was at balls at Marlborough House and wherever the Prince was invited.

When Lord Brooke succeeded to Warwick Castle, overlooking the Avon, the new Countess of Warwick remodelled a wing to give the Prince of Wales his own suite next to her bedroom and dressing room.

Alix faced many tribulations. Her eldest son, Eddy, died from pneumonia just after his 28th birthday. Eddy was backward from birth, bisexual, improbably rumoured to be Jack the Ripper, but Alix adored him. Colonel Oliver Montagu, commander of the Royal Horse Guards and an equerry to the Prince of Wales, now died at 48. He had served Alix with loyalty and a love just short of sexual expression. She was left desperately lonely.

Although Bertie and Daisy did not know it at the time, a lavish costume ball she gave at Warwick Castle in February 1895 was the beginning of the end of their liaison. The Socialist weekly, the *Clarion*, launched a stinging attack on the waste of resources for a 'few hours' silly masquerade' while too many citizens were worn down by grinding poverty.

Indignantly, Daisy took a train to London and marched off to the *Clarion*'s office to confront its editor, Robert Blatchford. Her ball, she told him, had provided work for half the county. 'Will you sit down,' he said, 'while I explain to you how mistaken you are about the real effect of luxury?'

She did not at once grasp all he said about the difference between productive and unproductive labour, but the seed was planted. Her broodings about Socialism began on the train back to Warwick Castle.

Before long she arranged a luncheon for the Prince to meet the crusading editor, W T Stead. Although Bertie came along only to please her, when she left them alone, the two men enjoyed exchanging viewpoints. The Crown Prince read little except the newspapers and would never be thought of as an intellectual like his youngest brother Leopold, the haemophiliac in the family, but he would have had no difficulty holding his own with the infamous radical.

For Bertie took a real interest in the world outside his circle and was politically informed. The Imperial Institute was his idea. A serious supporter of the visual arts, he was closely involved with English musical life, and was particularly fond of opera. He was not oblivious to the atrocious housing of the working classes, and was appalled when he broke loose from his minders to inspect slums. His most important speech in the House of Lords concerned the 'perfectly disgraceful' living conditions of the poor. Despite the Prince's raffish reputation, Prime Minister Gladstone longed to deal with him instead of the too often impossible Victoria.

Yet the Prince did not really want to spend his time with his mistress talking about the social evils that her new creed, Socialism, was addressing. He began to find Lady Warwick's limitless energy a little tiring. Nor was their sexual pleasure what it had been. His corpulence now interfered with passion, no matter that various methods were devised to approach intercourse. His affair with his darling Daisy began winding down.

Enter Mrs Keppel.

Having seen her at a distance, when she reappeared at the Sandown races, he asked for an introduction. She was 29 to his 56, tall with a delectable bosom, her thick chestnut hair heaped atop her head. Her voice soft and throaty, enchanted him, and she smoked cigarettes through an elegant long holder. She was widely and discreetly experienced with international financiers and other useful men, to whom her husband, Colonel George Keppel, turned a blind eye. The Prince sacrificed watching the horses to spend the day alone with 'Mrs George'.

In July 1898, he asked Vita Sackville-West if he and Alix could visit Knole House, along with the Countess of Warwick and 'his new friend the Hon Mrs G Keppel'. Somewhat daunted by having the Prince bring his wife and ex-mistress and presumed new mistress all at the same time, Vita took evasive action. 'He acquiesced and was nice about it,' she reported. He arrived with Alix alone and their usual entourage.

Alice Keppel captured his heart by her calm sex appeal, her kindness and her skill in conducting a triangular relationship with Alix. (Her great-granddaughter is Camilla Parker Bowles.) She had everything that Bertie wanted at this time in his life, when his obesity made his sexual desire stronger than his priapic prowess of yore. And she made an excellent partner at bridge, society's favourite card game in the nineties, the Tranby Croft scandal having eclipsed baccarat. It was widely remarked that the Prince was always in a congenial mood when Mrs George was present.

The Keppels had a perfectly good house in Belgravia, but Bertie decided that Mrs George's new status required a more elegant address in Portman Square, for which, of course, he would meet the costs. Separate bedrooms and bathrooms were tactfully arranged for husband and wife. Each day when the obliging Colonel had departed for his club, a green brougham (the Prince's least ostentatious carriage) drew up in Portman Square. Even when Mrs George was advanced in a pregnancy sired by the Colonel, the green brougham stood outside the door.

As Queen Victoria aged, her heir became less compliant to her demands. She had never liked Prime Minister Gladstone, and when he died at 89, the Prince asked the widow if he could be a pall-bearer. Learning of it, the Queen sent an outraged telegram from Balmoral asking by what precedent and by whose advice he proposed to be a pall-bearer. He replied tersely that there was no precedent and that he had taken no one's advice. Probably only Mrs Keppel knew whether he was genuinely fond of Gladstone or was trying to exasperate his mother. He even kissed the widow's hand before dispatching a more equable telegram to the Queen: 'Funeral just over, a most impressive and touching sight, very simple and dignified. Bertie.'

Despite his long neglect of Lady Susan, the Prince normally made sure his former intimates were provided for. He looked after the Court interests of Daisy Warwick's daughter and other ex-mistresses. Meanwhile Alix made herself scarce as the new love affair developed.

In January 1901, the Prince and the rest of the Royal Family gathered at Osborne House for the ancient Queen's impending death. Bertie had been heir apparent for sixty years. When the tracheal rales foreshadowing the end began, Victoria murmured to him: 'Kiss my face.'

Her small coffin was borne on *Alberta* through two lines of warships stretching from the Isle of Wight to Portsmouth, before the final journey to Windsor for the military funeral she wanted. Standing on the bridge of a cruiser following *Alberta*, the new sovereign demanded to know why the Royal Standard was flying at half mast. 'The Queen is dead, sir,' was all that the officer could find to say. 'The King of England lives,' replied His Majesty, and the flag was hoisted.

Winston Churchill wrote a rather unpleasant letter to his mother:

A great and solemn event: but I am curious about the King. Will it entirely revolutionise his way of life? Will he sell his horses and scatter his Jews or will Reuben Sassoon [one of an exotic Jewish family who were among Bertie's close companions] be enshrined among the crown jewels and other regalia? Will he become desperately serious? Will he continue to be friendly to you? Will the Keppel be appointed 1st Lady of the Bedchamber . . . I am glad he has his innings at last, and most interested to watch how he plays it . . .'

Punch, however, tossing aside its decades of criticism, pictured 'Mr Punch' saying to the sovereign, 'Your coronation awaits your Majesty's pleasure, but you are already crowned in the hearts of your people.'

At the coronation in Westminster Abbey, the new Queen was radiant, despite her long-held fear of reigning. Watching the ceremonies from what became known as 'the King's loose box' sat Alice Keppel and four of Bertie's former mistresses: Sarah Bernhardt, Lillie Langtry, Daisy Warwick, and the Italian Olga Alberta Caracciolo.

To Churchill's surprise, Bertie was an effective and popular monarch. He was an excellent linguist and informed on foreign affairs. By his enthusiastic visits to Continental capitals, he proved a sucessful middle man between hostile governments. His pro-French sympathies accorded well with Foreign Secretary Edward Grey's policies. He loved the role of constitutional monarch, yet he also understood the limits of royal authority.

Nine years after he became King, his health let him down: his pleasure in food and drink and smoking had taken their toll. Ill with bronchitis, he told the doctors who struggled in vain to keep him in bed, 'I shall not give in.' The Queen was visiting her brother the King of Greece. Alice Keppel and two friends played bridge with Bertie daily, Alice hiding her distress as she watched his condition worsen.

Alix, summoned home, arrived at Victoria Station and for the first time in their marriage he was not there to meet her; she feared the worst. She found him sitting in a chair, wearing a frock coat to receive his financial counsellor and battling for breath, defiantly lighting a large cigar he could not smoke. Later that day, semi-conscious in his chair, he learned that his horse, Witch of the Air, had won the Two-Year-Old Plate at Kempton Park. 'I am very glad,' he said, and lapsed into a coma.

In his final hours, Alice Keppel sent the Queen a letter that Bertie had written to her in 1901 before undergoing surgery for appendicitis. If he were dying, he wrote, he would want to say farewell to her, and he was 'convinced that all those who have any affection for me will carry out the wishes which I have expressed in these lines'.

The heroic Alix sent for her, and she was driven to Buckingham Palace where the Queen shook hands with her stiffly. 'I am sure you have always had a good influence over him,' Alix said and walked to the window.

In his bedroom, Mrs Keppel found the King comatose, and he did not recognise her. For the first time anyone could remember, she lost control of herself and had to be led from the room. He died that night.

Eight days would pass before Alix let him be taken from her. 'He was so wonderfully preserved,' she said later. 'It must have been the oxygen they gave him before he died. It was most extraordinary.' She summoned the King's lifelong friend and confidant, Viscount Esher, to say farewell. He found her moving quietly about the bedroom as if Bertie were asleep, his hats hanging on pegs where he had last put them.

She talked to Esher for half an hour 'with tenderness which betrayed all the love in her soul, and the oh! so natural feeling that she had got him there altogether to herself. In a way she seemed, and is, I am convinced, happy – it is the womanly happiness of complete possession of the man who was the love of her youth, and – as I fervently believe – of all her life.'

After the death rituals were completed – the lying-in-state at Westminster Hall, the state funeral in St George's Chapel at Windsor – Mrs Keppel's writing paper, like the Queen's, was bordered in black.

13

Oscar Wilde

1854–1900

'Oscar Wilde's greatest play was his own life,' remarked Frank Harris, braggart writer and editor. 'It was a five-act tragedy with Greek implications and he was its most ardent spectator.'

Act I. Oscar's golden childhood began in Dublin. His profligate father was a distinguished eye and ear surgeon, his mother an archdeacon's daughter who published her poems under the name 'Speranza'. Her salon was the most famous in Dublin.

At school in Enniskillen, Oscar's friends marvelled that he never seemed to do any work yet walked away with the prizes. He won scholarships to Trinity College, Dublin, and Oxford where he eschewed sport and all physical exercise and went on winning academia's prizes.

An apostle of the Aesthetic Movement which stemmed from Keats and the Pre-Raphaelites, he found its 'art for art's sake' suited to his temperament and talents. In open rebellion against the tastes of the majority, he was a debonair and popular figure at Oxford, admired for his unconventionality and high spirits, his generous nature and sparkling conversation. A collector of blue china and peacock feathers, he wore long hair, a languishing look, cobwebby shirts and velvet breeches – all too much for Oxford's philistines, who wrecked his rooms and threw him in the Cherwell.

Act II. Determined to be famous or infamous, he set off for London where his first book of poems was published, and his self-presentation as the arch-dilettante, a sunflower in his buttonhole, took London society by storm. His lover Frank Miles eased his entry into the cliques that frequented London's theatre circuit. Gilbert and Sullivan's opera *Patience* was so closely modelled on Wilde that in 1882 he went to America to publicise it in a succession of one-man shows. He arrived in New York with a 28-year old's vigour, and his tour was a triumph of showmanship, starting with his reply to the customs officer when asked if he had anything to declare: 'Only my genius.'

The Americans refused to take his dandyism seriously, and his ebullience and elegance made each show a spectacular success. In Boston he complained that he was disappointed by the Atlantic Ocean. In Salt Lake City he teased the Mormons about their polygamy. In Leadville he discoursed with miners on the secret of Botticelli, and descended into the silver mine, 'graceful even in a bucket', to open with a silver drill a new lode named 'Oscar' in his honour.

Act III. When he returned to England, having tired of being the Great Aesthete he now went about in fairly normal dress, perhaps with a practical eye to his life. For in 1884, he married Constance Lloyd, the violet-eyed rich daughter of a Dublin barrister. They settled in Chelsea. When their first son was born, Oscar's vermilion study decorated with peacock feathers became a night nursery.

For a time he seemed to have adjusted to domesticity, despite remarking that 'women spoil every romance by trying to make it last forever.' When Constance was pregnant with their second child, he found himself repelled by her body. Though husband and wife remained on good terms, their sexual relations were never restored. After his short period of virtue, he began again to dally with what he described as 'the raptures and roses of vice'.

At the same time, *The Picture of Dorian Gray*, his only novel, was published and caused a sensation: homosexuality was a scarcely veiled theme. In its preface Wilde wrote, 'There is no such thing as a moral or an immoral book. Books are well written or badly written. That is all.' Nonetheless it was almost universally condemned as a 'tale spawned from the leprous literature of the French decadents.'

In his anger at English critics for moralising rather than sticking to their brief, he went to Paris and wrote *Salomé*, a scandalous one-act tragedy which was produced by Sarah Bernhardt in Paris, but banned by the Lord Chamberlain in London. It was never performed on the English stage in Wilde's lifetime.

He returned to London to supervise rehearsals for *Lady Windermere's Fan*, the first of his brilliantly successful comedies of manners, followed by *A Woman of No Importance*. They served as a catalyst in creating the modern era; he used wit and humour to force Victorian society to re-examine its hypocrisies and the arbitrariness of many moral and social taboos. George Bernard Shaw wrote that Wilde's *An Ideal Husband* had 'the property of making his critics dull. Mr Wilde is to me our only thorough playwright.'

'Do you want to know the great drama of my life?' Wilde asked André Gide. 'It's that I put my genius into my life; all I've put into my works is my talent.' But even as he said it, the rumours about his personal life were threatening to overwhelm him.

Act IV. In 1893, during this his peak period, he met Lord Alfred Douglas, known as 'Bosie'. The young man aroused in Wilde emotions he had not experienced in his many other relationships. He was besotted with Bosie. Although this intense love affair consumed time and energy, he wrote what many consider his masterpiece, *The Importance of Being Earnest*, at this time; it opened in February 1895 to huge acclaim.

Weeks later, Bosie's father, the half-mad Marquis of Queensberry, who had persistently and publicly harassed Wilde, left his card at Oscar's club. On it was written his accusation that Wilde was 'a somdomite' [sic]. Any libel lawyer would have advised Oscar to do nothing: people have short memories unless a charge is brought to court. But Bosie was conducting his own battles with his father, and he persuaded Oscar to sue for libel.

The case came to court on 3 April 1895. Lord Queensberry's lawyers pitched their defence against Wilde's 'immoral, corrupting works' as well as his past relationships with working-class youths. Wilde's case against Queensberry was lost. Immediately afterwards, Oscar was arrested.

His trial for gross indecency began three weeks later. A succession of youths testified to presents and flirtations and 'acts of sodomy', which Wilde denied, though he readily admitted he was 'a lover of youth'. Once again his works as well as his private conduct were on trial. Never without courage, he delivered a magnificent defence of the 'love that dare not speak its name', and when he finished, the gallery burst into applause.

Friends urged him to leave at once for the Continent where sexual mores were more tolerant, but he said he would accept with dignity the consequences of his actions. Found guilty, he received the maximum sentence of two years' hard labour. The judge claimed it was the worst case he had ever tried. At forty, Wilde was incarcerated in Reading Gaol.

Act V. Constance stood by her husband throughout. She changed her surname to Holland and fled to the Continent, from where she sent him money. Prison was a harrowing experience for a man of Oscar's sensitive temperament. He started writing a 30,000-word letter, *De Profundis*, which is both a defence and a confession. In it he poured out his bitterness towards Lord Alfred who still 'walked free among the flowers'. It concludes: 'You came to me to learn the Pleasures of Life and the Pleasures of Art. Perhaps I am chosen to teach you something much more wonderful, the meaning of Sorrow and its beauty.'

After Wilde's release in 1897, he could not resist responding to a letter from his 'darling boy'. He changed his name, and in his wanderer's exile on the Continent, Bosie sometimes joined him. Constance continued to send money.

His final poem, *The Ballad of Reading Gaol*, was a grim account of prison brutality, a plea for reform. For me it is his most poignant and sincere work.

> And I and all the souls in pain
> Who tramped the other ring,
> Forgot if we ourselves had done
> A great or little thing,
> And watched with gaze of dull amaze
> The man who had to swing.

Wilde was broken. At the end of three years of absinthe and reckless sex, he was an almost unrecognisable derelict. He received the rites of the Roman Catholic church in a small left-bank hotel in Paris and died of cerebral meningitis. He was 46.

He was buried in the cemetery of Bagneux just outside the city. Lord Alfred Douglas was chief mourner.

14

Colonel Alfred Redl

1864–1913

Colonel Alfred Redl, the most famous counter-intelligence officer in the last days of the Austro-Hungarian Empire, began life sharing a bedroom with his thirteen siblings. His father was a minor freight clerk for the state railway which provided free housing and moved them about in the Austrian province of Galicia. Wherever they lived stank of cabbage and babies.

Alfred was of small build and more quiet than the rest. Blond, blue-eyed, with even white teeth, this apparently good boy could lie and swindle and successfully put the blame for his misdemeanours on one of his noisier siblings. Highly intelligent, he discovered at school that correct answers were great levellers of society.

The Lemberg army garrison was active in those years, and at fourteen Alfred easily passed the exams to cadet school, which was free. Obsessively seeking to break with his cabbage soup and smelly-babies past, at seventeen he chose a military career. He never looked back.

Some cadets thought the school a prison, but Alfred liked it: new clothes, the first he had ever owned, healthy food, a curriculum that taught you how to calculate. When the instructor called for solutions, Alfred provided them. At night when the dormitory was dark, another cadet called Hans led Alfred to the mattress room where a candle revealed boys writhing in sexual delight. Hans introduced

Alfred to exquisite physical pleasure. When all the boys were finished, they tiptoed back to the dormitory.

Sometimes Alfred looked across the classroom at Hans and tried to recapture the joy of their last night in the storeroom – in vain. Nor could he anticipate the next time. Instead he focused on his schoolwork to win the instructor's approval. He applied the same excluding concentration to each of his compartments.

In front of a mirror he practised the manner with which he accepted compliments from his teachers: a quick, shy smile before turning away in feigned embarrassment. If he failed at anything, his first instinct was to blame another, and when that proved impossible, his anger at his own shortcoming was all-consuming.

When he made a poor parry in fencing, he said that the floor had caused him to slip. The instructor replied coldly: 'You slipped because you were careless.' Alfred frowned slightly and said nothing. He practised the parry until he had mastered it, and he never ceased hating the man.

One night he discovered that Hans had a new lover. Alfred returned to his own bed, where, as it was dark and no one could see him, he cried himself to sleep. He never spoke to Hans again.

After he was commissioned, Lieutenant Redl performed extra duties with his usual thoroughness. 'Damn' fine officer' observed the senior military.

He was summoned to the Colonel who ordered him to sit down. 'Smoke? Cigarette? Cigar?'

'Cigar, sir, if I may.'

'Quite right,' said the Colonel. 'The officer's proper smoke. You use cigarettes as well?'

'Never, sir.'

When the Colonel told him he had been promoted to the General Staff as Battalion Adjutant, Alfred looked down. 'I do not know what to say, sir.'

'Nothing to say, Redl. You have earned it.'

Outside, Alfred gave a small smile, took out his cigarette case and lit up.

He was very popular with his comrades, making dry jokes as he picked up his share of bar bills. His well-cut uniform, paid for by borrowing from the Jewish moneylenders who swarmed about the garrison, was always immaculate, his boots gleaming. In frequent visits to a bordello, he acquired a reputation for virility, only his first prostitute knowing he had to be taught what to do with a woman and then found it infinitely less fulfilling than sex with men. The prostitute had been kind in her lessons, yet his climax with her brought to Alfred's mind the smell of babies and cabbage soup.

Intuitively he sensed which of his comrades shared his sexual taste, so embarrassment was avoided. He knew the dangers if his passion reached the ears of senior officers, but he counted on his intelligence to outwit them.

Then an unexpected thing happened: at a circus, he fell in love with Maria Montessi, 'the world's greatest acrobatic rider'. He waited outside her dressing room, and when she emerged he invited her to a late supper. To his delight, she accepted.

After their love-making he lay content, and while she slept he studied her small-breasted lithe body, not so different from a boy's muscular body. He showed her off to his friends, and they warmed to her. He discussed marriage with the gentle-faced Maria who always said the right thing; he knew she would be good for him.

She was expensive, and Alfred spent much of his borrowed money on their week of love. When the circus folded its tent to move on, he gave her a small diamond. Yet he did not miss Maria.

Soon afterwards, he noticed an unusual sore. 'I am sorry to have to tell you, Redl,' the doctor said, 'but you have syphilis.' He caught Alfred as he fainted. When he came round, he said, 'I spent a week with a circus rider.'

Most of them were whores, said the doctor.

'Will I go blind and crazy?'

'Not necessarily.' A new treatment was proving effective, but only if it was faithfully adhered to.

'Will it keep me from War College?'

'Not if you respond to treatment, though I will have to enter it on your record.' He filled a small syringe needle with mercury. 'Straddle the table and hold on hard. There will be pain.'

The excruciating agony that first day made Alfred cry out, 'God, oh my God, I hate her.' But slowly the three-times-a-week ordeal became bearable. Apart from the mark on Redl's record, it seemed that the only lasting effect was an increased hostility to women, which he took care to conceal. He told only his new lover, a young medical student called Arthur Schnitzel.

Graduating with honours from the War College, Captain Redl was at once appointed to the General Staff in Vienna. Not only could he uncover espionage activities, he could analyse them – in modern parlance, connect the dots. At a ball where he was presented to Emperor Francis Joseph, Alfred's watching commanding officer remarked: 'That young Redl is quite exceptional.'

Duty as a troop officer in Budapest followed. Then back to General Staff. Alfred was 25 when he was sent to St Petersburg to learn the Russian language. He was invited to have a vodka with a black-bearded officer on the Russian Imperial General Staff, Major Batjuschin. On his desk lay a report on the Austro-Hungarian Army's high expectations of Captain Redl. A second report concerned Redl's debts, so large that his Intelligence future would be blocked if they were known to senior officers on his own General Staff.

Batjuschin looked up from the reports and asked the young lieutenant, 'Have we penetrated the Vienna Intelligence Bureau?'

'No, sir.'

Major Batjuschin poured them each a vodka. He would bide his time.

At the start of 1900, the Russian desk in the Austro-Hungarian Intelligence Bureau became open. The Bureau Chief, Colonel Baron von Giesl, knew of Captain Redl's exceptional abilities, and Redl spoke the Russian language fluently. He transferred Alfred to the Intelligence Bureau of the General Staff in Vienna.

With his capacity to focus on a problem and his intuitive ability to assess people, Redl was soon able to lay his conclusions before von Giesl. 'I do not believe, sir,' he said with modest firmness, 'that we are getting the results that we should in this Bureau. Our counter-intelligence effort is no more than routine.'

As usual Redl's analysis was thorough and convincing, and he presented a coherent method of eliminating weaknesses. Von Giesl was only too happy to give him free rein.

Alfred worked hours that would have broken a normal man. Soon his capacity to calculate exposed five Russian agents who had infiltrated Austro-Hungarian Intelligence. Though he became famous among army and intelligence officers as the finest counter-intelligence officer in the Empire, he never abandoned his modest manner. Those who worked under him idolised him.

Alfred saw in a newspaper that Arthur Schnitzel, his earlier lover, had opened a surgery in Vienna. He invited him for a drink.

'How are you, Arthur? I had no letters from you. You received the money?'

'Yes, thank you.'

After a pause, Alfred lifted his glass and drank to their future – 'like old times'.

'That is all over, Redl.'

'But you took my money, my gifts.'

'I needed the money to get married.'

'Do you intend to repay me?'

'If you like. I can send the Chief of the General Staff a sum each month. With an explanation, of course. I would not sign my name. Your General Beck would not believe that anyone sends large sums of money as a joke.'

Alfred leapt to his feet. 'Get out of here, Herr Doktor.'

'If you wish. Pleasant seeing you again.'

In the silence that followed, Alfred mastered his rage. This was his first overt experience of blackmail.

Then an anonymous letter led Captain Redl to meet his correspondent in the Vienna hills. Pratt, as he called himself, was an undercover agent for the Russian Imperial General Staff. He was one of the most effective intelligence agents in the world. 'Major Batjuschin admires your work.'

'What do you want, Pratt?'

'An arrangement. You have many debts.'

'So? General Beck expects his officers to live well.'

'Would the General also understand the major reason for your debts?' He handed Alfred a file.

As he looked through it, a slight frown appeared on Alfred's face. 'You are very thorough, Pratt.'

'Shall we talk business?'

'It appears we must.'

Pratt told him he could give him more cash than Alfred had ever imagined. Of course, Major Batjuschin would expect something in return.

What Batjuschin wanted were the plans of three fortresses in the Austro-Hungarian Empire.

'And if I decline Major Batjuschin's offer?'

'I will mail a report directly to General Beck about your male lovers.'

Alfred gave a small smile as he pointed out that none of them would admit it and ruin their careers.

'What career has your servant Joseph to ruin? He is a stupid eighteen-year-old peasant. He always disliked your habit of dressing him like a woman before you made love to him.'

Alfred frowned again.

'If you look behind the stove in your bedroom, you will find the end of an open pipe. The other end comes out in my own sitting room. I have made interesting recordings of your conversations with Joseph and many others.'

'I need time to think, Pratt.'

It was then that Pratt spoke the lines that absolved Alfred from blame. 'I care nothing about your homosexual habits, Redl. It is society that has trapped you. I am offering you a way out.'

'Give me the envelope. I shall get you the plans.'

Alfred Redl now lived three lives: the superb counter-intelligence officer, the homosexual with transvestite tastes, the spy. It was the third life that brought him, as Pratt predicted, more money than he had ever dreamt of for himself. In his second life, he found the motivation to spend it all: a fourteen-year-old beautiful boy called Stefan Hromodka.

Stefan's father, a vegetable-seller, had heard the servant Joseph boast that his employer could get anyone into the army's cadet school. An appointment was made. When Joseph opened the door and Alfred saw Stefan, passion stirred.

Each time Captain Redl replaced one top-floor apartment with a better one, his furnishings, always feminine, became more extravagant. In his latest home he wanted fine surroundings for his 'nephew' Stefan who spent much time with him. Understandably proud of the youth's hard work and prowess at cadet school, Redl gladly pulled strings to smooth Stefan's path. The boy adored him.

Alfred never discussed his private life, and no one in Vienna society found anything strange in a forty-year-old bachelor taking his nephew on luxurious holidays. Homosexuality was a forbidden subject and rarely even crossed the minds of others. As for young Stefan, he could not guess the source of all this money; he just felt gratitude to his lover for opportunities and happiness.

When Alfred bought a custom-built scarlet Austro-Daimler with matching scarlet interior, he explained he had just received an inheritance. Nor did this unexpected display strike others as nouveau-riche vulgarity. Such was the reputation of the modest head of counter-intelligence that this sudden flashiness simply added to the glamour of a complex man.

But in his third life, as well as the increasing risks, there were moments of rage and sadness. He was summoned by General Beck and told the gravest news: the Austro-Hungarian Ambassador to St Petersburg had been informed by a sympathetic Russian diplomat that Russian intelligence was aware of Austro-Hungary's northern war plans. Redl was taut with anger. Was Batjuschin double-crossing him?

Cunningly he told General Beck that the worst interpretation was that 'we have a traitor in our section of the General Staff Corps.' Beck allowed himself a dismissive smile at this preposterous notion, and Redl knew he was safe. He welcomed Beck's order for him to go to St Petersburg to uncover what he could.

'So you distrust me, Captain Redl,' said Colonel Batjuschin.

'Do you wonder?' said Redl curtly.

Batjuschin blamed his compatriots' loquacity on too much vodka. Redl still was not pacified. But when the two men moved on to discuss practical ways to deal with the situation, they found common ground. The blame would have to be put on a Russian officer who was one of Captain Redl's best agents. Redl was shocked and genuinely saddened by the subsequent news of his agent's suicide.

Not long afterwards, General Beck recommended Captain Redl for a Military Service Cross. And in 1907, Major Redl began his new duties as Deputy to the Chief of the Intelligence Bureau.

Now an unforeseen hiccup occurred in Alfred's second life where his passion for his 'nephew' grew yearly. Stefan had reached his early twenties, his career in the Army advancing steadily, when out of the blue, he told Alfred he wanted to leave the military. He was in love with a young woman and intended to marry.

'Impossible!' Alfred told him. 'You have me to thank for everything that has come to you since you were fourteen. You have a splendid career guaranteed you. You are accustomed to luxury. Yet you think you can manage on a railway clerk's wages. You think love will last with a puling infant's demands.'

'I am sorry, Fredl, but I must do this.'

Alfred opened a desk drawer and took out a piece of paper. Stefan could see the heading on the paper: 'Austro-Daimler'.

'I ordered a custom-built automobile exactly like my own to be made for you – a surprise for your birthday. I shall cancel it tomorrow, along with your allowance.'

Stefan started to speak and then hesitated.

Alfred waited.

'You know it is only you that I really love, Fredl,' said Stefan. 'I shall not see her again.'

It was time for Major Redl to do a tour of military service as a troop commander. Soon he was the most popular officer in the regiment. 'Always dignified,' a young officer recalled, 'he was very friendly to junior officers. We worshipped him.'

In 1912, Colonel Redl was in Prague, drinking coffee with his General of old, Baron von Giesl. They were discussing the Intelligence Bureau in Prague. 'I know no one else whom I would trust with the job at this difficult time,' said the General. 'The Russians have been flooding the city with agents, as you know. To make your pay more palatable, I have arranged a private flat for you next door, if you want it.'

Alfred had borrowed heavily to furnish his top-floor flat elsewhere in Prague.

'I would appreciate that, sir. It would be convenient for my heavy workload. I wonder if I could take classified material to my quarters to study overnight? I would have a safe there.'

'Of course. It is splendid to have you with me again, Redl.'

The flat had three rooms, and Alfred soon had it furnished to his taste. In the bedroom stood a four-poster covered in red and rose silk. Closets held his remarkably extensive wardrobe. In a locked closet were women's kimonos and silk stockings. On a table stood the camera for photographing documents. Joseph lived in the flat. There were few visitors. Alfred did most of his entertaining in restaurants.

Normally he began his night's work with the ritual of unlocking his military desk and taking out his collection of pornographic photos. Of course he knew the dangers of keeping such material – some of his lovers wore dresses – but he knew his superior mind would protect him. In another drawer was Stefan's written promise not to marry, along with a small notebook in which the letters 'Nik. Nzt' recurred.

Early in the spring of 1913, Major Ronge of the Intelligence Bureau received a communication from his opposite number in the German Great Intelligence Service in Berlin. It enclosed a letter addressed to Herr Nikon Nizetas. After lying for many weeks uncollected in Vienna's General Delivery post office, it had been returned to the place of its postmark in Berlin where it was opened. Inside were 7,000 crowns in notes and a cryptic letter.

Major Ronge, who had been trained by his hero Redl, decided to look into it. Before long, two more letters to Nikon Nizetas arrived in Vienna's General Delivery. When Ronge opened them, he found 14,000 crowns and two more cryptic messages. He put the letters back in General Delivery and posted two detectives to wait within sight of the building. Weeks passed.

In his Intelligence Bureau flat in Prague, Colonel Redl received a letter that shook him. Stefan wrote that he was determined to resign from the army and marry. Alfred asked General Baron von Giesl for permission to drive to Vienna for the weekend. 'A difficulty with my nephew.' With him he took the sealed envelopes of copied intelligence secrets to post from Vienna.

In his room at Hotel Klomser, Alfred was joined by Stefan. A heated argument about Stefan's proposed marriage ensued, ending only when Alfred offered to advance 8,000 crowns to cover Stefan's latest gaming debt. 'No more girls,' Stefan repeated. 'Fredl, could you give me the money this weekend?'

Half an hour later, dressed in a trim, conventional grey flannel suit, Redl gave his name at the General Delivery counter: 'Nizetas. Nikon Nizetas.' The clerk pressed a button beneath the counter.

'I'm in a hurry,' said Nikon Nizetas.

The clerk pressed the button harder before handing over two thick envelopes.

Just after Redl stepped into his waiting taxi, the two detectives hurried into the post office. 'You are too late,' the clerk told them. They reached the pavement in time to take the licence number of the taxi before it turned a corner. Returning to the clerk they asked him for a description. 'An Austrian accent. Short. His hat was pulled down so I couldn't see his face.'

In the taxi, Alfred took out the sheathed knife that Stefan had given him for his birthday long ago. He slit open the two envelopes, read the messages and counted the money. Telling the driver to stop, he paid him. At a nearby taxi rank, he got into another cab: 'Hotel Klomser.'

The two detectives stood on the pavement, disconsolate, knowing they would be sacked. At that moment a miracle occurred: a taxi appeared and they hailed it. Then they recognised the licence number. Jumping in, they asked the driver where he had taken the man they were following. Looking down on the seat, one of them saw the knife sheath and picked it up.

At the taxi rank, an old man whose job was to dust the taxis, recalled the short, well-dressed man with his hat pulled down, and remembered that he had asked for the Hotel Klomser.

The detectives laid the sheath on the reception desk and instructed the manager: 'Ask each guest who comes downstairs if it belongs to him.'

Colonel Redl stepped from the lift and went to the reception desk. 'Ah, I wondered where I had left it.' As he put it in his pocket, he turned and caught the eye of the detectives. Colonel Redl knew his game was up.

He left the hotel. He had to walk: he had to think. He knew one man was following him. The other, on his way to report to his office, had picked up the scraps of paper that Redl had thrown away in an alley. Ten minutes later he reported to his chief who phoned Major Ronge: 'We have made the pick-up, sir. The man is Colonel Redl . . . That is correct: Colonel Redl. On your way here, sir, will you stop by the post office and pick up the receipt he signed?'

At the other end of the phone, Major Ronge thought he was going to be sick.

The detective laid the scraps of paper on the desk and he and his Chief began piecing them together.

In his room at Hotel Klomser, Alfred Redl was writing two letters. The first was to his patron General Baron von Giesl. The other was to his brother Heinrich. The letters were similar: in both he saw himself as a victim of life, moved like a pawn by circumstances beyond his control. When he had sealed the envelopes, he wrote the time on each.

They would be coming for him soon. He had to die, yet he still did not understand himself. He sat smoking, trying to dig out of his brain the key to his life. He looked at his watch again. Picking up Stefan's knife, he knew the fear of all who want to kill themselves: supposing he failed, and the knife missed his heart. He looked up at the curtain and cut a long piece from its cord. Standing on a chair he tied one end over the curtain rod, the other around his neck, and kicked the chair from under him. As the fixture came away from the wall, he fell to the floor. When he loosened the cord around his neck, his eyes filled with tears. Then he looked at his watch.

He washed his face, brushed his short hair, checked that his moustache was as he liked it and sat down to wait for the knock at the door. When it came, he opened it to four senior officers.

'I know why you have come. I am guilty. I would like to speak to Major Ronge alone.'

Ronge nodded and the others stepped outside, closing the door.

'I do not know how it all began, Ronge. For God's sake, help me. Give me a pistol.'

The two stood looking into one another's eyes. Ronge wanted to feel outraged hatred, but all he felt was leaden sorrow pressing down on him.

'I beg you to do this last thing for me. Give me a pistol.'

'We must interrogate you.' Ronge opened the door and the others came in.

Whom had he worked for?

'Russia. Not very long,' Alfred lied.

Each officer scribbled notes.

Who were his accomplices?

'I had none. Only a fool has accomplices. My nephew, Lieutenant Hromodka, has had nothing to do with my activities.'

What did he betray?

'Not much,' Alfred lied. 'A General Staff manual. An Order of Battle.'

And?

'I photocopied the Eighth Corp mobilisation plan.' He pressed his fingers into his forehead, shielding his eyes from Ronge's gaze. 'You will find it all in my desk in Prague.'

When they were done, Major Ronge laid a small pistol beside the sealed letters. Unspeaking, the four left the hotel room to wait outside.

Alfred held the pistol in his hand to test its weight, and as he did so he felt something in his brain shift, as if a clamp had been released. At once there was an agreeable surge through him, rather like adrenalin, only he knew it was something else. Euphoria. Ah, the relief of discovering himself before he died, the joyous relief of *knowing*. He was not a victim of circumstances, as he still believed when he only a little earlier wrote the two letters. No one else was to blame for his treachery. He alone was responsible for his crimes.

Laying the pistol aside, he sat down and began writing feverishly, covering sheet after sheet of paper. His long confession ended, 'Passion and levity have destroyed me. Pray for me. I repent my sins by my death.'

He signed it simply 'Alfred' and wrote beneath his name, 'It is 1.45. I shall now die. Pray for me.'

Almost ecstatically he placed the pistol's small muzzle in his mouth, pressed it hard against the roof and pulled the trigger.

Colonel Redl's large scented apartment in Prague, its decoration feminine and lush, yielded up vivid evidence of his transvestite homosexual practices which his colleagues would have preferred not to know. Long afterwards, when Major Ronge encountered the same perfume again, he retched. He and his fellow officers were already deeply shaken by unlocking the military desk in the official flat and discovering that Redl had told them only a tiny fraction of his betrayals. That he had sold out his own spies to Batjuschin was particularly repugnant.

Now in these scented rooms more evidence of the far-reaching effect of Redl's perfidy spread itself before them. All attempts to hush up the scandal proved useless. The Austro-Hungarian Intelligence Bureau in the run-up to the First World War was still reeling from the devastating treason.

On 28 June 1914, the Emperor's nephew Archduke Francis Ferdinand and his wife were assassinated at Sarajevo, and the Great War began. Most of Austria's shattering defeats by the Russians were but one direct result of Redl's betrayals. Echoes reverberated throughout other European intelligence services, which never again enjoyed the esteem they had known before Alfred Redl was unmasked.

15

Eleanor Roosevelt

1884–1962

On President McKinley's assassination in 1901, Vice-President Theodore Roosevelt succeeded him automatically. The eccentric, bellicose scion of an upper-class New York family, Teddy Roosevelt had already made his name in the Cuban War as commander of 'Roosevelt's Roughriders', twirling one of his moustaches before bellowing 'Charge!' His portly figure was always in the fore of the battle.

Eleanor was born on one of the Roosevelt estates that look over the Hudson River. Her father, Elliott, was Teddy's younger brother. Part hedonist, part Puritan moralist, he was adored by everyone – most of all by his shy little daughter. He was the golden ray of light in her miserable childhood.

Her mother was a celebrated beauty. She called Eleanor her ugly duckling. What made this most painful for the child was her knowledge that she *was* ugly – her mouth too large for that day, her chin almost non-existent. Her glamorous mother coined the nick-name by which Eleanor was known throughout her childhood: 'Granny'. Only her father cared for her.

Then heartbreak. His alcoholism led the family to send him south to keep him away from his children. He and his daughter exchanged what can only be called love letters. Instead of criticising her as everyone else did, he told her stories and described how he wanted her to be when she grew up and they could set forth together – 'truthful, loyal, brave, well educated'. Meanwhile, she was starved of affection from anyone else.

She was eight when the beautiful mother who had rejected her died from diphtheria and she was sent to live with her maternal grandmother in a sombre house further up the Hudson. This formidable lady was as humourless as she was domineering; her house was rigidly run and life there would have been grim for any child, not least an unconfident one. When Eleanor was ten, the adored father in exile died in New York City in the arms of a mistress.

Not until, at the age of fifteen, she was sent to Allenswood, a distinguished English boarding school run by a freethinker, did the awkward ugly duckling begin to come out of herself. To her amazement, she was popular with the girls at school. At eighteen, speaking excellent French, German and Italian, she returned to America and the dreaded debut where she was certain she would be a wallflower.

Then a funny thing happened. A distant cousin, Franklin Delano Roosevelt, took a liking to her. His branch of the family was less grand than hers – 'the sort of person you wouldn't ask to dinner, but for afterward,' Teddy Roosevelt's sarcastic daughter said of Franklin. He was handsome, charming, spoiled by his mother and ambitious. He wanted the highest post in the world, currently occupied by his uncle Teddy.

Franklin was rather intrigued by 'Granny'. Unlike other debutantes, she was serious, high-minded and ambitious not only for him but for herself. Her letters to him discussed the advancement of blacks (whom in that day – 1902 – she called 'darkies') and she did a U-turn from her prejudice against Jews. She had acquired the qualities that her dead father had dreamt of for her. Yet her confidence was still crippled. Unlike some whose childhood is blighted, Eleanor did not turn to therapists to listen to her woes. Instead she identified with others who were familiar with suffering and threw her energies into helping them.

Nearly six feet tall, she was slender and graceful; the fact that her profile was marred by the near absence of chin seems not to have bothered the handsome Franklin. He displayed a mixture of idealism and pragmatism. They talked about their shared desire to make it possible for America's poor to get on their own feet. He decided she would make the perfect political partner in marriage. Alas, we do not have his letters to her: not many years later she destroyed them.

In 1903, when Eleanor was nineteen, Franklin twenty-one, they became engaged and two years later married. She was given away by the President, her uncle Teddy Roosevelt, who dominated the show – to Eleanor's amusement and Franklin's acute annoyance.

His mother continued to run the Hyde Park mansion where he was raised, and now his wife moved in. The mother-in-law insinuated herself into every corner of their lives. Eleanor determined to emancipate herself. By the time Franklin was made a state senator and they moved to Albany, she had thrown off her despondency and her overbearing mother-in-law. 'No one can make you feel inferior without your consent,' she said to a friend. In their zestful life in Albany, it was quickly noticed that the dapper new senator's wife was his greatest political asset.

Behind the scenes, the powerful political couple shared little physical or emotional joy. Despite bearing six children, Eleanor later confided to a daughter that she didn't like sex. Perhaps Franklin's active love life with another was inevitable. The bond between husband and wife depended on the knowledge she acquired about politics and America's wider social structure.

When he became Assistant Secretary of the Navy during the First World War, the popular couple settled in Washington, DC. It was when he became gravely ill with pneumonia and she was sorting out some files for him that she came on the love letters. Thus she discovered that her husband and her secretary, Lucy Mercer, were conducting an intense love affair. The betrayal by a young woman who was her friend as well as her social secretary was as grievous a blow as was her husband's betrayal. She was crushed. That is when she destroyed his pre-marriage letters.

Shattered as she was, she nonetheless made a cool proposal: if her husband truly loved his mistress, he should be free to marry her – she would give Franklin a divorce, but Lucy would have to bring up the five surviving children. This was not at all what the lovers had in mind. Lucy was a Catholic; Franklin was pursuing a glittering political career. The *coup de grâce* was delivered by his mother: knowing that divorce would blight his career, she told him she would cut him off without a cent if he left his wife. Painfully the lovers decided to put their affair on ice. The Roosevelts were reconciled, but Eleanor never slept with her husband again.

They moved back to New York, and he ran unsuccessfully for Vice-President of the United States. The next year he was struck down with polio. He was forty. For three years he lay paralysed. He would not walk again. At meetings and dinner parties, he was always seated at his place when the others entered the room.

Eleanor came into her own. She tended him devotedly. A trusted and tireless reporter, she became his eyes and his ears. She took on active work in Democratic politics to keep Franklin's interest alive. Under the tutelage of his most trusted adviser, Louis Howe, she learned the art of making speeches and moulded herself into an articulate and knowledgeable alter ego for her husband. The 'old crowd' talked of how elegant she had become.

At the same time she found her own voice. With her grit and stamina and her sensitivity to others' exclusion and suffering, she began what would be her lifetime work for the underprivileged of all races and religions.

Without her, the crippled man could never have made his successful campaign in 1928 to become Governor of New York. Four years later he ran for the presidency against Herbert Hoover. During the campaign, Eleanor's febrile relationship began with Lorena Hickok, a 38-year-old reporter for the Associated Press, whose intuitive sense that Eleanor was unhappy made an immediate bond between them.

On a midnight train to New York, the Democratic candidate's 48-year-old wife poured out her anxieties to the younger woman. The AP report led other press members to pick up Eleanor's reluctance to go to the White House. The next day she asked 'Hick', as she now called Lorena, to join her on the drive to Albany when she confided more than she ever had before. She had never, she said, pushed Franklin towards the presidency, 'even though some people say my ambition for myself drove him on'. She glanced at Hick. 'You don't quite believe me, do you?'

Franklin was elected President. By then Eleanor's emotional emancipation was so complete that her wings could not be clipped. She insisted that she would not be shadowed by security men, and she scorned having her own driver, usually driving herself – adding to her reputation for fearlessness. In the interregnum period following Franklin's victory, Mrs Hoover invited the new First Lady to call on her and look over the White House. Eleanor had breakfast at the Mayflower, intending then to walk to the White House. The chief of protocol, a cousin of Franklin's, turned up with a limousine and tried to dissuade her. 'But Eleanor, darling, you can't do that. People will mob you.' To no avail. She liked to walk, Miss Hickok would accompany her, and that was that.

She was afraid that once in the White House, she would be a prisoner in a gilded cage. The press confirmed her fears: 'She will have nothing to do except stand in line and receive visitors and preside over official dinners.'

The day before the inauguration, Hick collected her in a cab, and they drove together to Rock Creek Park where they walked to Saint Gaudens's haunting memorial to his wife. They sat on a stone bench facing the hooded 'Grief'.

'When I was younger,' Eleanor said as much to herself as to Hick, 'sometimes I'd be very sorry for myself. I'd come here alone and sit. I'd always come away stronger.' Hick sensed that the wound left by the Lucy Mercer affair was still open.

After the inauguration, it was Hick who suggested the First Lady hold a press conference for women. Franklin agreed. Two days before his own first press conference, Eleanor held hers for 35 women reporters. Soon she was lecturing throughout the country and had her own radio programme. Her syndicated newspaper column was published six days a week (except the four days following her husband's death).

The President's confidante in decision-making, she urged on his New Deal to meet the post-Depression economic crisis, striving to ensure that the measures applied equally to women and men. No First Lady had ever been so active. Travelling widely, she gradually

discovered the insidious effects of racism and anti-Semitism and
sought to rid herself of these prejudices. Idolised by some, she was
reviled as 'that woman' by others.

Unsurprisingly, the Republican Party were incensed by the First
Lady's power. Mrs Hoover had stayed apart from the political game.
Eleanor seemed to be everywhere. A union official remarked to the
press, 'Previous Presidents sent their Labor Secretary to negotiate
with us. This President sends his wife.'

There was not a drop of coyness in her make-up. Nor was she
domineering or arrogant. She approached the mostly men-only
negotiating table as if she were a teacher, and time after time she was
persuasive. Those who had never met her often disliked the *idea* of
her. Close up the alert blue eyes and ready smile enchanted.

About now Lorena Hickok realised that her tight bond with
Eleanor was affecting her detachment as a journalist. She resigned
from the AP to work for Harry Hopkins in the new relief
administration. Her intimacy with Eleanor continued. Perhaps it was
in response to her husband's betrayal that Eleanor initiated her own
extra-marital relationships with other women. She craved affection
and jealously held on to her friends. A number of them were
journalists. Living in Val-Kill cottage on the Hyde Park estate made
discretion possible, but inevitably gossip began. It was not an era
when same-sex relationships were acceptable, yet the President
tolerated his wife's personal life. What else could he do? Did he
care? Her role in his life had become solely that of acute political
adviser and champion for the liberal policies he pursued.

For sexuality and relaxation, he turned to his social secretary,
Missy LeHand. She and Eleanor had a cordial relationship, and
Eleanor was delighted to have someone else take on the 'hostess'
role that she herself despised. Like many wives, she knew and didn't
know how close her husband was to another.

When he had no engagements, he and Missy passed the evenings
in his bedroom. Franklin, a gourmand, had intensely disliked
Eleanor's hairshirt attitude to his meals (a penance?) and to no avail
sent his wife memos complaining that he was 'getting sweetbreads
about six times a week. I'm getting to the point where my stomach
positively rebels and this does not help my relations with foreign

powers. I bit two of them today.' Now Missy directed the cook to produce delicious suppers, which were brought upstairs to his bedroom for their shared delight.

Fulton Oursler, who published *Liberty* for which both Eleanor and Franklin wrote, came to dinner on a hot night and was disconcerted by Missy's vital role in FDR's life: 'She was young and attractive, and should have been off somewhere cool and gay on a happy weekend. Yet month after month and year after year she gave up date after date, keeping company with a very lonely man.' Oursler underestimated women's attraction to Franklin. Despite their separate lives, Eleanor never stopped loving him.

Sometimes Eleanor was prepared to wound Hick deeply, mischievously even. In the 1936 re-election campaign, riding in Eleanor's car was a petite blonde. The press gawped. Was this a femme fatale sharing the First Lady's car in presidential parades? Finally a woman reporter was delegated to ask the question.

'Oh, she's Mayris Chaney – Tiny – a dancer and friend.' They had planned to go on holiday together, and when instead the campaign trail unfolded, Eleanor asked Tiny to tour with the presidential party. After the election, Eleanor kept a small hideaway apartment in Greenwich Village. There Tiny could stay with her.

When FDR's second term neared its end in 1940, he put himself in purdah. In the daily struggle between those who wanted him to go for an unprecedented third term and those who were obsessively against it and lobbied for Henry Wallace instead, Franklin confided in no one except Missy LeHand.

He was deeply troubled at the prospect of going against American custom. Yet he desperately wanted to help the Allies and knew that he was the only person who could bring the American people into the Second World War. On the home front, the New Deal remained dependent on him. Eleanor told him there was still time to groom a successor. She thought he had done enough, that he had served his place in history.

Lorena Hickok, now working for the National Democratic Committee, kept her beloved friend informed of disaffections in the party. At the Democratic convention things got out of control. Eleanor was scheduled to speak. Hick panicked, saying it was folly to put the First Lady into this mayhem. Eleanor stood up. The delegates caught her mood and gravity and fell silent. 'They were like lambs,' she said afterwards. The next day's United Press report was headlined: 'MRS ROOSEVELT STILLS THE TUMULT OF 50,000'.

FDR won the third term. Of the Allies who in 1939 had entered the Second World War against Hitler, only Britain still held out, despite the Blitz on her cities that sometimes killed more than 3,000 British civilians in a single night. Churchill longed for America to come into the war.

On 7 December 1941, Japanese carrier-borne aircraft bombed the US naval base at Pearl Harbor in Hawaii, decimating the fleet and killing 3,300 service personnel. The following day, America, Britain and Australia declared war on Japan, and the Anglo-American special relationship began.

Out of the blue, Missy LeHand had a stroke. 'A much greater loss to the country than the loss of a battleship,' said an aide. Probably Missy was unsurprised that Franklin never visited her. She had told Fulton Oursler that the President 'was really incapable of a personal friendship'. Yet she never begrudged this fascinating man's concentration on himself and his objectives. When on Christmas Eve Eleanor went in to Franklin to ask if had phoned Missy, he replied he had not and was not planning to do so. But he altered his will to provide that Missy's medical expenses should be taken care of out of up to half of the income from his estate, the remainder going to Eleanor.

As the war lurched on, Eleanor became known as 'the GIs' friend'. But her impending visit to the South Pacific cut little ice with commanders in the field, notably Admiral William S Halsey, who would ultimately conquer the Japanese fleet. He 'dreaded' the First Lady's visit, looking on her as a 'do-gooder'. Most of the troops lying in hospitals in the Fijis were casualties from the great battles in the Solomons.

On her arrival at the Admiral's headquarters in Noumea, he briskly suggested that she proceed at once to Australia and New Zealand. Nervously she produced a letter from the President declaring that the decision about her itinerary should be made by the Area Commanders. 'She is especially anxious to visit Guadalcanal and at this moment it looks like a pretty safe place to visit,' the President concluded.

'Guadalcanal is no place for you, Ma'am,' the Admiral snapped.

'I'll be entirely responsible for anything that happens to me,' she replied.

'I'm not worried about the chances you'd take,' he answered. 'I know you'd take them gladly. What worries me is the battle going on in New Georgia at this very minute. If you fly to Guadalcanal, I'll have to provide a fighter escort for you, and I haven't got one to spare.'

She looked so crestfallen that he heard himself saying, 'I'll postpone my final decision until your return from Australia. The situation may have clarified by then.'

When she returned, he let her know that he was ashamed of his original surliness. In his report on her visit, he wrote:

> Here is what she did in twelve hours: she inspected two Navy hospitals, took a boat to an officers' rest home and had lunch there, returned and inspected an Army hospital, inspected the 2nd Marine Battalion (her son Jimmy had been its executive officer), made a speech at a service club, attended a reception, and was guest of honor at a dinner given by General Harmon.

She then pecked away at her typewriter in the dead of night, writing her column.

The Admiral's report continued:

> When I say she inspected those hospitals, I don't mean that she shook hands with the chief medical officer, glanced into a sun parlor and left. I mean that she went into every ward, stopped at every bed, and spoke to every patient: What was his name? How did he feel? Was there anything he needed? Could she take a message home for him? I marveled at her hardihood, both physical and mental, she walked for miles, and she saw patients who were grievously and gruesomely wounded. But I marveled most at their expressions as she leaned over them. It was a sight I will never forget.

Her New Zealand visit had included a Maori welcome. The Maoris were bewitched by her simplicity and friendliness, and called her 'Kotoku' – 'White Heron of the One Flight'. Back in the southern United States, photographs of her rubbing noses with her Maori guide were seen as proof of the First Lady's 'nigger-loving' propensities.

By late 1944, on the eve of FDR's fourth term, it became evident that his health was failing. Missy died and a statement issued at the White House in Roosevelt's name was an encomium. He moved to Warm Springs, Virginia for a rest. Unknown to Eleanor, Lucy Mercer (now Mrs Rutherford) stayed with him, concerned to make this overburdened man's life as pleasant as possible. A message came from Eleanor: on his return from Warm Springs, she wanted to see him 'before you begin to look weary!' He was in no hurry to see her.

At his fourth inauguration, only a few intimates joined him in the Green Room. Eleanor stood for hours at the receptions, shaking hands with his supporters until she was drawn and exhausted. Two days later he left for the crucial Yalta Conference where he and Churchill and Stalin decided on their separate areas of influence after the fast-approaching Allied victory in Europe. Eleanor asked to accompany him, but the President turned her down. 'Franklin felt that I would only add to the difficulties as everyone would feel they had to pay attention to me.'

The travellers returned to Washington. The President addressed Congress sitting down because of the weight of his braces. His doctor said he must have half an hour a day of relaxation and perhaps a drink. Eleanor could not bear that he become an invalid, and kept pestering him with advice he no longer had the strength and patience to thrash out with her. On one occasion his daughter Anna was mixing cocktails when her mother came in yet again with an enormous bundle of letters that she wanted to discuss with him immediately and have a decision. 'Father blew his top. He took the bundle of letters and pushed it over to me. "Sis, you handle this." '

Throughout March he longed to return to Warm Springs and to Lucy. Soon after he arrived there, Eleanor was holding her regular press conference in Washington when a call came from Warm

Springs to say that the President had fainted and been carried to his bed. It was decided that she should keep her next engagement so as not to set the rumours going. She would fly down to Warm Springs later in the day. When she returned from completing her engagement, she was told that the President had died. After a pause, she entered upon her responsibilities. She sent for Vice-President Harry Truman.

'Harry,' she said quietly, putting her arm around his shoulder, 'the President is dead.'

Too stunned initially to speak, he at last said, 'Is there anything I can do for you?'

'Is there anything *we* can do for *you*?' she asked. 'For you are the one in trouble now.'

To reporters outside the White House she said: 'The story is over.'

She was wrong. Within a year she began her service as American spokesman in the United Nations. Not until her 77th birthday did she admit: 'I suppose I should slow down.' She died the next year and was buried in the rose garden at Hyde Park next to her husband.

Eleanor told Lorena Hickok and other women friends that she had not been in love with Franklin since her discovery of the Lucy Mercer affair, and that she had given her husband a service of love because of her respect for his leadership and faith in his goals. One of her friends remarked: 'That was her story. Maybe she even half believed it.'

16

Roscoe 'Fatty' Arbuckle

1887–1933

Roscoe was born into a poor Kansas family constantly on the move, always looking for something better, who eventually reached California. He was always fat and was still a young boy when other children gave him the name by which he was forever known. Unfazed, in his late teens he became a singer in dance halls. Then he began to dance as well, for he was unexpectedly light on his feet.

In 1912 Mack Sennett, owner of the fledgling Keystone film company, watched Fatty and realised he would be perfect as a slapstick comedian in silent two-reel movies. He was made one of the leads in 'The Keystone Cops'. The public loved him, that great bucket of lard with his solemn face and big blue eyes and a large sensual mouth. His light-footedness made the joke funnier.

Soon he was cast in *Fatty and Mabel* with Sennett's glamorous girlfriend Mabel Normand. Fatty was in heaven. He had a roving eye for beautiful women. By now pretty girls were stampeding to the mission-style huts among the orange groves that made up Hollywood in its early days. Fatty's immense bulk was not a deterrent on the 'casting couches' scattered among the huts: would-be stars regarded fornication as they did shaking hands.

In 1916 he defected to Paramount Pictures where he had been offered the unique privilege of having complete control over his movies. By 1921 Fatty was making seven-reel features. Paramount was so certain of his goldmine potential that they gave him a three-year contract at the unprecedented rate of $1 million per year. He was 34. The fat boy could not put a foot wrong.

But he was exhausted. In the first eight months of 1921 he made nine feature films for Paramount. He was desperate for a break. One Saturday morning in September, on a whim, he decided to start his break in San Francisco. It would give him a chance to run in his new $25,000 custom-made Pierce-Arrow, with two Hollywood cronies as his passengers. A second car streaking up the Coast Highway bore several showgirls whom Fatty put up in the Palace Hotel. He and his male friends checked into the lavish St Francis Hotel where they took over three suites – ready for the frolics to commence.

It was the era of Prohibition. So the first call was to Tom-Tom, the bellboy with a bootleg connection. Drink was rolled in. Jazz on the radio was turned high. And the girls arrived. Among them was a raven-haired beauty, a part-time actress with the ominous name Virginia Rappe. Fatty's eye had been on her for some time. True, she had given crabs to half the company in her last film. But crabs, while creepy and itchy, were no big deal: they were easy to cure. And Virginia *was* beguiling.

It was Labor Day weekend, and the party begun on Saturday was still going strong on Monday. Though it was a toss-up who was the drunkest, the mood was good, despite some rooms looking as if a tornado had swept through and turned the Louis-XVI-style furniture into kindling wood. Fatty took the drunken Virginia by the hand, looked back at the crowded suite and gave his film-famous leer. He locked the bedroom door behind them.

What happened next was wildly disputed. Was Fatty, exceptionally well endowed, so drunk he could not distinguish one part of Virginia's anatomy from another? Was he embarrassed and angry at finding himself impotent from drink and resorted to a bottle neck to give Virginia a good time? Or a combination of the two?

What is certain is that dreadful screams came from the bedroom, followed by moaning. The revellers pounded on the door, and when it opened, Fatty sauntered out in torn pyjamas, Virginia's hat on his head, and told the girls, 'Go in and get her dressed and take her to the Palace. She makes too much noise.'

Two showgirls went in and found Virginia groaning and half-naked. It was impossible to dress her because her clothes were in shreds. Writhing in pain she cried out: 'He hurt me.'

At the exclusive hospital where she was taken, she murmured to a nurse: 'Fatty Arbuckle did this to me. Please see that he doesn't get away with it.' She lapsed into a coma and died from acute peritonitis on Friday. What had led to her blood poisoning?

It would have remained a mystery had not the San Francisco Deputy Coroner received a telephone call inquiring about a post-mortem. Something in the caller's manner made him suspicious, and he went around to the hospital to see for himself what was happening. He arrived just as an orderly stepped from the lift carrying a glass jar with Virginia's injured female organs, and headed for the incinerator. The Deputy Coroner demanded the organs and the orderly had no choice but to hand them over. Thus it became public knowledge that Virginia's bladder had been ruptured by some form of violence, which led to peritonitis.

Detectives were soon grilling the uneasy hospital staff to find out who was covering up what. Two days later Roscoe Arbuckle was charged with Virginia Rappe's rape and murder. Newspapers around the world went wild. Until her death, Virginia Rappe was an unknown, but all cinema audiences knew and loved – until now – Fatty Arbuckle. He was charged with murder by excessive 'external pressure' during sexual dalliance.

As the actor sat in a grim San Francisco jail awaiting trial, Adolph Zukor, who had millions at stake on Arbuckle, tried to bribe the District Attorney. Other prominent Hollywood figures ran a campaign to blacken Virginia's name, claiming she was a lush who had slept her way up and down the western hemisphere. None of these interventions cut any ice with the District Attorney.

The trial began in November. Arbuckle's lawyers fought to get the charge reduced to manslaughter. His solemn face impassive, Arbuckle denied all charges, and appeared entirely indifferent to the fate of Viginia Rappe. The forty witnesses had been so drunk at the time of the incident that their evidence was hopelessly conflicting. No evidence of a bottle was found – though that didn't stop cartoonists drawing a grand hotel with a bottle sailing out of an open window; sometimes it was a Coca-Cola bottle, sometimes a champagne bottle. The jury disagreed and a mistrial was declared.

It took three trials before Fatty Arbuckle was acquitted. Even so, Paramount cancelled his contract. To pay his lawyers' bills he had to sell his elegant English-style home in Los Angeles and his fleet of opulent cars. His unreleased films were shredded. He was banned from acting. The only friend to stand by him was Buster Keaton, who suggested Fatty change his name to 'Will B Good'.

Hollywood's first major scandal had besmirched its name for all time. The self-appointed newspaper moral arbiters, the public and the film colony itself now knew that anything could happen, however grotesque, among its fresh-faced stars.

In later years Fatty Arbuckle adopted the name of William Goodrich in order to get work as a gag writer. That did not stop Los Angeles workmen whistling 'I'm Coming, Virginia' when they recognised him in the street.

He drank heavily. One time when police stopped his car, he tossed a whisky bottle out of the window into tall grass, chuckling, 'There goes the evidence!' All he asked was to be allowed to act again. Finally, by 1932, he had worked his way back in front of a camera. It was too late. He died of a heart attack in 1933. He was 46.

17

Edward and Mrs Simpson

1894–1972/1896–1986

'You'd think that we'd all come straight out of *Tobacco Road*,' said Wallis Warfield's Aunt Bessie, who acted as her chaperone at the time of the Abdication of King Edward VIII. This comment stemmed from the fact that Wallis's mother had run a boarding house in Baltimore, Maryland. My grandmother did the same for a while: her boarders were her relations who, like her, had left Southern Maryland where their original land grants came from Charles I; their leisured life growing tobacco was wiped out by the Civil War.

Wallis's parents were the poor relations of two distinguished 'old families'. They knew poverty and insecurity, but no one had ever before questioned their breeding. Her unmarried Uncle Sol was a prosperous Baltimore banker who assisted her widowed mother. Wallis would observe in him and the other well-to-do Warfields that while an 'old family' gave one standing, money was rather a useful addition. Presumably that is when her obsession with wealth began.

Educated at a good private school, paid for by Uncle Sol, from the age of fourteen she deliberately attracted boys and soon was known as 'fast'. No one has ever fathomed her first marriage to Winfield Spencer Jr who was in the air arm of the US Navy. A striking-looking, burly man, he had neither money nor a glittering future, so we can assume the attraction was sexual. And at twenty Wallis wanted to get away from home.

On their wedding night, Win Spencer turned ugly and started drinking heavily. This could have been in response to his own frustration. Much later Wallis said that she stopped short of intercourse with her first two husbands. Win Spencer became violent to his wife. Nonetheless, she followed him to his posting in China where it seems her husband sent her to a brothel to be trained in obscure sexual techniques.

On returning to Baltimore, a cultivated but insular city, she told her mother she wanted a divorce. Uncle Sol was predictably outraged: 'I won't let you bring this disgrace upon us! The Warfields in all their known connections since 1662 have never had a divorce. What will the people of Baltimore think?'

His niece was undeterred. But thenceforth, she had to cajole money out of him – enough for a small apartment in Washington and for occasional shopping trips in New York. On one such trip she met Mr and Mrs Ernest Simpson. He was an American-born Englishman whom she describes in her autobiography *The Heart Has Its Reasons*: '. . . a good dancer, fond of the theatre, and obviously well read, he impressed me as an unusually well-balanced man. I had acquired a taste for cosmopolitan minds, and Ernest obviously had one. I was attracted to him and he to me.'

Then Uncle Sol died and left only a small trust fund for his niece, which would cease if she remarried. Her Aunt Bessie took Wallis on a trip to Europe. Lo, they found that Ernest Simpson had divorced and moved his business to the London office of his father's firm. A year later, he and Wallis married.

Comfortably off, they lived in a pleasant flat in Bryanston Square and seemed happy together, sharing a passion for antiques. For the first time in her life she could indulge her love of beautiful things. Soon the flat and her cuisine were 'fit to entertain a king'. Wallis's perfectionism – she drew diagrams for the butcher of how she wanted a T-bone steak cut – made her dinner parties flawless. But whom to ask?

Ernest's sister took Wallis under her wing and soon she had friends of her own among rich American expatriates. They included Lady Furness, the married mistress of the Prince of Wales. In the autumn of 1930, Lady Furness introduced Mrs Simpson to the

Prince. Wallis had the unabashed confidence of a woman who knows she has strong sex appeal.

Not long afterwards, Mr and Mrs Ernest Simpson were invited to Fort Belvedere, favourite home of the Prince of Wales. He designed the gardens, and like many a keen gardener he loved the hard work, personally clearing the laurels and cutting the paths through woods. In the morning, Ernest Simpson – unused to tough exercise – found himself conscripted with the other male guests to clear the undergrowth in the Prince's woods.

Never beautiful, Wallis was an exceptionally attractive woman with a magnetic personality. She had vivacity and wit and an uncalculating manner; she was kind and thoughtful to those at the Fort. Many more visits followed, Lady Furness always present and acting as hostess.

Physically slight, blonde, handsome, the Prince was famously charming to one and all when he wished to be. At forty, he had accomplished much in modernising the work of royalty, adding lustre amd wide popularity to the House of Windsor. Young women were in love with the very idea of him. In his two important affairs, with married women – with Mrs Dudley Ward and then Lady Furness – only in the most trivial ways was he unfaithful. He did not have the nature of a testosterone-charged hunter.

In June 1933, he gave a birthday party at Quaglino's for Mrs Simpson, who was two years younger than himself. During July he dined for the first time at the Bryanston Square flat. Six months later Lady Furness sailed to New York for a two-month visit. Before she left she invited Wallis for a cocktail and said, laughingly, to her friend: 'I'm afraid the Prince is going to be lonely. Wallis, won't you look after him?'

By the time Lady Furness returned, London society was agog with gossip about the Prince and Mrs Simpson. He was now dropping in routinely for a drink at Bryanston Square where Wallis was at home to her friends after six. One evening he stayed so long that she included him in the family meal. Soon he was arriving for informal dinners with the Simpsons, Ernest afterwards retiring to his upstairs study to work on his papers, leaving his wife to entertain the Prince.

Focused on his obssession with Wallis, the Prince became impervious to decorum or his friends' feelings. Lady Furness found that her former lover would not speak to her on the telephone. Her invitations to the Fort were a thing of the past. The Prince's previous and most important mistress, Mrs Dudley Ward, with whom he had been desperately in love for years, had remained a close friend and he visited her and phoned almost daily. Now when she rang him, the telephonist she had known for years said: 'I have something terrible to tell you. I have orders not to put you through.' She would never see him again.

Always dressed in chic severe clothes, Wallis now dazzled with costly jewels. Each week more precious stones bedecked her. A letter from Lady Colefax to a friend gives a pro-Mrs Simpson picture:

> . . . people are speaking in a very horrid way of the poor Prince and Mrs Simpson. It's awfully unfair, and pure jealousy on the part of the women he has liked in the past . . . Almost all of them had lovers and of course that made him feel wretched. Mrs Simpson is quite a different sort of woman. She doesn't pose as being young and in fact must be nearly forty. She is clever and intelligent and is interested in everything that interests the Prince, including gardening.

In her autobiography, Wallis wrote with characteristic candour:

> Over and beyond the charm of his personality and the warmth of his manner, he was the open sesame to a new and glittering world that excited me as nothing in my life had ever done before . . . It seemed unbelievable that I, Wallis Warfield of Baltimore, Maryland, could be part of this enchanted world.

To those around them it was apparent that the Prince was in complete subjection to her. It was widely believed that she was the only woman to satisfy the physical side of his nature. Yet the bond went far beyond this. In addition to the Prince's sexual dependence, his close friend, Walter Monkton, said that there was 'an intellectual companionship, and there is no doubt that his lonely nature found in her a spiritual comradeship.'

When he asked Mrs Simpson to marry him, she supposed it was in his gift to make her Queen. This man whose popularity was enormous throughout the United Kingdom and the Empire, who had always defied tradition, who publicly sympathised with the plight of unemployed miners, who would soon be enthroned as 'Defender of the Faith' (and the Church of England did not accept divorce), this man was so besotted with a woman who had two husbands living that he thought he could 'get away with it'. He was obstinate and, when he chose, a formidable personality.

In February 1935, the Prince invited Mr and Mrs Simpson to accompany him on a skiing holiday in Kitzbühel. Ernest declined on the grounds of business in New York. Because the Prince could not bear to return home, the holiday was extended to Vienna and Budapest. When Wallis returned to the Bryanston Square flat, she found that things had changed with her husband: love had passed.

King George V was dying. Most of his family believed that his death was hastened by the Prince's worship of 'that woman'. On 20 January 1936, hardly had the King stopped breathing than his widow, Queen Mary, kissed the hand of her eldest son: 'The King is dead, long live the King.'

The new King had come to the throne intending to reform and democratise the monarchy. His ambition was thwarted by his determination to make Mrs Simpson his wife and Queen. Prime Minister Baldwin did little to conceal his certainty that she was unsuitable to be Queen of England – unacceptable to the Establishment, unacceptable to the people, no matter how much the King was loved.

Not a word appeared in the British press. Yet as 1936 advanced, rumour spread by word of mouth. In the summer, King Edward and Wallis holidayed together on the yacht *Nahlin*, accompanied by two destroyers as they voyaged through Greek waters to Turkey. At each port of call mobs awaited them, shouting in their own language: '*Vive l'amour!*' Instead of being anxious at this unheralded publicity, the King and Wallis were like excited children. Photographs of them that appeared in Continental newspapers were censored in Fleet Street.

By September, the American press was in full cry, daily becoming more scurrilous about Mrs Simpson. Canadians reacted first with disbelief, then with horror. In Britain, readers who subscribed to American newspapers found their copies censored.

Ernest Simpson by now wanted to marry someone else. The case for divorce was to be heard at Ipswich Court on 27 October. The King summoned the newspaper baron Lord Beaverbrook and asked his help in suppressing publicity. In the time-honoured custom, the husband would be the one charged with adultery, and the evidence of Ernest Simpson's adultery was provided by the usual device at a hotel in Bray where he stayed with a lady called Buttercup. Mrs Simpson received a decree nisi, which would be made absolute on 27 April 1937, just in time for the King to marry her before his coronation in May.

By November there was only one topic in London. Chips Channon, the celebrated diarist, wrote, 'We are faced with an impasse. The country, or much of it, would not accept Queen Wallis, with two live husbands scattered about.' The House of Commons was openly talking of abdication.

A morganatic marriage was now put forward as a solution: the King would legally marry Mrs Simpson but she could never be Queen. Wallis, at last aware of the true situation that they had entered so gaily, was in favour of this solution. Above all she did not want the King to abdicate. For probably the only time in their life together, he ignored her wishes: his wife, he repeated, had to rule by his side as Queen.

Wallis and her Aunt Bessie were now sheltering at Fort Belvedere. The King was with them when the British press broke its long silence. Whereas in America and France the prospect of abdication and marriage was presented as True Love, most Britons saw the abdication as an incomprehensible and selfish dereliction of duty.

Wallis said she must leave the country and not see Edward again. The King agreed with only her first intention. His friend Lord Brownlow and his personal detective accompanied her to Cannes where she stayed with friends.

On 10 December, the Instrument of Abdication was signed and witnessed by the King's three brothers. The next day he invited his friend Winston Churchill to luncheon to wish him goodbye and show him the draft of his speech. During this luncheon he ceased to be King. There were tears in Churchill's eyes when they parted.

That evening the ex-monarch dined with his assembled family at Royal Lodge. Then another companion, Walter Monkton, drove him to nearby Windsor Castle from where, following the announcement 'This is Windsor Castle, His Royal Highness Prince Edward', he made his famous broadcast:

> . . . You all know the reasons which have impelled me to renounce the throne. But I want you to understand that in making up my mind I did not forget the country or the Empire which as Prince of Wales, and lately as King, I have for twenty-five years tried to serve. But you must believe me when I tell you that I have found it impossible to carry the heavy burden of responsibility and to discharge my duties as King as I would wish to do without the help and support of the woman I love . . .

After the broadcast he returned to Royal Lodge to say farewell to his family. As he bowed to the new King George, the Duke of Kent, another younger brother, cried out: 'This can't be happening!'

Later that night, the ex-monarch boarded *Fury* waiting at Portsmouth. *Fury* sailed at once and anchored in St Helen's Roads for the night, arriving at France in the morning. Prince Edward drove directly to the villa in Cannes where Wallis waited for her first glimpse of the man who had been King.

Erstwhile friends of the ex-King and Mrs Simpson scuttled. More surprisingly, the British people accepted the Abdication calmly. King George VI and Queen Elizabeth were crowned and anointed.

On 3 June 1937, Edward and Wallis were married in France. He longed for his family, especially his mother, to be at his wedding, but Buckingham Palace turned its collective back. His new title had already been settled. The best man, Fruity Metcalfe, had the unenviable task of bearing a letter from King George VI. In it he informed his elder brother that: '. . . the Duke of Windsor shall, not withstanding his Abdication . . . be entitled to hold and enjoy for himself only the title, style or attribute of Royal Highness, so however that his wife and descendants, if any, shall not hold the said title or attribute.' In short, the Duke of Windsor was to be HRH; his wife was not.

In the years to come, the Duke of Windsor would receive many more blows from Buckingham Palace and the Establishment, but for mean vindictiveness none would match this gross discourtesy to his wife. Understandably, Queen Elizabeth blamed Mrs Simpson for the monarchical convulsion that cast her shy, stammering husband, happy in his family life, into a role for which he was unprepared and fearful of falling short.

As well, Queen Elizabeth said many years later, she had first been in love with the older brother. (Strangely, though love has gone, jealousy often lingers on.) Inside the Queen's velvet glove was a hand of steel. She needed to boost her husband, and his charismatic brother was a threat and an interfering one.

Unfailingly supported by his wife, King George managed to cure the worst of his stammer. He and the Queen quickly came to be respected and loved, not least by staying on at Buckingham Palace during the Blitz, and walking among their people in the bombed-out rubble.

Inevitably angered by the chance she had missed, the Duchess of Windsor commented: 'The reign of George VI is a split-level matriarchy in pants. Queen Mary runs the King's wife and the King's wife runs the King.'

In vain did the Duke of Windsor ask to put his years of training into a job that might be useful to his country. In vain did he ask to return to England. With England on the brink of war, he bombarded the harassed Prime Minister with claims that his wife should receive her rightful title.

He and Wallis paid a warm and sympathetic visit to Adolf Hitler and senior Nazi officers in the misguided belief that he, the Duke of Windsor, could find a way to avert war. The meeting was, unsurprisingly, resented and criticised in Britain. At last the Duke was allowed to return to England with his wife, imagining he could give welcome advice to his brother, but the Palace appeared not to know the Windsors were in the country.

Finally Prime Minister Churchill decided the best course of action was to give the Duke a job on the far side of the Atlantic – as Governor of the Bahamas. It was stipulated that he should not set foot on American soil without permission from the English government.

As they sailed to Bermuda, the Windsors were miserable at the prospect of exile in a place where, except for the winter holiday season, the heat was insufferable and the society provincial. Even in Nassau, they felt the humiliation of the Duke only receiving a curtsy – apart from native children in pigtails curtsying to the Duchess.

However, the Windsors excelled at anything requiring charm, and Wallis applied her flair and perfectionism to entertainment at Government House. They were rather less able at the duller side of a governor's duties, though they both worked hard. In London the Minister for the Colonies relented on his initial ban on their visiting the United States, and in New York and Palm Beach they were received with honour and offered lavish hospitality by sophisticated Americans.

Everyone noticed that the Duke was more in love with his wife than she with him. Hers seemed to be a maternal love; his was adoration. If she left the room, his gaze lingered on the door, and his face lit up when she returned.

He resigned as Governor of the Bahamas in March 1945, near the end of the war in Europe and five months before his term was up. Wallis described Bermuda as their Elba and St Helena. When the Windsors reached Paris in September, they found their house in the Boulevard Suchet had been undisturbed by the German occupation. By chance or by Nazi command in appreciation of their earlier congenial visit to Hitler?

The Duke was now allowed to return to England to visit his mother and brothers, but his wife remained unrecognised by them. In February 1952, King George VI died. At once the Duke of Windsor travelled to London and took his place with the family. The following year his mother, Queen Mary, died, and again he played his part in the ceremonies of mourning. Both times he was compelled by Buckingham Palace to be alone.

During this same period, something unlikely occurred. In 1950 when the Windsors were returning from New York on the *Queen Mary*, Wallis fell in love with another first-class passenger. At 54, she was still in her prime. Jimmy Donahue was 34. He was one of the Woolworth family, first cousin to the famously rich Barbara Hutton.

Witty and entertaining in New York society, Jimmy was a homosexual who increasingly favoured rough trade. He was the kind of prankster who on giving a luncheon party for the Marquess of Milford Haven, whom he found dull, seated a dozen brightly turned out young women and men at the table, not mentioning that they were all prostitutes. After lunch our prankster invited the guest of honour to see his mother's collection of bronzes in the next room. There he inflicted on the Marquess the spectacle of half a dozen naked black men, their bodies oiled and arranged in erotic positions.

The Windsors and Jimmy became a threesome. Because of Jimmy's homosexuality, for some time no one suspected that he and Wallis were in love. Gradually their apparent delight in each other's company, the body language when they danced, made the truth evident. In the party life that they all enjoyed, the Duke would retire to bed at twelve or one. Wallis and Jimmy joked and confided until four or five. When the Duke had to be away, Wallis and Jimmy were together non-stop.

The biographer Michael Bloch, who has done enormous research on the Duchess of Windsor, asserts she had a vaginal deformity that made full penetration impossible. Jimmy Donahue's biographer, Christopher Wilson, claims she was half delirious with love for Jimmy because he gave her the first sexual ecstasy she had ever known. Her inability for copulation seems to have suited the Duke who preferred Wallis to minister to him. For all those years she had done so, giving him bliss while she herself experienced only vicarious pleasure.

Jimmy applied himself with skill, and her response was overwhelming, Wilson asserts. It was impossible for the Duke to remain ignorant, but however humiliated, nothing could lessen his love for his wife. It was like an addiction. Four years went by before

Wallis was surfeited and able to see that Jimmy was not quite as amusing as she had thought and more shallow than she had realised. Once more she enjoyed her dominant role with her husband, which fitted so well with his gratification at being subservient to her.

In 1966, the young Queen Elizabeth II ended thirty years of her family's refusal to meet the Duke of Windsor's wife: she invited both of them to the unveiling of a plaque to Queen Mary. The Duchess curtsied to the Queen, and the media was beady-eyed to see whether she would curtsy to the Queen Mother who had long scorned her. She bowed instead.

The following year, I wrote to the Duchess as a fellow Baltimorean, asking for an interview for the *Sunday Express*, then the most influential middle-brow broadsheet in Fleet Street. In November I met her in the suite at Claridge's where they were staying while they did their Christmas shopping.

She was far more attractive than her photographs, her hair reddish-brown, her eyes a very bright blue. Apart from words like 'terribly' being pronounced in a cut-glass English accent, she retained her light Southern speech.

'I'm quite aware that some people assume I'm the boss,' she said. 'They've forgotten how subtle the Duke can be!' Unlike the Queen who refers to her consort as 'my husband', the Duchess always spoke of 'the Duke'. She talked humorously – except when the subject was the HRH that her marriage normally would have accorded her.

'I suppose they must have had very good reasons for withholding it,' she said sardonically, swinging her crossed leg impatiently. 'The Duke has been hurt very deeply. I always know the things that have hurt him because he never mentions them.'

I flew to Paris for my second interview. The Windsors' home in the Bois de Boulogne, like their previous French houses which she decorated, was elegantly splendid and also inviting. The Duke, a slender figure, strolled across the drawing room to welcome me. When he smiled, his narrow handsome face remained etched with sadness.

After he had left to play golf, the Duchess said of the abdication, 'He *did* want to be King. It still seems to me that something could have been done. I do sometimes feel: "What a pity." I mean, you can't help looking across at a person who has given up such a colossal amount and *thinking*.' She paused before adding: 'I don't mind for myself. All I can do is dedicate my life to making His Royal Highness happy in little domestic ways.'

The Duke of Windsor died in 1972. In death he received the pomp and ceremony he had forgone in life. The Queen invited his widow to stay at Buckingham Palace. The public, feeling he had been shabbily treated, flocked by the thousands to St George's Chapel at Windsor where he lay in state for two days. At the family funeral in the Chapel, the Duchess sat with the Queen. The Queen Mother offered her condolences but nothing more, her face remaining stony.

The Duke's coffin was interred, as he had wished, in the royal burial ground at Frogmore. It was announced that on her death the Duchess would lie beside him. She pointed out that the space reserved for her was extremely small, and subsequently a hedge was moved to allow her more room.

She lived in their Paris house for the rest of her life, keeping everything – even his clothes and cigar boxes – exactly as he had left them, while she grew frailer. On her death in 1986, Buckingham Palace made arrangements for her body to be flown to England with military honours.

The funeral was in St George's Chapel where from beginning to end her name was not mentioned. Then she was interred in the royal burial ground, at last given her rightful place alongside her husband.

18

Lord Boothby

1900–86

With fairy godmothers crowding round his cradle, Robert Boothby began life with brains, beauty, imagination, a strong body and extraordinary charm. While still in his twenties, he was talked of as a future Prime Minister. This he found a splendid idea: his vanity was always Olympian. In the event, he never rose above the most junior of ministers at the Ministry of Food. What went wrong?

A combination of things:

* He saw no virtue in restraint and refused to be respectable.
* He was ambitious only up to a point; beyond that point, he preferred the good life to struggling the rest of the way.
* Some sort of staying power was missing. He would stand up boldly in the front line and make a courageous speech, but then he would wander off somewhere for convivial and prolonged refreshment.
* His sense of right and wrong was personal and spontaneous.
* He was always a reckless gambler who did not confine his risk-taking to Deauville's baccarat tables, though heaven knows he spent enough time there.
* An exceptionally generous man, he would have hated to get out of debt at the expense of an individual. But he did not worry too much where an impersonal institution was concerned.

All of these 'flaws' made him wildly attractive to both men and women – most notably to Lady Dorothy Macmillan, daughter of the Duke of Devonshire and wife of Harold Macmillan, the Prime Minister.

Bob Boothby was born in Edinburgh, an only child. His father was a prosperous, much-respected Scottish banker who played the piano beautifully and collected seventeenth-century Dutch paintings. His wife was a tiny woman who alone could dominate her spoiled son.

Ludovic Kennedy, a cousin, who often visited the family in their fine house outside Edinburgh, told me how he watched, fascinated, one morning as Boothby arrived home off the morning sleeper to be greeted by his diminutive mother with the words: 'Bob, your breath is smelling of drink and your shirt is filthy. Go upstairs and clean your teeth and change your shirt *at once.*'

'Very well, Mother,' replied her son in that deep gravelly voice and went upstairs to obey. He was then forty.

His mother kept him at home until he was ten, when he embarked on a conventional upper-class education. He hated Eton but enjoyed Oxford where he began his friendships with Labour intellectuals – John Strachey in particular. They liked him for being a radical and rebel; they admired his unorthodox economic arguments; and they delighted in his indiscretions as he lovingly dissected the frailties of his fellow Tories. Boothby was never really at home in the Tory party. His intellect baulked at many of its policies.

Even when John Strachey left the Labour Party for Communism, he loved Boothby above any other man, despite his occasional belief that Boothby might lead the Tory party. 'You are one of the very few people in the world whom I have *felt* about – felt in a way that no rational consideration affects at all ... If you become king of the cannibal islands, I shall still have, until I die, the same depth of feeling towards you.'

From university Boothby went into the City, where his up-and-down career began in rollicking fashion. 'He's the cleverest man I know,' said a more staid financier, 'but his judgement is bad. Anything Bob says he's buying, I sell as fast as possible.'

Boothby was 24 when he entered the House of Commons. Starting with only a small majority in East Aberdeenshire, he had built it up to 12,000 by the time he left after 34 years for the House of Lords.

He talked endlessly about his constituents' porridge oats and herrings, and waged battle with the Russians themselves to protect the fishing rights of his electorate. They in turn adored him and didn't care tuppence what he did elsewhere.

Never modest about his undoubted grasp of highly complicated subjects, he was forever writing lengthy letters of advice – often unasked and unwanted – to successive Prime Ministers.

At 26 he became Parliamentary Private Secretary to Winston Churchill, then Chancellor of the Exchequer. 'It was my first big mistake,' Boothby said when I interviewed him in 1973 for a *Sunday Times Magazine* profile. 'Oswald Mosley warned me against it: "If you join Winston, he will demand total allegiance. When a difference of opinion arises between you, he will accuse you of disloyalty and betrayal." And he did. With Winston there could be no other god. Unfortunately, I'm not cut out to be a henchman.'

Yet throughout the thirties, when Churchill was in the political wilderness, Boothby was a good friend to him when few others were. Together they spoke out against Chamberlain and appeasement and the Tory party's attitude towards Nazi Germany.

If Boothby's political heresy made him suspect to most Tories, so did his private affairs. The liaison central to his life became known to a widening circle, but when I interviewed him he asked that I refrain from naming the lady. Though she had died in 1966, her husband, Harold Macmillan, was still alive. Boothby wounded Macmillan grievously, yet he also had good manners.

Macmillan's biographer, Alistair Horne, said that while 1929 was a year of disaster throughout the world, 'it was also one of the most wretched in Harold Macmillan's life.' He lost his seat in Parliament and his wife to another man.

The Macmillans had been married for nine years. Lady Dorothy was both bored and highly sexed. Robert Rhodes-James wrote that her sisters rated Macmillan 'as the most stupendously boring man they had ever met, and they could not understand why the vivacious and attractive Dorothy had ever married him.'

The Macmillans and Boothby met for the second time at a house party. Not long afterwards, Boothby invited them to a shoot on his father's estate. Rhodes-James described what happened next: 'It was on the second day on the moors, when Boothby was waiting his turn to shoot, that he was startled to find his hand being squeezed affectionately, and turned to see a beaming Dorothy beside him. That was when it all began.'

Each was mad about the other. Born into a formidable clan, Dorothy saw no reason not to do what she wanted. As well, there was a streak of cruelty in her. She made not the slightest effort to conceal Boothby's letters to her, and if her husband came into the room while she was on the telephone to her lover, she simply carried on her conversation.

Macmillan was profoundly humiliated by the affair. In 1931 he had a complete nervous breakdown and was sent to a Munich clinic to recover. The previous year, Sarah Macmillan was born. She was widely believed to be Boothby's daughter.

In September 1932, when Boothby and Dorothy were on holiday together in Portugal, he wrote to his friend Cynthia Mosley: 'I love Dorothy. As much as I have ever loved her ... She said to me tragically yesterday: "Why did you ever wake me? I never want to see any of my family again. And without you, life for me is going to be nothing but one big hurt." '

In the early fifties, Sarah Macmillan and Tony Crosland (in what he called his 'dukes' daughters period') fancied one another. By then, Sarah talked freely about the sadness in her life. She had become pregnant in her teens, and her mother had insisted on an abortion so as not to damage Macmillan's career. He had regained his seat at Stockton, and Dorothy knew his constituents would be shocked by an illegitimate grandchild. Not until later did Sarah learn at a college dance that Boothby was her father. From then on, she frequently visited him at his Belgravia flat.

All Dorothy's children seem to have suffered one way and another from their confused upbringing. Each had a problem with alcohol, particularly Sarah. Boothby said he could never forgive Dorothy for ruining Sarah's life: she discovered when she married that the abortion had left her unable to have children.

Boothby's mother believed that Dorothy ruined his career. A curious fact in those pre-permissive days was that the opprobrium rubbed off only on Boothby. Other men increasingly thought him a rascal. A friend, A J P Taylor, pointed out an obvious explanation: 'All those poor chumps who had got married and had to pay for their fun resented the fact that Boothby didn't.'

Dorothy, impervious to the pain she caused, kept her grip on both men. She was in daily contact with Boothby and travelled everywhere with him. At the same time she ran the Macmillan home at Birch Grove, entertained for her husband, and did what was expected of an MP's wife.

Intense as the love affair remained, sometimes Boothby rebelled. He put down the failure of these rebellions to the Devonshire clan. 'Once you get into the clutches of any member of that family, by God, you haven't a hope,' he said. 'I fled to France, to America; once I even went to Africa. It was no use. I was pursued. They are the most tenacious family in Britain.'

In his half-hearted efforts to break off the affair, he got engaged a couple of times. 'But it was only to try to break out of the web, not because I really loved anyone else.'

At 35, he even got married – to Diana Cavendish, a niece of the Duke of Devonshire. As he soon returned to Dorothy, it was the briefest of marriages, formally terminated by divorce two years later, he and Diana remaining friends.

When Boothby's hero, Churchill, after his ten-years' isolation, became Prime Minister and the nation's wartime hero to boot, Boothby had reason to expect a challenging job. Under Churchill, he could have been a brilliant and forceful minister. But Churchill showed no great eagerness to reward his small band of loyal supporters. He made Boothby Parliamentary Secretary at the Ministry of Food.

Boothby told me:

The whole of my career has turned on jealousy. Churchill and I always had a love-hate relationship. He resented my popularity – which he never shared himself except in 1940 when he was the war hero. He resented my popularity in Scotland; he himself kept losing constituencies. Above all he resented my popularity on radio and television.

Did he paradoxically resent the fact that Boothby had been loyal to him when others had not? 'Of course,' said Boothby. 'Still, in the end, he gave me a KBE. He said: "He has rendered great service to the country." '

The following year, 1954, Sir Robert, as he now was, played a leading role in setting up the Wolfenden Committee on homosexuality and prostitution. When many politicians were wary of taking a public stand in favour of reforming the laws on homosexuality, Boothby campaigned openly – 'as a kind of non-playing captain', said his friend Michael Foot. Nonetheless rumours of active bisexuality attached themselves to Boothby.

And Harold Macmillan? Permanently seared by his wife's open love for another man, he flung himself with a vengeance into his career. Later he admitted: 'All this personal trouble did strengthen my character.'

Partly because he was (like Boothby) unwilling to follow the party line, partly because his air of intellectual superiority irritated senior colleagues, Macmillan remained a backbencher until 1940 when Churchill gave him a foothold on the ministerial ladder as Parliamentary Secretary to the Ministry of Supply – exactly the same rank that he gave Boothby at Food. Macmillan, however, kept climbing. In a succession of posts he proved an effective administrator, and when Eden resigned the premiership in 1957, Macmillan emerged as Prime Minister. That would show Boothby and Dorothy.

Macmillan made himself into a different public personality with a dry wit and a flair for optimistic expressions, as in the slogan for the 1957 General Election: 'You've never had it so good.' His popularity soared, and he became affectionately known as 'Supermac'. Yet underneath, he remained the shy man whose unworldliness ill-equipped him to deal with the scandals that engulfed his government in 1962–3, culminating in the Profumo scandal.

During Macmillan's six years in office, he and Dorothy grew closer, and he came to value her advice, despite the fact that her affair with Boothby continued until her death.

Being Boothby, he was always a magnet for apocrypha (as well as author of a good many himself). The story was widely told that in

1958, when he was summoned to Prime Minister Macmillan's office, he expected to be appointed First Lord of the Admiralty. 'Macmillan,' goes the oft-told story, 'had an old score to settle with Boothby. "My dear Bob, I think you'd make an admirable life peer, and I want you to go to the Lords." For a politician, the kiss of death.'

When he went to the Lords, he resigned the Tory whip and settled his burly self on the crossbenches as Baron Boothby of Buchan and Rattray Head. He had wanted his title to include the names of practically every place in his constituency. 'Come, come, come,' said the College of Heralds, 'you can only have two.' He was most upset.

He became Rector of St Andrews University, one of the most coveted honours in Scotland. And he continued to give incomparable performances on radio and television. He was cut out for both media. Essentially a showman, his majestically rusty voice, his splendid indiscretions, his outrageous boasting, all endeared him to a growing audience, as they still endeared him to Harold Macmillan's wife.

Boothby's flamboyance made him beloved by the press, but in 1964 the *Sunday Mirror* ran a story whose banner headline he would not have chosen: 'PEER AND A GANGSTER; YARD INQUIRY'. A few days later the *Daily Mirror* proclaimed: 'THE PICTURE WE DARE NOT PRINT', which the paper then described as 'a well-known member of the House of Lords seated on a sofa with a gangster who leads the biggest protection racket London has ever known.'

Rumours cascaded. Homosexual practices between a peer and clergymen in Brighton, Mayfair parties with East End gangsters, blackmail – all good racy stuff. Boothby with immense boldness took the bull by the horns. With the help of two lawyers, the great and good Lord Goodman and Gerald Gardiner (soon to become the impeccable Lord Chancellor in the Labour government), Boothby wrote a letter to *The Times*.

He spelled out the rumours, about himself, one by one. Then he refuted them:

> I am not a homosexual. I have not been to a Mayfair party of any kind for more than twenty years. I have met the man who is alleged to be 'King of the Underworld' only three times, on

business matters, and then by appointment at my flat, at his request, and in the company of other people. I have never been to a party in Brighton with gangsters – still less clergymen. No one has ever tried to blackmail me.

Was some of this bluff? He would not be the first politician to indulge in occasional risk-taking in the company of homosexual thugs.

In any case, five days later the *Mirror* carried a humble apology and paid Lord Boothby £40,000 for any embarrassment he might have suffered.

Nonetheless, I asked him, could he really be quite so innocent? Why on earth did he wish to be photographed with anyone like Ronald Kray, who, incidentally, was the homosexual of the twins? Surely the most naive of men would be wary. He replied:

Ronald Kray came to see me with his lawyer and two other men to ask whether I would become director of some project in Nigeria. As they were leaving, Kray said: 'I have a passion for being photographed with celebrities. Do you mind?' I said: 'Go ahead.' After all, the man's lawyer was sitting there. I didn't give it a thought.

Could even a man with sublime vanity have thought nothing of it? I asked Lord Gardiner his view. 'I don't think it had anything to do with vanity. This sort of bad luck can happen to particularly polite people.'

Half a year after the Kray scandal, Boothby outraged the House of Lords by speaking in the twins' defence. He had long campaigned against people being held indefinitely without trial. The Krays were arrested in January 1965 and were still in jail awaiting trial three months later. His words were largely lost amidst a hubbub of protesting Lords and Ladies who found it a gross impertinence for Boothby even to mention the name Kray.

All of this, of course, gave much delight to Dorothy Macmillan. Until her death in 1966, she wanted the fascinating Boothby's company, but did not wish him to compete too much with her husband's career. She wanted to have her cake and eat it. And she did.

In 1967 there were more headlines and photographs. A striking young Sardinian woman with flashing white teeth and long jet black hair had taken matters in hand: this man twice her age must settle down. And he did, in a way. Amid a fanfare of flashbulbs and a battery of television cameras and microphones, Lord Boothby at 67 embarked on marriage in the exuberant expectation of living happily ever after.

The last time I saw him was six years later. He was thriving. While herself prepared to tease him, his wife would not have a word said by anyone – himself included – which suggested that he might not be the greatest man since Napoleon.

'If anyone implies I'm not sublime, she becomes a tiger,' he boomed in that rusty voice, beaming.

19

The Duchess of Argyll

1913–93

This was too much. Three weeks earlier in June 1963, Prime Minister Harold Macmillan's government had nearly been brought down by his Secretary of State for War, John Profumo. Profumo had to resign when it was discovered that he had lied to the House of Commons about his intimacy with Christine Keeler, an unusually enticing call girl who at the time was also sharing her bed with a Russian diplomat. Now another Cabinet Minister, Duncan Sandys, son-in-law of Winston Churchill, announced in Cabinet that he was about to resign because of a widely circulated rumour about *him*.

Protesting his innocence, he was enraged that certain of his closest colleagues believed the story that he was the 'headless man' in the Duke of Argyll's divorce case. The Duke held one of the most distinguished titles in Scotland. The Duchess was a celebrated promiscuous beauty. 'This will be the end of the government,' said Number Ten's chief press officer.

In his wife's absence in Australia, the Duke had travelled to London, and in her Mayfair home he searched her writing desk where he found she had entered details of her manifold affairs in her diaries. Then he came across four Polaroid photographs. The Polaroid instant-developing camera was a new invention and became a status item for the rich. The four photos were taken, presumably with a self-timer, in the Duchess's mirrored bathroom.

Apart from her pearl necklace, she was naked, fellating a standing man in different states of arousal, his face outside the picture. The captions read: 'before', 'thinking of you', 'during – oh' and 'finished'.

The Duchess's boudoir revealed a further set of pictures which showed a man masturbating. Again the image was 'headless'. It was assumed that they were the same man. The two sets of pictures formed the central exhibit in the Duke's divorce case in 1963, the longest and most sensational case to be heard in Britain.

Margaret Argyll had been brought up as a spoiled little rich girl. Her father, a Scottish self-made millionaire, spent lavishly on his only child to make up for the lack of background. Margaret had plenty of suitors, among them Aly Khan. Her social-climbing father felt the line had to be drawn somewhere. A Pakistani! So Aly Khan went off and married Rita Hayworth instead.

Although Margaret became engaged to the Earl of Warwick, she already had her eye on a rich American stockbroker, Charles Sweeny, whom she married. During the war years, she suffered a terrible injury from stepping into an empty lift shaft. Afterwards, her appetite for men became insatiable. (Do not ask me how this cause and effect transpired.) The Sweenys were divorced in 1947.

Ian Campbell, heir to the Dukedom of Argyll, spent most of the war in a German prison camp and returned with a drink problem. Good-looking and charming, he was a renowned reprobate and cad, with virtually no cash. Still, he was a duke. Margaret wanted a grand title; he knew her cash value. On his divorce from his second wife in 1951, he married Margaret. Initially, each was smitten with the other, but essentially it was a marriage of convenience.

In his court action, the Duke cited 88 men whom he suspected of being his wife's lovers, including two government ministers and three royals. The Polaroid photos were produced as evidence of the Duchess's promiscuity. Duncan Sandys was rumoured to be both headless men.

He was persuaded not to resign by the Prime Minister, who promised that Lord Denning, the nation's most senior law lord, would investigate and report on the rumours. Sandys then took himself to a Harley Street doctor who examined the minister's pubic hair and pronounced that it was not like the pubic hair in the masturbation photos – the only set that Sandys, cunningly, had brought with him.

Denning's report was unequivocal: 'It has been demonstrated to my entire satisfaction that the "unknown" man in the photographs was not this Minister.' The minister, he went on, offered to be examined by a medical man 'who proved conclusively . . . that the physical characteristics of the "unknown" man differed in unmistakable and significant respects from those of this Minister.'

So who then was the headless man? Of the 88 men cited by the Duke, Lord Denning narrowed the field down to five and invited them to the Treasury. Each had to sign the visitors' register. A graphologist had no difficulty in saying which man had written the captions to the pictures.

He was the swashbuckling American actor Douglas Fairbanks Jr who lived with his wife in a mansion in The Boltons and was a habitué of London high society. Though neither he nor Sandys was named in the report, implicating Fairbanks in the investigation effectively put Duncan Sandys in the clear in the public's eyes – for the time being.

The presiding judge, Lord Wheatley, could not bring himself to speak of fellatio, referring to it as 'sexual association'. Granting the Duke a divorce from his wife, the judge said: 'There is enough in her own admissions and proven facts to establish that, by 1960, she was a completely promiscuous woman whose sexual appetite could only be satisfied with a number of men.' For good measure he added that she was involved in 'disgusting sexual activities to gratify a basic sexual appetite.'

Recent evidence now makes it virtually certain that the two sets of Polaroids showed two different men. Duncan Sandys was the standing man on whom the Duchess was performing fellatio, and his masturbating rival was Fairbanks. How Fairbanks must have chuckled as he wrote the four captions on the photos of Duncan Sandys. Neither man ever admitted involvement.

Though the Duchess remained silent on the pictures that shredded her reputation, just before her death at 80 she told a friend: 'Of course, sweetie, the only Polaroid camera in the country at this time had been lent to the Ministry of Defence.' In 1957, when the pictures were taken, Sandys was a minister at Defence. It was as if she wanted someone to know.

In the divorce case, the Duke and Duchess abandoned their class discretion. Margaret was stripped in public. After the case, the Duke took to showing the Polaroid photos around his club. Charles Sweeny, Margaret's first husband, was also a member of the club. Being an American, he had better manners than the Duke and had him expelled.

The Duchess's end in a nursing home was ignominious and impoverished. Nothing could put her reputation back together again. Out of human kindness, Charles Sweeny – who died not long before Margaret – arranged that she be buried in the same grave with him.

20

King Farouk

1920–65

Few kings have a more determined reputation for hedonism than Farouk I of Egypt. Yet his reign began so well. When his father died, the new King was a slim, stunningly handsome youth of sixteen. He devoted himself to schemes for his country's economic development and land reform. These worthy personal aims would be short-lived.

Born in Cairo, Farouk was raised in the royal palaces among women – his overbearing glamorous mother, Queen Nazli, his four beautiful sisters and their female attendants. The newly arrived British High Commissioner, Miles Lampson, physically a giant, was a prime example of Foreign Office arrogance in the days of Empire. His patronising of the King made a mockery of Egypt's new independence from Britain.

Lampson decided this well-mannered boy should go to Eton and learn to be an English gentleman. Without any previous formal education, his concentration span short, Farouk was turned down by Eton but studied at the Royal Military Academy, Woolwich. Neither English nor Arab, he was a Muslim who picked and chose which Muslim customs he observed. He never drank spirits or wine, so whatever he got up to was undertaken in stone-cold sobriety.

When he was eighteen, his mother selected his bride, Farida, wrongly supposing that the elegant patrician teenager would be 'manageable'. A national holiday was declared for the wedding day.

Kept in purdah while her father and Farouk completed the business part of the deal, Farida quickly showed herself to be a thoroughly modern young woman, ignoring the Muslim edict against photography by lifting her veil and smiling at the cameras. The pictures were soon hanging in every shop in Cairo. The public saw Farouk and Farida as the perfect couple.

Not for them the tradition of a wife kept in a harem. He took her everywhere, each day surprising her with a new jewel or painting. Contrary to the Muslim proclamation against the graven image, he put her portrait on postage stamps. The people loved it.

Farouk's happiness would be complete if he had an heir, and at the end of November 1938, Queen Farida gave birth. Alas, the Palace guard fired 41 salvos rather than the desired 101: the child was a girl. Farouk and his Queen would have to try again. But there was a problem known only to them. Not only was the King's equipment undersized, he was undersexed. Nonetheless, Farida became pregnant – and gave birth to another daughter.

Farouk's next disappointment was still more humiliating: his teenage wife fell in love with another man. Normally sweet-tempered, the King exploded in anger. His daily gifts to Farida were replaced with quarrelling. Yet he did not want to divorce her: their 'fairytale romance' was an important ingredient in his popularity with his people. To compound his anger, his mother, Queen Nazli, began a discreet love affair with his adored tutor. As if that were not enough, by 1940 the domineering British Ambassador, the now elevated Sir Miles Lampson, was slyly denigrating the King to one and all.

Farouk had earlier signed a treaty of alliance with Britain, whereby the British retained rights in the Suez Canal zone. Now Egypt joined the Allies in the Second World War. In 1942, the German Field Marshal Rommel was sweeping across northern Africa, and Egypt was about to be overwhelmed. At 22, wherever he looked, Farouk faced nothing but disaster. That is when he took the decision that the only thing certain in his life was a capacity for pleasure. He embarked on hedonism and never looked back. When the British Eighth Army won the decisive battle of El-Alamein, Egypt was saved from German invasion. But the King's priorities were by now fixed on his own delights.

Any young woman was a prospective mistress. Two early 'official mistresses' were a beguiling Alexandrian Jewess, Irene Najjar, and a self-willed English 'intellectual's moll', Barbara Skelton. The latter femme fatale was married (twice) to the celebrated and usually broke man of letters, Cyril Connolly, and worked in the British cipher office in wartime Cairo. Connolly voiced his approval of Barbara's long Farouk adventure with the immortal words: 'After all, a King's a King.'

In her memoirs, Skelton describes one of her royal lover's little foibles. 'I am deadly tired and ache all over from a flogging of last night on the steps of the Royal Palace. I would have preferred a splayed cane, but instead had to suffer a dressing-gown cord which created a gentle thudding sound over an interminable period.'

Skelton grew very fond of the monarch, finding his childish side endearing. In a *roman-à-clef* about Farouk and his dressing-gown cord's tassel, she describes a flourish which I expect is practised by few flagellants:

> The cord made a dull, thudding plop when it met her skin and her whole body tingled. As the blows rained harder, his breath fanned her neck and at each stroke a cool current of air passed over her back. Tensely she awaited each thud with a forlorn feeling which was not unpleasant. His heavy breathing increased. 'It's coming faster,' he bellowed, until with a prodigious roar he gave a final lash and somersaulted across the bed to the floor. 'I did enjoy that. Will you let me do it again some time?'

By now the British concluded that their cipher clerk had grown much too intimate with the King.

> They were convinced Farouk was setting me up just to get information from me. What they never could understand was that Farouk couldn't have cared less . . . There was absolutely nothing political about him then. In the end, though, the British simply wouldn't have it. They decided to ship me out.

Among Farouk's pleasures were his two hundred red motor cars. When he was unable to sleep, he would roar down the corniche to some gambling club. Lest police, failing to recognise his car, made themselves tiresome, however briefly, he had a law enacted permitting only Palace cars to be painted red.

His greatest joys, however, were women and food. His reputation for sexual experiments with girls went side by side with giving them little sexual satisfaction. But as Skelton testified, his company was stimulating and amusing. And as Connolly had cynically and rightly observed: 'After all, a King's a King.' Farouk never lacked female companionship, be it with princesses or belly-dancers.

To the Egyptians' dismay, in 1948 Farouk said to the lovely, cultured Queen Farida, mother of his three daughters: 'I divorce you. I divorce you. I divorce you.' As far as Koranic law was concerned, that was that. He spotted a petit-bourgeois sixteen-year-old commoner called Narriman and decided she might be the one to produce a male heir. Though no one else could see anything particularly desirable about her, Farouk had fallen in love.

He sent her to Rome to be polished up. Pregnant by her wedding day, she gave her husband his ultimate happiness: she produced a boy, Prince Fuad. Farouk's royal blood line was secure. Or so he thought.

In 1952, disgusted by the incompetence and corruption of Farouk's rule, Gamal Abdel Nasser and General Neguib plotted a successful *coup d'état* and forced the King to abdicate. Nasser's Free Officers voted by one vote not to execute Farouk at this time. The ex-King and his family, the new King in Narriman's arms, boarded *Mahroussa* and set sail for Italy. Fuad was for a few years the boy King in exile, but he never returned to Egypt. Monarchy, which had held power from the Pharoahs to Farouk, was at an end.

With his family, Farouk lived the high life in Italy. In 1965, alarmingly bloated by his three hundred pounds, his blood pressure high, he was enjoying a midnight banquet with one of his endless girls. Having polished off his usual dozen oysters, lobster thermidor, roast lamb and a few other courses, he leant back in his chair to light one of his huge Havana cigars, clawed at his throat and fell over dead.

His excesses could, of course, have killed him. But almost certainly he was assassinated. Nasser, now President of Egypt, was paranoid that the people of Egypt might demand Farouk's return and thus destabilise the Republic. The poison – thought to have been administered in Farouk's lobster thermidor – would have been alacontin, which would stop his heart but not show up in an autopsy. In any case, on orders from the Italian secret service, there was no autopsy.

He was 45.

21

Lana Turner

1920–95

Schwab's Drug Store in Los Angeles became a Mecca for screen-crazed girls. It was there, perched in an upfront posture on a fountain stool and sipping a soda, that Lana Turner was discovered by a Hollywood talent spotter. She was passed from one mogul to another until Mervyn LeRoy arranged a screen test. Dubbed 'The Sweater Girl', soon afterwards she appeared in the aptly named 1937 film *They Won't Forget*, wearing a figure-hugging cashmere sweater and skirt. Lana = sex. She exuded the stuff.

Every soldier's pin-up and every schoolgirl's fantasy (the craze for a tight sweater and skirt swept through the nation), in few of Lana's films was she allowed to show how good an actress she might have been. Her roles involved *chemistry*. Mix three parts Clark Gable with two parts Turner and you had a winning movie cocktail. He was her favourite leading man. They played together three times.

The chemistry was what put the dynamite in *The Postman Always Rings Twice* when street tough John Garfield came up against bleached blonde small-town girl looking for money and love in that order. In some ways Lana was playing herself, though personally she would have put money and love on a par.

She had started life in Wallace, Idaho. Her father was murdered for gambling debts. When she was fifteen, her family moved to Los

Angeles where she attended Hollywood High School, surrounded by would-be actresses. She was sixteen when she presented herself at Schwab's Drug Store.

In the 1940s she became one of the ten highest-earning women in the United States, and by the fifties she was queen of MGM. Her seven husbands (all celebrities) included beefcake 'Tarzan' actor Lex Barker and band leader Artie Shaw, a relative highbrow. Lovers abounded – Sinatra, Howard Hughes, Tyrone Power, Fernando Lamas, to name a few. All of these frolics managed to stay on the acceptable side of Hollywood's moral boundary and simply added to her sex-symbol status. But her own life was not happy. Only one man had stirred her, Tyrone Power, and her possessiveness had ruined that affair. She was always searching for another love to equal this one.

A gangster provided an outlet for her passion. Johnny Stompanato, alias Johnny Valentine, former bodyguard of big-time criminal Mickey Cohen, was startlingly handsome even by Hollywood standards. He was much sought after as a gigolo, like Porfirio Ruberosa making great play of his outsize penis, which was known as 'Oscar' in reference to the foot-high Academy Award. Everyone in America knew that Lana Turner had just separated from Lex Barker, and Stompanato guessed that she might be lonely. He got hold of her private number and proposed a blind date, mentioning mutual acquaintances and dropping a hint about 'Oscar'.

The blind date proved the start of a sado-masochistic affair in which Lana found herself increasingly infatuated with Johnny's calculated violence. While filming in England, she sent him letters about her longing for the 'happy aches' he skilfully caused, and became so desperate for them that she sent him a plane ticket and set him up in a big house in London.

His cockiness was supreme. 'When I say HOP, you'll hop. When I say JUMP, you'll jump.' He threatened to mutilate her so savagely that she would have to stay hidden for ever. He came to the set and waved a pistol at Lana's co-star, Sean Connery, warning him to keep away from Lana. Connery threw a punch that floored Stompanato. The studio contacted Scotland Yard who ordered him out of England.

She wrote begging letters to him, longing for his caresses, 'so fierce that they hurt me – it is beautiful and yet it is terrible – I am yours and I need you.'

When filming was finished, the two went to Mexico where other guests at the Hotel Via Vera complained of the noise from their SM activities. When they returned to Hollywood, Lana's only child, Cheryl Crane, was waiting at the airport. Like many stars' teenage children, fourteen-year-old Cheryl was disturbed.

One evening the rumpus at the big house in Bedford Drive was noisier than usual. Lana had threatened to stop paying Johnny's gambling debts. At the same time as hurting her he shouted: 'I'll cut you up and I'll get your mother and your daughter too. That's my business.'

Cheryl ran into the kitchen and grabbed a nine-inch butcher's knife and rushed back to her mother's aid. Stompanato swaggered in front of her to block her way. 'It all happened so quickly,' Lana later testified in court, 'that I did not even see the knife in my daughter's hand. I thought she had hit him in the stomach with her fist.'

Stompanato stumbled forward, then turned and fell on his back. Minutes later, Jerry Geisler, the film colony's most famous lawyer, answered his phone. 'This is Lana Turner. Something terrible has happened. Could you please come to my house?'

He found Lana in tears and the teenage killer in hysteria. When he stepped into Lana's pink boudoir, he was confronted by the bloodied corpse stretched out on the thick carpet.

In the courtroom Geisler acted for mother and daughter. Lana needed his physical support as well when she continued her testimony, weeping. 'Mr Stompanato choked, his hands on his throat. I ran to him and lifted up his sweater. I saw the blood. He made a horrible noise in his throat. I tried to breathe air into his semi-open lips, my mouth against his . . .'

She was near fainting. A bailiff brought her a glass of water. She could barely speak when she concluded: 'He was dying.'

After twenty minutes, the jury returned their verdict of justifiable homicide. The press were over the moon and declared it: 'Her best performance'. Lana's prodigious love-life was put under a micro-scope. Stompanato's thug friends ransacked his house to find her love letters which were promptly sold to the highest bidder. For two days they were on front pages across the land.

Columnists denounced her as a dissolute, unnatural mother. Psychiatrists, clergy and sociologists all got in on the act. Sometimes Cheryl was defended, other times condemned. Walter Winchell was the only major columnist to speak out against the threat to deprive Lana of her child:

> She is made of rays of the sun woven of blue eyes, honey-coloured hair and flowing curves. She is Lana Turner, goddess of the screen. But soon the magician leaves and the shadows take over. All the hidden cruelties appear . . . And of course it is outraged virtue which screams the loudest. It seems sadistic to me to subject Lana to any more torment.

She rode out the storm and later that same year won an Academy Award for her role in *Peyton Place*. In movie theatres when she first came on screen, audiences applauded and shouted: 'We're on your side, Lana!'

Back in demand, she made some of her most successful films and remained a queen until she retired at 53. In the hiatus between acting and her death – 22 years later – she became a recluse.

Cheryl grew up to write a book about her traumatic childhood and, perhaps unsurprisingly, opted to live in adult partnership with her lesbian lover.

22

John Profumo and Christine Keeler

1915–/1942–

My first newspaper job was for the great John Junor on the then influential *Sunday Express*. In March 1963, my editor asked me to interview Valerie Hobson, a distinguished actress whose second husband was John Profumo, Secretary of State for War in Harold Macmillan's government.

'There is reason to believe that the marriage is in rough waters. She may soon divorce Profumo. Try to bring the conversation around to that,' said my editor. I thought: 'Oh, great.'

I phoned Valerie Hobson and asked for an interview on how she combined the stage with marriage to a senior Cabinet Minister. With friendly self-confidence, she suggested I come to her home for tea. 'We can put our feet up and have a just-girls' talk – off the record until you have checked the quotes with me.' Disappointing, but better than nothing.

On the agreed day, I was reading the cuttings on both Profumos when Valerie Hobson's secretary phoned. She was extremely sorry, she said, but she would have to cancel my interview with Mrs Profumo. Something had come up that made it impossible.

I suggested we fix another date.

'I'm afraid that Mrs Profumo does not want to make any arrangements with the press just now.'

That afternoon a senior reporter came back from lunch with his face bright crimson. Nothing so strange in that except he was waving a publication and regaling his colleagues with what he had just read in *Westminster Confidential*, an authoritative weekly newsletter that normally featured inside information on the economy. As well as including a highly embarrassing passage from a letter signed 'Jack' on the stationery of the Secretary for War, the article said:

> ... the allegation by this girl was that not only was this minister, who has a famous actress as a wife, her client, but so also was the Soviet military attaché, apparently a Colonel Ivanov. The famous actress wife would, of course, sue for divorce ... Who was using the girl to 'milk' whom of information – the War Secretary or the Soviet military attaché? – ran in the minds of those primarily interested in security.

As the newsletter had small circulation, Profumo decided not to sue. Had he seen the excitement in the office of the *Sunday Express*, he would have known his days as a leading Cabinet Minister were numbered.

Initially, the press could only circle round the story for fear of libel. Then the *Daily Express* went at the thing with a degree of subtlety. Coincidentally, a criminal case was before the courts: in 1962, a West Indian drug-dealer, Johnny Edgecombe, with whom a young prostitute, Christine Keeler, was having an affair, had tried to shoot out the front door lock of Dr Stephen Ward's flat where Miss Keeler was living. At the time, the case had little publicity, but the *Express* now ran a story on the current trial of Edgecombe at the Old Bailey: the principal witness had disappeared, and it was rumoured that she had been got at. Immediately above a photograph of the ravishingly pretty missing witness, Christine Keeler, was an article headed 'War Minister Shock', which claimed that Profumo had offered his resignation for personal reasons.

Five days later, Colonel George Wigg, probably the Labour Opposition's most poisonous member, took advantage of MPs'

privilege to raise in the Commons a contentious matter without fear
of the law of libel:

> ... There is not an hon. Member in the House, not a journalist
> in the Press Gallery who, in the last few days, has not heard
> rumour upon rumour involving a member of the Government
> Front Bench. The Press has got as near as it could – it has shown
> itself willing to wound but afraid to strike ... I rightly use the
> Privilege of the House of Commons – that is what it is given me
> for – to ask the Home Secretary ... to go to the Dispatch Box
> – he knows the rumour to which I refer relates to Miss Christine
> Keeler and Miss Davis [*sic*] and a shooting by a West Indian –
> and, on behalf of the Government, categorically deny the truth
> of these rumours ...

A more amiable Labour colleague, the eccentric fox-hunting
Reginald Paget, remarked: 'What do these rumours amount to? They
amount to the fact that a Minister is said to be acquainted with an
extremely pretty girl. As far as I am concerned, I should have thought
that was a matter for congratulation rather than an inquiry.'
That night Macmillan told Profumo he must repeat to the
Commons the denials he had made in private. At 11 a.m. on Friday
22 March, the Secretary for War began his reckless personal statement to a crowded House. As is normal for caught-out husbands, he
made repeated reference to his wife. I thought of Valerie Hobson's
evident ignorance until two weeks earlier of the political fall-out.
It had been alleged, Profumo said,

> that people in high places might have been responsible for
> concealing information concerning the disappearance of a
> witness and the perversion of justice. I understand that my
> name had been connected with the rumours about the
> disappearance of Miss Keeler ... I last saw Miss Keeler in
> December 1961, and I have not seen her since. I have no idea
> where she is now ... My wife and I first met Miss Keeler at a
> house party in July 1961 at Cliveden. Among a number of
> people there was Dr Stephen Ward, whom we already knew

slightly, and Mr Ivanov, who was an attaché at the Russian Embassy. The only other occasion that my wife or I met Mr Ivanov was for a moment at the official reception for Major Gagarin at the Soviet Embassy. [So far, true.] My wife and I had a standing invitation to visit Dr Ward. Between July and December 1961 I met Miss Keeler on about half a dozen occasions when I called to see him and his friends. There was no impropriety whatsoever in my acquaintanceship with Miss Keeler . . .

I now go back to that weekend in July 1961 when the lead characters in this story first met at Cliveden, Lord Astor's palatial estate in Buckinghamshire. His Lordship had a dicey back, and had made a straight barter with Dr Stephen Ward, a well-known society osteopath: in exchange for the use of a cottage at Cliveden, Dr Ward would treat the Astor back. The principal guests that weekend were the Secretary of State for War, John Profumo, then 46, and his 37-year-old wife, Valerie Hobson. Educated at Harrow and Oxford, Profumo came from aristocratic Italian stock and was independently rich. On the first evening, Lord Astor took the Minister for a stroll in the splendid gardens. Lo, a naked girl with a Mona Lisa face and shiny shoulder-length dark hair was splashing in the pool. Her escort, Dr Stephen Ward, had hidden her bathing costume.

Lord Astor, who always liked his guests to enjoy themselves, introduced Profumo to Dr Ward. As well as being a fashionable osteopath and talented artist, fifty-year-old Ward often had one or another pretty young prostitute sharing his flat in Wimpole Mews. Wanting to please the rich and famous, he was happy to pimp for them.

Christine Keeler, then nineteen, had come to London at sixteen to make her way as a topless showgirl in Soho. That's when she met Stephen Ward and Mandy Rice-Davies, a cocky impish blonde who had turned her back on her Birmingham council estate. Both girls based their activities in Ward's flat.

Astor invited Dr Ward and Christine to join the house party on Sunday. Along with everyone else, Valerie Hobson saw that her husband was fascinated by Christine. They both disappeared from view when he gave her a tour of the sumptuous mansion, which ended in hide-and-seek in the bedrooms – all quite innocent, of course, he would have assured his wife.

An attractive Soviet naval attaché turned up, and soon a water piggy-back race was under way in the pool, Astor astride Colonel Eugene Ivanov, Christine on Profumo. Later when she sold her story to the *News of the World*, she spoke of her disappointment at not being on Ivanov's shoulders instead. Profumo may have been generally regarded as an elegant, well-built man, but the burly, balding Ivanov was more to Christine's taste. 'He was a *man*,' she explained to the Sunday tabloid. 'He was rugged with a hairy chest, strong and agile.'

Later Christine told the *Daily Express* how she had met Profumo's wife by the swimming pool at Cliveden. 'She was charming and we chatted for quite a while.' Not for nothing was Valerie Hobson an actress. She must have felt quite ill at what was unfolding before her eyes.

The Soviet Colonel stole a march on his rival by driving Christine back to Ward's flat in Wimpole Mews. After they drank a bottle of vodka, she found herself in Ivanov's arms. 'He was a wonderful lover, so masculine . . . We left serious discussion [*sic*] and I yielded to this wonderful huggy bear of a man . . .'

By the end of the week she found herself also in the Minister's arms. As Profumo was totally smitten, I am sorry to say that she described their meetings as 'screws of convenience'.

'Unlike Jack,' she told the world, 'Ivanov was a party boy and loved to take me to the bright spots, wining and dining me. Jack never took me anywhere, except for drives all over London, and even then he was so anxious to be discreet that he used to borrow a big black car from Mr John Hare, the Minister of Labour.' I dare say that would have been more comfortable than Profumo's Mini Minor, another venue for their couplings.

Sometimes they met at Ward's flat. Mandy Rice-Davies regaled friends with the French farce of Profumo, who had no idea he was sharing his mistress, leaving the flat and a few minutes later Colonel Ivanov walking in. Almost inevitably, I suppose, Profumo took his mistress to his home while his wife was away: there has always been an attraction for errant husbands in 'defiling' the marriage bed.

Besotted, he lavished presents on Christine. For her, she said, the liaison meant no more than 'a look across a crowded floor'. It could have been a story by Balzac.

Meanwhile, Dr Ward whose complex nature included a taste for espionage, had contact with MI5. Early in 1961, MI5 had encouraged Ward to set up a 'honeytrap' once Ivanov had fallen for Christine Keeler. But by now the security services were more than a little concerned by the pillow talk of the Soviet Colonel *and* the British Secretary for War.

In August 1961, the head of MI5, Sir Roger Hollis, went to the Cabinet Secretary, Sir Norman Brook, and told him that Profumo could be severely embarrassed by the honeytrap operation. Brook passed on the warning to Profumo. The Minister continued to see Christine until December; when he wanted to set her up in a discreet London flat, but she refused to leave Stephen Ward's home in Wimpole Mews.

1962 seems to have been a noisy year in Christine's life. She alternated her favours between two West Indian black lovers, who in October had a knifefight over her, 'Lucky' Gordon suffering a slashed face. Christine moved in with the other one, Johnny Edgecombe. When she left him in December to return to the comforts of Wimpole Mews, the enraged Edgecombe followed her and shot out the lock of Ward's front door. He was charged with attempted murder. His three-year sentence was quashed on appeal.

This was too much for Dr Ward, who had so far kept a respectable front over his sideline activities. He told Christine she would have to go. After that, loyalty was cast to the winds. Keeler, as I intend to call her now that her beguiling side has gone out the window, told several people, including a journalist and a Labour MP, that Ward had asked her to find out from Profumo when the Germans were given atomic secrets. In January 1963, thirteen months after she had last seen Profumo, she met a *Sunday Pictorial* journalist and showed him a handwritten note from the Minister, which she had foresightedly kept against just such an opportunity. As financial negotiations dragged on, Ward tried to kill the story by telling the government. Profumo then attempted – in vain – to get MI5 to block the story on security grounds.

Ward next told Keeler that if she did not sign up with the *Pictorial*, he would pay her the same money. She claimed £5,000 had been offered. When Ward's solicitor gave her £500, her outburst was so vindictive that Ward decided the best thing was to tell the *Pictorial* that Keeler's story was a pack of lies. Already nervous about libel, the *Pictorial* dropped the whole thing.

Outraged that her old friend had spoiled her meal ticket, Keeler made a series of accusations about him to the police, including that he procured call girls for rich clients.

On returning in February from a trip to Italy, poor old Prime Minister Macmillan was told the whole sordid story. For who knows what reason, he did not act on it before things got worse. Instead he wrote:

> Profumo had behaved badly and indiscreetly, but not wickedly. His wife ... is very nice and sensible. Of course, all these people move in a selfish, theatrical, bohemian society, where no one really knows anyone and everyone is 'darling'. But Profumo does not seem to have realised that we have – in public life – to observe different standards from those prevalent today in many circles.

It was on 8 March that my fellow journalist on the *Sunday Express* rushed into the office, excitedly brandishing *Westminster Confidential*.

Things then moved rapidly. The government, MI5 and the police joined together to make Dr Stephen Ward the scapegoat. Mandy Rice-Davies, Keeler's friend who had also lived at the Wimpole Mews flat, resisted police attempts to get her to implicate Dr Ward. They then charged her with possessing a false driving licence, setting bail at £2,000 for this pathetic offence, jailing her for ten days on remand, and eventually fining her £42. She went to Spain. On her return, her passport was confiscated and she was arrested for stealing a television set, a charge later dropped. After more such police tactics, she agreed to testify against Stephen Ward.

By this time, the police had scared off many of the osteopath's rich clients by subjecting them to questioning about his other activities.

Lord Astor had withdrawn the use of his cottage at Cliveden. So-called friends did not return Ward's calls. Macmillan at last questioned his Secretary for War: Profumo did not budge from his story.

Close to emotional disintegration, Ward fired off letters to the Home Secretary, to his MP, and finally to Harold Wilson, Leader of the Opposition, protesting about police harassment and claiming that Profumo had been lying. Wilson passed the letter to the Prime Minister, and the two men met on 29 May. Macmillan agreed to set up an inquiry under Lord Dilhorne.

On 4 June, Profumo was recalled from his holiday with his wife in Venice to appear before the Dilhorne inquiry. Unable to face cross-examination, he confessed to Macmillan's PPS and the Chief Whip that he had lied. He at once resigned as a Minister, as an MP, and as a Privy Councillor. His letter of resignation was published the next day:

Dear Prime Minister,

You will recall that on 22 March, following certain allegations made in Parliament, I made a personal statement. At the time rumour had charged me with assisting in the disappearance of a witness and with being involved in some possible breach of security.

So serious were these charges that I allowed myself to think that my personal association with that witness, which had also been the subject of rumour, was, by comparison, of minor importance only. In my statement I said that there had been no impropriety in the association. To my very deep regret I have to admit that this was not true, and that I misled you, and my colleagues, and the House.

I ask you to understand that I did this to protect, as I thought, my wife and family, who were misled, as were my professional advisers.

I have come to realise that, by this deception, I have been guilty of a grave misdemeanour and despite the fact that there is no truth whatsoever in the other charges, I cannot remain a member of your Administration, nor of the House of Commons.

I cannot tell you of my deep remorse for the embarrassment
I have caused you, to my colleagues in the Government, to my
constituents and to the Party which I have served for the past
twenty-five years.

Yours sincerely,

Jack Profumo

The Prime Minister replied:

Dear Profumo,

The contents of your letter of 4 June have been com-
municated to me, and I have heard them with deep regret. This
is a great tragedy for you, your family and your friends.
Nevertheless, I am sure you will understand that in the
circumstances I have no alternative but to advise the Queen to
accept your resignation.

Yours very sincerely,

Harold Macmillan

Press, public and politicians had a field day. The affair, and
Macmillan's handling of it, would contribute to the Tories' electoral
defeat the following year. Another Cabinet Minister, Lord Hailsham,
Leader of the House of Lords, blew a fuse on television:

'A great Party is not to be brought down because of a squalid affair
between a woman of easy virtue and a proved liar . . . He lied to his
friends, lied to his family, lied to his colleagues, lied to his solicitor,
lied to the House of Commons . . . We have all been kicked in the
stomach . . .'

Profumo's brother-in-law, Lord Balfour of Inchrye, wrote to *The
Times*: 'Lord Hailsham had no mercy . . . Yet surely such a proud
and powerful Christian as Lord Hailsham could have shown some
element of Christian charity in his denunciation of a man with a
shattered life.'

Ten years later, writing a *Sunday Times Magazine* profile of Lord
Hailsham when he was Lord Chancellor, I asked him if he regretted
his savagery to a man who was down.

'No man who has an ounce of intellectual honesty,' he replied, 'will attack a man for being unchaste. Most men are unchaste, if only in their imagination. But you must not tell lies in public life.

'I think one's private life is one's own, though I doubt if I could get away with adultery as Lord Chancellor. If it was found out, I think I'd be for it. Lord Chancellors are meant to be above that sort of thing.

'But public men must be irreproachable about telling the truth to the best of their ability. You would expect a soldier to be brave and disciplined. Different walks of life require different emphases in conduct.

'I was incensed that people should use Profumo to do down the Party.'

Matthew Parris, who has studied the matter in depth, says in his *Great Parliamentary Scandals* that he believes Profumo knew he was finished if his affair with Keeler was found out, and – having nothing to lose – tried lying. 'This approach,' Parris adds drily, 'has not always failed in politics.'

Though Profumo's career was finished, the scandal spread like bushfire. Keeler's second West Indian boyfriend, 'Lucky' Gordon, came to trial on the same day that the Minister resigned. Gordon was charged with assaulting Keeler outside a friend's flat. Keeler arrived at the trial in a chauffeur-driven Rolls-Royce.

Conducting his own defence, Gordon said of Stephen Ward: 'He gets his delight from seeing people get aggravated.' And he also accused Keeler of giving him VD.

Three days later, when Desmond Wilcox interviewed Dr Ward on television, Ward said: 'The key point for me to clear my name was to indicate that I had not encouraged the relationship between Miss Keeler and Mr Profumo . . . As tactfully as possible, I had informed the Security Service . . . knowing that I had a friend in the Soviet Embassy, I think I was rightly disturbed about it.'

The next day Stephen Ward was arrested, charged with 'on diverse dates between January 1961 and June 1963 having knowingly lived wholly or in part on the earnings of prostitution at 17 Wimpole Mews, W1.' (One would have thought he had no earnings as a society osteopath.)

Britain seemed to go a little mad with all this sexual excitement. Mandy Rice-Davies skilfully fed the flames with her accounts of debauchery in high places: 'There was a dinner party where a naked man wearing a mask waited on table like a slave. He had to have a mask because he was so well known.'

My colleague at the *Sunday Express* looked as if he might have a coronary from excitement: a story was also circulating, he announced, about another man in a mask (a Royal??? gasp, gasp) who waited on table wearing only a small square, lace apron. At once reporters were sent out to discover which royal belonged to the Freemasons.

Stephen Ward's eight-day trial at the Old Bailey in July provided a second climax to the Profumo scandal. A New Zealand paper was fined for indecency merely for reporting it. Mandy Rice-Davies, when it was put to her that Lord Astor denied her allegations about him, made her immortal reply: 'He would, wouldn't he?'

When the judge, Sir Archie Pellow Marshall QC, began his summing-up to the jury, Ward knew he had reached the end of the road. He said to one of his few remaining friends, Tom Mangold, the *Express* reporter: 'This is a political revenge trial. Someone had to be sacrificed and that someone was me.'

Without waiting for the judge to complete his summing-up the next day, Ward went back to the Chelsea flat of another remaining friend, Noel Howard-Jones, and swallowed a massive overdose. Before it took effect, he wrote a letter of great style and elegance for a man who had been systematically ruined:

Dear Noel,

I am sorry I had to do this here! It is really more than I can stand – the horror, day after day in court and in the streets. It is not only fear, it is a wish not to let them get me. I would rather get myself. I do hope I have not let people down too much. I tried to do my stuff but after Marshall's summing-up, I've given up all hope. The car needs oil in the gearbox, by the way. Be happy in it.

Incidentally, it was surprisingly easy and required no guts. I am sorry to disappoint the vultures.

I only hope this has done the job. Delay resuscitation as long as possible.

Dr Ward was taken in a coma to St Stephen's Hospital. The following day the jury found him guilty on two charges of living on immoral earnings. Sentence was delayed and in the event never passed: Stephen Ward died in hospital on 3 August.

There were six mourners at his funeral and two wreaths, one from his family. The other was made up of 100 white carnations, sent by Kenneth Tynan, John Osborne, Annie Ross, Dominick Elwes, Arnold Wesker, Joe Orton and Penelope Gilliatt. The card read:

'"To Stephen Ward, Victim of Hypocrisy." You cannot apologize to the dead and nobody in British public life seems to apologize anyway, but there are people alive today (not Profumo) who wronged Stephen Ward badly. Some indication of remorse would have been refreshing.'

A day or two after the Ward trial, Christine Keeler was jailed for six months for not being present as a witness at all of Lucky Gordon's trial.

John Profumo demonstrated atonement for the next 25 years, working at Toynbee Hall in London's East End, devoting his talents to the homeless. In 1975 he was awarded the CBE for his charitable work.

Sometimes I think of Valerie Hobson. If it was true that in early March she was considering leaving her husband, once he was ruined what else could a decent, sensitive woman do but stand by him? The Profumos continued to live together until her death in 1998.

23

PAMELA CHURCHILL HARRIMAN

1920–97

Born at Minterne in Dorset, Pamela was the eldest of four daughters of the eleventh Baron Digby. Not only was the family's wealth declining, but a brother was born and inherited the lot. Brought up in aristocratic luxury yet having no money of her own, even as a girl Pamela Digby was obsessed with acquiring riches. To that end she used her bed to network.

Often she read to others from a biography of her 'wicked' Victorian forebear, Lady Jane Digby (see Chapter 10). But Pamela deceived herself in claiming her ancestor as her role model. The infamous Lady Jane was driven by her hormones, not Pamela's lust for lucre. Lady Jane was wildly spontaneous, Pamela calculating and manipulative. But the two Digbys shared a determination to do as they wished, whatever the world said about them.

Pamela's lifelong habit of shamelessly embellishing her past – a domestic science certificate from Downham School turned into graduation from 'Downham College', several months at the Sorbonne in Paris were transformed into two years with the implication that she received a good degree – mean her life story as told by herself is suspect. Those who knew her during her progess are frequently more reliable.

Pamela was a plump teenager nicknamed 'Miss Fat'. At school she was more hardworking than intelligent. When she came out, her London Season was not a success. Yet she had aristocratic assurance and was the apple of her mother's eye: whatever Pamela did was praised by Lady Digby.

She came under the tutelage at the romantic Leeds Castle of its glamorous American-born owner, Lady Baillie. Pamela was a close observer. She watched Olive Baillie's grace and attractiveness. At nineteen Pamela began reinventing herself as a femme fatale.

Most of her flings were with older men because they were more likely to have money. She was oblivious to the fact that Sir Philip Dunn, for instance, heir of an enormously rich Canadian industrialist, had a wife, Lady Mary Dunn, who was her own friend. Sally Bedell Smith, one of Pamela's distinguished biographers, recalls the Earl of Warwick's description of the form when one was having an affair with Pamela: 'She would arrive at your house, sit down, push a pile of bills across the desk, and say, "What am I going to do with these?" Of course they would be paid.'

In late August 1939, Germany and the Soviet Union signed a non-aggression pact, and days later the Anglo-Polish alliance was signed. On 1 September, Hitler invaded Poland. Two days later, Prime Minister Neville Chamberlain, the longtime appeaser, announced: 'This country is at war with Germany.' Winston Churchill was recalled to government as First Lord of the Admiralty. He was the coming man.

His son, Randolph Churchill, on forty-eight-hours' leave from his regiment, ran into Lady Mary Dunn at the Ritz and asked her to dine with him that night. She had an engagement and suggested a blind date. Pamela was due at her flat that afternoon. 'If you want to have dinner with a red-headed whore, go round to my flat and you will find her waiting for me from two o'clock onwards.'

He phoned the flat and Pamela agreed to meet him for dinner. 'What do you look like?' he asked. 'Red-headed and rather fat, but Mummy says that puppy fat disappears.'

At 28, Randolph had already made his mark as a part-time journalist and bad drunk – loud, boorish, boastful of his philandering. Convinced that he soon would be killed, he wanted a son and heir. He had proposed drunkenly to a number of women – on one evening, three – all of whom turned him down. Pamela had failed to get any of her lovers to marry her and tarnished her reputation in the process. She needed the Churchill name. Over dinner Randolph proposed and she accepted. Neither was remotely in love.

He took her to meet his parents at Chartwell, their home in Kent, where Winston and Pamela were charmed by one another. He and Clemmie were unaware that she was an adventuress, perceiving her as a fresh young girl more wholesome than Randolph's usual worldly women.

The wedding was two weeks later, Randolph having used the Churchill influence to evade the thirty-day waiting period. The fashionable church St John's in Smith Square was crowded with smart people, most carrying a gas mask in a canvas case. Winston Churchill gave the reception at Admiralty House. Just a year later, German bombers would destroy St John's, Smith Square, in the Battle of Britain.

The first months of marriage could have been worse. True, living near Randolph's barracks in Yorkshire was not agreeable for either of them, Randolph unpopular with his fellow Fourth Hussars and brooding because he had not already been sent abroad to show off the courage he was always bragging about. Pamela was unprepared for his belligerent drinking. But the Churchill name brought compensations, not least weekends with the recently ennobled press baron, Lord Beaverbrook, at his country house, Cherkley Court, in Surrey. The magnetic Beaverbrook's dining table gave Pamela her first taste of power politics.

In January 1940 she became pregnant, and several months later, Lady Luck took her by the hand. Randolph was sent to training camp without her, for Winston and Clemmie invited Pamela to live with them. They included her in everything, even official dinners, and she met anyone of importance in London. With her father-in-law she perfected the beguiling flirtatiousness which would be her trademark in seducing older men. Perhaps unsurprisingly, Randolph's sisters saw Pamela as the cuckoo in the nest.

In April, Hitler's armies descended on neutral Norway and Denmark. A month later, Nazi invaders overran Holland, Belgium and France. Bombs fell on Kent. On 10 May, Chamberlain resigned and Winston Churchill was the new Prime Minister. Pamela's reckless marriage had paid off in spades.

When the Prime Minister moved into Downing Street, Pamela went too. Her weekends were divided between Lord Beaverbrook's house parties at Cherkley and the Prime Minister's country house at Chequers. Each of her hosts enjoyed the gossip she brought about the other. If Randolph had leave and could come too, he was now superfluous, and his drunken ranting made him a hazard at Chequers.

On the day the Blitz began, Pamela was at Blenheim for the christening of a son of the Duke of Marlborough, Winston's cousin. To her horror, the baby was named Winston, the name Pamela intended if she had a son. She begged Churchill to get the Marlboroughs to change their child's name. Most unwillingly, they bowed to Churchill's instruction.

Out of the blue, Randolph at last got into Parliament. Three times before the war he had tried and failed to win a seat. Now the Conservative MP for Preston in Lancashire died, and the party leaders there asked the Prime Minister's son to be their candidate. A wartime agreement between the parties meant there would be no contest. When Lieutenant Churchill took his seat in the House of Commons, Clemmie and Pamela beamed down from the gallery.

Two nights later, Pamela went into labour at Chequers. In London, Randolph was in bed with the wife of the tenor Richard Tauber, eventually arriving at Chequers after his wife had given birth to their son.

Not the least maternal, Pamela entered a new phase. She had lost weight and turned into a beauty, photographed by Cecil Beaton for the cover of *Life*, looking like a red-headed siren instead of a mother, no matter that baby Winston was included in the picture. Other publicity followed, each come-hither photograph enjoyed by the Prime Minister.

Meanwhile the thorn in the flesh was at last shipped abroad. Randolph spent his time at sea playing cards for high stakes. Immediately on landing in Egypt, he telegrammed his wife asking her to pay his debts in any way she could – but not tell his father. Pamela went to Beaverbrook for help. Even with his large cheque, she still had to sell some of her wedding presents, particularly begrudging her diamond earrings. That's when she realised she could manage better without Randolph.

The war brought a new liberty to women. Beaverbrook said that baby Winston and his devoted Nanny Hall could live at Cherkley, and Pamela went to work at the Ministry of Supply. She took a room at the Dorchester, whose construction of modern steel and concrete made it more fashionable during the Battle of Britain than the Ritz. There were nightly parties in the Dorchester's private suites, and in the way of these things there were none of the tiresome food ration cards that afflicted normal souls outside the rich hotels. Pamela alternated her weekends between Chequers and Cherkley.

Enter Averell Harriman. In March 1941, he arrived in London as President Roosevelt's special war-aid representative in Britain. It was his first prestigious government post. He was 49, humourless, diligent, rich, given to love affairs despite his buttoned-up emotions, and his delightful and versatile second wife, Marie, had remained in New York. With his black hair and dour, gaunt face he brought to mind an undertaker, and his wide smile was the more engaging for being unexpected.

Averell was not from one of America's 'old families'. His self-made father, E H Harriman, was among the Robber Barons. He made the bankrupt Union Pacific Railroad into one of the great transport systems.

Averell grew up in a large house on Fifth Avenue and a 20,000-acre estate called Arden on the Hudson River. Like some other seriously rich Americans of that era, E H called this hundred-room stone castle his 'cottage'. Educated at Groton, at school and at home Averell had a strict and sombre upbringing, his father drumming into him the responsibility of wealth to achieve greater wealth. To that end, no expense was spared. E H brought a legendary crew coach to Arden to teach Averell and his brother to row. By the time Averell graduated from Yale he was a sportsman with a mid-Atlantic patrician accent.

With his father dead, he made a few false starts. Then he became chairman of the declining Union Pacific and ordered top-to-bottom modernisation, fussing over every nut and bolt. Cleverly he exploited tourism to help pay for the railroad, developing the Sun Valley ski resort in Idaho. It lured Alpine skiers to the United States, and soon was a mecca for international socialites and Hollywood.

Early in the 1930s, when he was in his forties, he decided to move into politics at the top. An opportunist rather than an ideologue, he left the Republican Party in which he was raised and joined the Democrats: that's where the action was by then. Soon he was known as 'FDR's tame capitalist'.

A few weeks after Harriman's arrival in London, he met the twenty-one-year-old Pamela at Chequers. It didn't hurt that he had a multimillion-dollar fortune, but what particularly attracted her was reading in *The Times* that he was the most important American in London. He had taken a suite of rooms at the Dorchester, and several encounters followed. In mid-April, both were at a private dinner party in the Dorchester when 450 bombers descended on London.

The raid lasted from 9 p.m. until five in the morning, one explosion nearly knocking over the dinner guests. They went down to the relative safety of Harriman's third-floor suite, and when the party broke up, Pamela was still there. Shortly afterwards, she and Harriman were in his bed.

In all his liaisons, he made it clear that work came before romance, just as he made it evident in bed that his own gratification occupied him rather than his partner's. This latter trait did not disappoint Pamela unduly: she regarded sexual intercourse primarily as a means to an end. If it was physically gratifying for her as well, that was a bonus.

Some years earlier, his stunning and irreverent wife Marie had ended their sexual intimacy because she found it unpleasant. (Instead she had affairs of her own.) But they remained deeply devoted, as their regular letters to one another made clear. Throughout Harriman's life he was reticent about his fling with Pamela. As she was flirtatious with everyone, her manner with him after their affair began was not at first conspicuous.

Then the perfect cover turned up. Harriman's twenty-three-year-old daughter Kathleen moved to London to work for Hearst's International News Service (INS). She and Pamela hit it off at once. Their friendship brought Pamela into Harriman's life on a closer basis, and before long all three moved to a spacious flat in the Dorchester, with two sitting rooms and three bedrooms and over-looking Hyde Park.

Next Harriman rented a weekend house for the two girls, close enough to Cherkley for them to join Beaverbrook's house guests. Sometimes Harriman went with them. Kathleen had long been aware of her father's extra-marital activities, and was entirely unfazed by his relationship with Pamela. They simply didn't discuss it.

Randolph was in Cairo where Harriman went on a fact-finding mission, and Winston had written asking Randolph to try and see him. Afterwards, Randolph wrote to Pamela about how impressed he was with Harriman, finding him 'absolutely charming . . . He spoke delightfully about you . . .'

In April 1942, the Harrimans moved to a sunny flat at 3 Grosvenor Square, taking Pamela with them. The three kept their habit of separate bedrooms.

With America's entry into the war, American soldiers burst on to the London scene, passing out nylon stockings and cosmetics and cigarettes. Pamela left her job at the Ministry of Supply to join the Women's Voluntary Services (WVS). In her green uniform, her red curls slightly disordered, she served as a guide for American VIPs. And she developed her talent for planning and organising. At the flat in Grosvenor Square, she and Kathleen entertained a succession of American generals.

When Randolph returned to England for treatment after a car crash, there was a quick turn-around at 3 Grosvenor Square. His sister Sarah moved into Pamela's room at No 3 and lent her own flat to her brother and sister-in-law. At his London Club, White's, Randolph learned that Harriman was cuckolding him. Although he pursued women the entire time he was in Cairo as well as having a regular mistress, he was outraged that Harriman had, as Randolph saw it, taken advantage of his friendship with Winston.

In fact, Winston had encouraged his daughter-in-law's affair with Harriman as a means of access to Roosevelt. Meanwhile, the senior Churchills took Pamela's side in the marital disputes. She could scarcely bear to be in the same room with her gross, spotty husband.

Previous page

**Duchess of Argyll,
1963**
*In his 1963 divorce
action, the Duke of
Argyll cited 88 men as
his wife's lovers,
including two
government ministers
and three royals. The
presiding judge could
not bring himself to
speak of fellatio,
referring to it as
'sexual association'.*

Above: King Farouk
*In 1942, as the German Field Marshal
Rommel was sweeping across northern
Africa, Farouk decided the only thing
certain in his life was a capacity for
pleasure. He embarked on hedonism and
never looked back.*

Left: Barbara Skelton
*English 'intellectual's moll' and femme
fatale author, she described her royal
lover's joy in flagellation: 'I am deadly
tired and ache all over from a flogging of
last night on the steps of the Royal Palace.'*

Right: Lana Turner in the aptly named _The Bad and the Beautiful_, 1952
Among the highest-earning women in the United States, the original 'Sweater Girl' found time for seven husbands (all celebrities) and an infamous gigolo, who died on the floor of her boudoir with a knife in his chest.

Below: Christine Keeler, 1963
The Mona Lisa-faced prostitute infatuated and ruined the Secretary of State for War, John Profumo. The affair (and Prime Minister Macmillan's handling of it) helped bring down the Conservative Government.

Pamela Churchill Harriman (Ascot, 15 June 1948)

An English aristocrat obsessed with money, she used her bed to network. Once she acquired the Churchill name in a loveless marriage to the wartime Prime Minister's boorish son, Randolph, all doors opened. Next, Pamela pursued a career as a great courtesan, nabbing broadcaster Ed Murrow, playboy Prince Aly Khan, American Ambassador to Britain Averell Harriman, Fiat heir Gianni Agnelli, to name but a few. And then…

Sir Laurence Olivier and Marilyn Monroe in *The Prince and the Showgirl*, 1957
With her new husband, playwright Arthur Miller, Marilyn arrived in London to film with Olivier. Her heavy consumption of barbiturates led to her showing up on set two, four hours late or not at all. Olivier became bemused and hostile. Six years later in her Los Angeles bedroom, having overdosed she believed her recent lover, Attorney-General Robert Kennedy, would save her. She was wrong. She died with the telephone still in her hand.

Aristotle Onassis, Jacqueline Kennedy and Caroline Kennedy at the wedding on his private Ionian island of Skorpios (20 October 1968)
Four months after the assassination of Jackie's great love, Robert Kennedy, she tied the knot with the Greek shipping owner. The American public felt betrayed: their idol was marrying a coarse foreign tycoon who looked like a toad.

Jeremy Thorpe MP campaigning in North Devon (1974)
It might be a black comedy had the consequences been less dire. The Liberal Leader had homosexual tendencies at the time that he met Norman Scott, but did he deserve to have his public life destroyed by an hysterical, fantasising creep – not to mention the antics of Thorpe's friends who tried to shut Scott up?

Above: Monica Lewinsky (*About Schmidt* première at the 40th New York Film Festival, 27 September 2002)
Clinton protested that while she had sex with him, he did not have sex with her. Salman Rushdie provides a culturally satisfying explanation for the paradox.

Left: Monica Lewinsky and President Bill Clinton *in the picture used by the Starr Report as part of the evidence to prove that they had an affair.*

With the marriage in its death throes, Pamela's protector Beaver-brook conferred with Harriman about his financial obligations to Pamela. She in turn went to see her father-in-law in the Cabinet Room to ask his approval for her to seek a divorce on the grounds of desertion.

In November, Randolph left for good, returning to the Middle East. Harriman was visiting his wife in New York, for she had learned of his affair with Pamela. It was the public knowledge that angered Marie. She offered her husband a divorce, but he told her he wanted to stay married to her.

At this moment Pamela was moving into a luxurious top-floor flat at 49 Grosvenor Square, around the corner from No 3. Beaverbrook had arranged to be the middleman so that Harriman could pick up the tab for Pamela's flat discreetly. (Harriman's financial contributions would continue for decades after he and Pamela parted.)

No 49 had a second bedroom, and baby Winston, now two, reappeared with Nanny Hall. Thus a sense of propriety was imparted, though even Beaverbrook expressed doubts at the wisdom of raising the child amidst his mother's goings-on at the flat. Then Nanny Hall disappeared. The sixty-year-old woman had complained about carrying the child downstairs and into the air-raid shelter each night. Pamela sacked her for insubordination and hired a governess, Bobbie, instead.

The flat was decorated with Harriman's help, and he gave Pamela a racy Ford. His American friends kept Kathleen and Pamela supplied with chic clothes and luxuries unobtainable in England. Pamela was not a quick-witted hostess like Emerald Cunard and Mrs Ian Fleming, but she knew how to put men at ease, though any wives who came to No 49 were made to feel uncomfortable.

As Harriman had chosen to stay married to Marie, he could not complain when she began walking out with Jock Whitney, who arrived in London in the summer of 1942, a US Army captain, recently remarried, with even more money than Harriman. The two men got on well enough despite their affairs with Pamela running simultaneously. Whitney too arranged for Pamela to receive an ongoing allowance.

Watching her at work – the sincere gaze, throaty laughter, whispered asides – annoyed London's social arbiters, especially the females; this made not the slightest difference to Pamela. When Roosevelt appointed Harriman as Ambassador to Russia, he did not want to go so far from 'the action', but the President insisted that Harriman was needed in Moscow to help persuade Stalin to come into the war against Japan. Kathleen left her job with INS to accompany her father. In mid-October they departed.

Six weeks later, Pamela was on the arm of thirty-five-year-old CBS Radio broadcaster Edward R Murrow. Ed Murrow was a different cup of tea from his worldly, promiscuous predecessors. Puritanical, melancholy, he did not go in for girlfriends. Moreover, his wife, Janet, was with him in London. Undaunted, Pamela set out to nab him. He was not rich, but he was a renowned American whose authoritative voice was known to all. It was not long before Murrow was infatuated.

In the early months of 1944, German bombers resumed pounding London. The Prime Minister had little Winston and the governess Bobbie move to Chequers. This made 49 Grosvenor Square convenient for Pamela and the besotted Murrow. Being Pamela, and perhaps to keep Murrow on his toes, she also had affairs with his CBS boss, William Paley, who was more her type, and Major General Fred Anderson, the American bombing commander.

Finally Janet Murrow, who had behaved with great dignity, had some sort of collapse and returned to New York to convalesce. During this period Pamela pressed Murrow to divorce Janet and marry her. Finally Murrow discussed it with Bill Paley who was adamant that neither Murrow nor Pamela would stay in such a marriage. Paley admired and enjoyed Pamela's skills as a courtesan, but he knew she would be bad for Ed. When Murrow remained unconvinced, Paley pulled rank and ordered him not to divorce Janet.

In their emotional turmoil, the Murrows went to Texas for a complete break and when they returned to London in the spring of 1945, Janet was pregnant with their first child. Murrow continued to see Pamela. On 8 May, Churchill announced Germany's unconditional surrender. Throughout the wild celebrations of VE Day, Ed Murrow was broadcasting from Piccadilly.

In July a general election was called. The great wartime Prime Minister was defeated by Labour, and Clement Attlee became Prime Minister. Pamela knew that Churchill's loss would directly affect her own power contacts. And post-war London was grey. Her interest in Ed Murrow now had a desperate edge. Then his son was born, and the overjoyed father flew to New York to negotiate his transfer to a job at CBS headquarters.

The next day his wife Janet read in a London newspaper that Pamela had just flown to New York. It proved to be her last crack at persuading Murrow to get a divorce and marry her. He refused. Always resilient, never showing disappointment publicly, Pamela flew directly to Palm Beach to stay with her friend, Kick Kennedy, one of JFK's sisters, in the Kennedy compound.

Her next port of call was Bermuda. Beaverbrook's mistress had died, and he asked Pamela to be hostess at the cottage he had rented. While there she heard that on 24 March, 1946 President Harry Truman had nominated Averell Harriman to be Ambassador to Britain. She returned to London and when he arrived in April they resumed their affair.

At the same time Beaverbrook offered her a job on the London *Evening Standard* – to make her an 'independent woman', he said, apart from the handsome subsidies she received from lovers. Now divorced from Randolph, she was more assertive than Harriman wished, but he knew things would change when his wife Marie joined him in September.

Before that could happen, Truman fired Henry Wallace, the Secretary of Commerce. The President asked Harriman to take over the job. Without an instant's hesitation he accepted: at last he would be at the centre of power. Days before Marie was due to sail for London, Harriman moved back to the United States. It was the end of his affair with Pamela.

She was twenty-six and there was no man in her life. What to do? She turned her attention to Paris where she could stay with the Duff-Coopers at the magnificent British Embassy, once the home of Napoleon's sister Pauline Borghese, herself no dud at self-display. Pamela's milky skin and red hair seemed to be particularly enticing to Frenchmen and Latins. She decided to resettle on the

Continent. Her child would live at 49 Grosvenor Square with the Scottish housekeeper and spend his weekends with the Digby or Churchill grandparents. Pamela's career as a Continental courtesan began.

Her first notable success was with Prince Aly Khan, playboy son of the billionaire leader of fifteen million Ismaili Muslims in Asia and Africa. Aly had an international reputation as a lover. Famed for his sexual technique, called 'imsak', of staying erect indefinitely, thus giving much pleasure, he often left the woman uneasy because he never reached a climax himself.

He would fall madly in love with one woman for a fairly limited time and then fall madly in love with another. While Pamela had her turn, she lived like a rich woman with the run of his home on the Riviera, Château de l'Horizon. Though he was not known for giving large sums of money to his 'harem', he flew Pamela wherever she liked in his twin-engined Dove airplane – London, Paris, and so forth.

When Aly fell in love with Rita Hayworth, he was desperate to get Pamela out of l'Horizon, but he hated confrontations. Instead he flew Rita Hayworth to Spain while Pamela remained rejected and alone at l'Horizon. Lo, a power launch from a yacht arrived below the terrace where Pamela dawdled, uncertain of where to turn, and a smiling young man got out. Enter Gianni Agnelli.

There are many versions, not least Pamela's, of what happened next. Agnelli's sisters insisted: 'It was a big joke. Gianni picked up a girl for the day and she never left.' In any case, Pamela departed l'Horizon (thus making way for Aly Khan to return to his own home with Rita Hayworth) and was installed in Agnelli's rented villa, Château de la Garoupe, farther along the coast.

He was twenty-seven, a year younger than Pamela, and thought her glorious. He did not believe in love: he saw women as conquests. His austere provincial grandfather had founded Fiat in Turin, and as usual each generation became more self-indulgent. Gianni was exceptionally attractive and charming.

He was invited to bring Pamela with him to visit Count Rudi Crespi in Capri. They arrived late and went to their adjoining bedrooms. As arranged, the Count joined Gianni for breakfast in his bedroom where Gianni sat naked on the bed as he normally did in hot weather. He shouted to Pamela to join them, and in she strolled, also naked, and walked straight over to Crespi who kissed her hand and observed the pubic evidence that she was a natural redhead, after which she sat on the bed and crossed her legs demurely.

Gianni had endless girlfriends, but Pamela was recognised as his *maîtresse en titre*. He was always generous, yet the affair was leading nowhere. She became pregnant. He told her she must have an abortion, which was performed in Switzerland.

Gianni's sister Susanna told her he would never marry a non-Catholic. Pamela operated on the principle that success requires luck and enterprise: neither is sufficient alone. She began the complicated process of conversion, flying back and forth to London in Gianni's plane. In 1950, in the Farm Street Church in Mayfair, Father Joseph Christie received her into the Roman Catholic Church. Next she obtained a 'decree of nullity' from the Vatican, thus annulling her marriage to Randolph. (This went down poorly with their suddenly 'bastardised' son, Winston.) All to no avail.

Pamela turned thirty. Gianni bought another home on the Riviera, La Leopolda, for her to decorate, and she called in her favourite Paris decorator, Boudin. Unlike her comportment in the Count Crespi incident, her manner now was that of the grande dame, behaving as if she owned the house. Gianni's sisters saw her simply as a golddigger.

Trying to provoke Agnelli's jealousy, she had affairs with the Marquis de Portago, a rich man with an old Spanish title, and a Greek shipping heir called Andre Embiricos. Gianni took no notice. Never wishing to be offensive, he did not know how to get rid of her.

In August 1952, he was involved in a fearful car crash, shattering one leg in seven places. Pamela rushed to his hospital bedside. So did his sisters. He developed gangrene, and the doctors said they must amputate the leg. Gianni refused to let them. They cut out the gangrene and a mass of flesh around it, leaving him bedridden for nine months. During that time his sisters brought the daughter of a Neopolitan prince and an American to his bedside, and in 1953 they married, Agnelli walking with two canes, Marella three months pregnant. After five years with Gianni, Pamela had to accept it was the end of the road.

With virtually all of her lovers, she remained friends after they rebuffed her. By making them feel guilty, she was more likely to receive a consolation prize; Gianni Agnelli left her with an apartment in Paris and a Bentley, as well as an exceedingly generous financial settlement.

But she was in a bad patch socially. When she went to Biarritz, she found that the eminent hostess Ann Fleming [she began life as Anne but later became Ann, so Ann it is] had ridiculed her as 'international flotsam and jetsam'. In Paris she was *persona non grata* at the British Embassy during Oliver Harvey's tenure, then when Sir Gladwyn Jebb was ambassador. At the St Moritz carnival ball, her escort was her twelve-year-old son. She was desperate to find a man.

A rescuer was about to ride over the hill. In Paris several bankers organised for Baron Elie de Rothschild to meet Pamela. Rothschild was a prominent and spoiled fifth-generation member of Europe's most celebrated banking family. On this particular evening, his wife Liliane was away convalescing after giving birth and grieving for her sister's recent death. Like Pamela, Elie was on the prowl. They quickly became lovers. He was three years older than Pamela and greatly taken with her.

True to form, she began pressing Elie to divorce Liliane and marry her. When her husband showed signs of wobbling, the feisty and popular Liliane would have none of it. If she saw them out together, she sent rude notes to them. When Pamela was driving Elie somewhere in her Bentley, Liliane bashed it with her Austin Mini. At a Paris dinner in 1954, she was seated beside the Duke of Windsor who asked her: 'Which Rothschild is the lover of Pamela Churchill?' 'My husband,' Liliane replied deadpan. Instead of being a serious rival, Pamela was turned into a joke that went the rounds of international salons.

With Elie still hovering in the background, lesser mortals came and went as lovers. When she bedded Stavros Niarchos to impress Elie, he dismissed the Greek shipowner as vulgar and revolting. In 1956, during one of her annual trips to New York, Pamela had a hysterectomy. Elie de Rothschild paid for it and was mildly irritated to discover that Agnelli and Niarchos had done the same.

During her long convalescence on Long Island where one friend, Betsey Whitney, stood by her, Pamela read about prominent Americans, studying the scene. As she focused on her present position – a courtesan who had lost her cachet – she decided that the best way to reclaim status would be to marry a well-known American. After her notorious career in Europe, the likelihood of an advantageous marriage there appeared remote. When she returned to Paris, her life seemed to be frittering away in the shadow of Elie de Rothschild.

In October 1958, Betsey Whitney phoned Babe Paley from London: she was trying to fix up dates for her friend, Pamela Churchill, who was coming to New York. Although Babe Paley was disconcerted to learn that the Englishwoman who had had an affair with her husband, Bill Paley, was back in the picture, the upshot was that the Paleys took Pamela to the theatre. Babe rang her friend Slim Hayward and asked if she could borrow Slim's husband to go to the theatre as Pamela's date.

Leland Hayward, a reserved Midwesterner, was a distinguished theatre producer whose career had its ups and downs. He and Slim lived at the centre of a *galère* of Broadway stars and East Coast socialites. They did everything first class. When they decided to move to Hollywood, they immediately became part of Humphrey Bogart and Lauren Bacall's circle.

Hayward's career did not flourish in Hollywood, though he remained a multimillionaire from the royalties of his earlier Broadway productions of *Mister Roberts* and *South Pacific*. In 1958, he resumed work on Broadway, and his career took off afresh.

Even so, he was frequently depressed. He was 56, he overworked compulsively, he had problem children, and his third wife Slim – against Lauren Bacall's advice – had insisted on telling him about her love affairs. Lately she turned her acid wit on him in front of others. Pamela offered care and comfort.

Early in 1959, just after her 39th birthday, he proposed. She stalled. When he screwed himself up to tell his wife of his intention, Slim replied: 'Nobody *marries* Pam Churchill.'

Meanwhile Pamela, not yet uprooted from Paris, still had hopes of netting Elie de Rothschild. She gambled on an ultimatum: 'Leland Hayward wants to marry me. It is now or never.' Elie replied:

'Never. My son wins.' On that sour note, they parted. Pamela sold the flat Agnelli had given her, put her furniture up for auction, and gave her dog to the maid.

In New York, she rented an apartment at the Carlyle so she and Hayward could live together. Slim was being distinctly awkward about a divorce. Pamela made herself Hayward's theatrical help-mate, and in November 1959, *The Sound of Music* with Mary Martin opened on Broadway. It was Pamela's formal debut as Hayward's fiancée.

The new year began with Hayward family dramas. Leland's second wife Margaret Sullivan committed suicide three hours before she was due on stage in New Haven for the opening of a new play, leaving the Hayward children more disturbed than they already were. Leland's daughter Brooke conducted open warfare with Pamela. Slim refused to be the one to sit it out for six weeks in Nevada to obtain a divorce that Leland wanted. Leland said oh-all-right-he-would-do-it, and Pamela found herself playing slot-machines with him in Las Vegas. With nothing else to do except eat she put on fifteen pounds. Occasionally Hollywood VIPs flew to Nevada to meet Pamela and were uniformly charmed.

But after two years without a day off, mostly Leland slept. Pamela tended his every need. Like a geisha, she took pride in knowing how to cosset a man and make him comfortable. They were not in love, but they suited each other, and she was grateful. Only hours after the divorce was finalised on 4 May 1960, they flew to Carson City where the Chief Justice of the Nevada Supreme Court performed the marriage. At last Pamela had things in order.

She continued to look after Hayward devotedly. When he came back to their Fifth Avenue apartment tired, visitors were intrigued to see his new wife kneel down, take off his shoes and put on his slippers. Lady Mary Dunn had just arrived from London for a visit when Hayward came home grey with fatigue. Pamela said: 'Darling, you haven't got a lot of time to change.' 'Oh Christ, are we going out?' She said: 'To dinner with Jack and Jackie.' 'Do we have to?' 'Of course not. I'll ring them up.' She came back with his slippers and said: 'I've just ordered supper on two trays. We will eat quietly.' 'Alone,' she added to Lady Mary.

His sixtieth birthday was not auspicious. His much anticipated *Mr President* was a flop and proved to be his last major production on Broadway. He flung himself into various forms of theatre but had run out of good luck. His writer and director Marshall Jamison commented: 'Here was a guy with everything in the world. He had been lionised and loved by people, and all of a sudden he wasn't.' Deeply demoralised, Hayward wrote to a friend: 'Bad luck plagues me.' His drinking became a serious problem, though it was known only to close friends and Pamela. He was not a truculent drunk like Randolph.

As with her previous men, she mugged up on Hayward's interests and brought them into dinner-party conversation. When his daughter Brooke telephoned him, she found their conversations were three-sided, Pamela on an extension offering suggestions. An acute attack of pancreatitis stopped Hayward's drinking, and royalties from earlier successes began running out.

Though Pamela never let up on spending, they were able to maintain some of their lifestyle by selling the opulent Fifth Avenue apartment and a number of antiques from it, and living full-time – 'for Leland's health' – in their Westchester County house, Haywire, forty miles north of Manhattan. There Pamela applied her per-fectionism to their Sunday luncheon parties, fussing over each of their thirty guests.

When he was 66, Hayward suffered his first stroke. After intensive physiotherapy, he largely recovered. Now crotchety, he was not easy to live with, but Pamela rolled with the ship. Two more strokes put him in hospital. As his moments of lucidity faded, she took him home to Haywire to die. Friends came to say goodbye. In mid-March 1971, he died at the age of 68.

Following their eleven years of marriage, Pamela was still known as a man's woman. She was 51, plump in a curvy way and pretty. But there was little in the way of cash. What there was led to ugly feuds with the Hayward children.

She retreated to England, flying economy class for the first time in her life. Sir Winston Churchill was dead, and she found London emptied of her old friends. After several unhappy weeks, she decided she was now more American than English and flew back to New York where she went to ground in Haywire and pondered what to do next.

A friendly neighbour, Lally Weymouth, was the divorced daughter of *Washington Post* publisher Katherine Graham. Lally, who wanted to do something else, asked her mother if Pamela could come in her place to a grand dinner her mother was holding. Pamela flew to Washington. Who should be at the dinner but Averell Harriman, now nearly eighty. Since he had joined Truman's Cabinet in 1946, he had held influential jobs under successive presidents, been sent abroad to administer the Marshall Plan, conduct various negotiations, and so on. Harriman said of himself that he was 'more a fixer than a strategist'.

Hoping to fulfil a longtime dream, he twice ran for President, but was heavily defeated both times. However, in 1954 he became Governor of New York, 'elected instead of selected', he said proudly. For the rest of his life, he insisted on being addressed as 'Governor'. He and his delightfully eccentric wife, Marie, settled into a sexless but warmly compatible marriage. As a leading hostess in Washington, she provided the Governor with the company he craved. A year before Katherine Graham's momentous dinner party, Marie died. Averell was heartbroken and desperately lonely.

When most of the guests had gone home on that hot August night, Pamela and Averell were still talking in the garden. His gloomy appearance notwithstanding, he was a very physical man, and they were soon lovers again. In early September he stayed a weekend with her at Haywire. On leaving, he asked her to visit him in his Georgetown house to which she replied: 'I will never set foot in Washington except as your wife.'

They were married on 27 September, six months after Leland Hayward's death. The private service was in Our Lady's Chapel at St Thomas More Roman Catholic Church in Manhattan. Thronged receptions were held in Harriman's New York apartment and his Georgetown house.

Pamela's role as Mrs Averell Harriman was the second and crucial stage in her creation of a post-courtesan self. Humourless, she saw no irony in Averell's wedding gift of George Romney's portrait of an earlier notorious courtesan, *Lady Hamilton as the*

Vestal Virgin. Her present to him was her promise to become an American citizen.

At the same time as pampering her husband, gradually she took control. Averell had commissioned a biography of the remarkable Marie, his wife for forty years, and given many interviews to the writer. The contract was awaiting his signature when he married Pamela. It was never signed. All traces of Marie were removed from Harriman's homes. Her fine collection of Impressionist paintings, which covered the walls of the Georgetown house, were given to the National Gallery of Art.

The Governor was famous for his parsimony, no matter his generous settlements on Pamela. She coaxed him to part with his money. She was persuasive rather than demanding. She was patient. She cajoled him into giving her son Winston a large bequest for his 31st birthday and convinced Averell of her worries about Winston using a single-engine plane to fly back and forth to his constituency. Harriman helped him buy a twin-engine Piper Seneca. An even greater triumph was bringing her husband round to buying a Westwind jet for themselves.

Pamela's acceptance by Washington society leaders was two-faced. As Averell's wife, she was received hospitably, while behind her back her courtesan career provided sardonic mockery.

Being a perfectionist hostess to backroom congressmen began to pall. She persuaded the Governor to let her hire an ambitious political fund-raiser as her personal assistant, and Janet Howard became indispensable. During Ronald Reagan's supremacy, with the Democratic Party in disarray, the Harrimans set up their own political action committee (PAC) to raise money and distribute it to candidates.

At 89, Harriman knew he lacked the energy to lead it. Pamela was nervous about making political speeches, and he hired media coaches to tutor her. He wanted to stay at the centre of things, and his nearly thirty-years-younger wife would be his way to do so. Their committee was instantly nicknamed 'PamPAC'.

Averell's second home in N Street was used for PamPAC, Pamela directing, the formidable Janet Howard organising. Instead of fund-raising in a hired ballroom, they gave dinner parties in N Street, the

Governor serving as chairman. These personal and superbly arranged dinners brought in major contributions.

In 1986, Averell's health deteriorated. After Pamela's Fourth of July party, they flew in their jet to Haywire (renamed Birchgrove after Brooke Hayward called her bestselling vengeful memoir *Haywire*). He died on 26 July. Pamela had already organised what would be, in effect, a state funeral in New York and a memorial service in the National Cathedral in Washington.

He was to be buried between his mother and Marie at his childhood home in Arden. Instead of watching his coffin interred, the last the mourners saw of it, it was sitting beside the freshly dug grave. Two months later, the *Washington Post* was tipped off that Harriman was not buried beside Marie: following the charade orchestrated by Pamela, he was still refrigerated in a funeral home, awaiting the preparation of a grave elsewhere in Arden. After the *Post* ran the story, it was a long time before the widow spoke to its proprietor, Katherine Graham.

Pamela was alone. But this time she didn't need a man to bail her out: she had status and financial security. Harriman's will left her $115 million and made her trustee of the rest of his estate which was supposed to go to his children. (She spent so much of it that the Harriman heirs sued her.)

Sporting 'the best facelift in the entire world', at 66 she re-embarked, lavishing money on the Democratic Party which was still out of office. The Director of the National Gallery, John Carter Brown, became her considerably younger escort and lover of sorts – a liaison useful to both, combining her money with his cultural prominence. In 1992, she opened her house for the campaigning Democratic presidential candidate, Bill Clinton, to hold meetings.

When Clinton was elected, Pamela was riding high in her own right. Of course he knew that she had been a professional courtesan in France. He didn't care. He wanted to reward her for her generosity with the money Averell had left in trust. He appointed her as Ambassador to France. Naturally there was *sub voce* ridicule among the diplomatic corps. But Ambassador Harriman took advice, worked hard, and made her dinner table an effective hub for international networking.

Pamela never grew old in the normal way. While swimming in the pool at the Ritz, she had a massive stroke and was dead three days later. The French bestowed on her the Grand Cross of the Legion of Honour. Her funeral was in the Washington National Cathedral. Everyone who was anyone was there.

24

MARILYN MONROE

1926–62

When I was writing a column for the *Sunday Times* and male sexual deviations were much in the news, I interviewed a psychoanalyst on the subject. He said that, unlike men, women have few deviations. Unless you count lesbianism, the most common is narcissism: their sexual gratification comes not from the sexual act in itself but from making men desire them.

Norma Jean Baker aka Mortenson was born out of wedlock in Los Angeles. Her mother's life was divided primarily between changing lovers/husbands and stays in mental institutions. The child was moved from one foster home to another, and when a foster family wanted to adopt her, the mother, in her current asylum refused permission. Along the way Norma Jean was placed in an orphanage. She could read the sign – Los Angeles Orphans' Home – yet she knew that her mother was alive. She had to be dragged through the front door, screaming: 'I'm not an orphan!' It was in the orphanage that she became a habitual liar, finding it the best way to keep things pleasant.

When she walked down the street in her teens, males of all ages lusted afer her. It was her walk that drove them crazy. She didn't use scent: she preferred the smell of her own body as did any male who got close to her, for her pheromone was in a constant state of activity, her musk, silently calling out to the male. By now she was living with her mother's best friend, Grace Goddard, and an older woman called Ana Lower. Ana was the first person to love the girl.

When Norma Jean was fifteen, Ana decided that the sooner she got married the better. The youth chosen by the adults was a neighbour's son, Jim Dougherty, an attractive, amiable twenty-year-old aircraft plant worker who already had a girlfriend. The first time he was asked to take Norma Jean to a dance, he thought he was robbing the cradle, but they married the following year.

Later, in Hollywood, she was rumoured to be frigid. Dougherty described her as friendly in bed, the passive recipient more concerned for his pleasure than for her own. She worked hard at being a good wife. When the war took him to sea, she moved in with his family and got a job in a defence plant with her mother-in-law. Norma Jean was liked by her employers. Her fellow workers couldn't stand her and were outraged when an army photographer, looking for an appealing defence worker, chose Norma Jean. That's when her modelling career began.

The war ended and Dougherty returned to a wife who sat on his lap, kissing him unselfconsciously while Ana rocked in a chair nearby. When Dougherty went back to sea, Norma Jean set off on a modelling trip with a Hungarian photographer called André de Dienes. He had difficulty getting her into bed – there had been no one except Dougherty, she told him – but once there 'she was lovely and very nice. It was something she allowed me to do to her.'

She told him she had never had an orgasm before. As she would say the same thing to successive men, the statement is unreliable. By the time the trip ended he was in love with her. His friends thought him batty: 'She's not that remarkable.' When they returned to Los Angeles, he discovered she was going out with other men.

Except when he was photographing her, she and André drifted apart. And after four years of marriage, she and Jim Dougherty were divorced, but he continued to speak well of her. She was not troubled by these endings; when she wasn't focused on a camera, she often seemed like a sleep-walker.

By now her brown hair was bleached blonde. She was appearing on magazine covers. Her name was changed to Marilyn Monroe, and she was given a part in a third-rate film. She fell in love with a divorced older man, Fred Karger, who was her singing coach on the film. As well as making love to her (she wore a bra in bed at night to compensate for wearing no support for her breasts during the day), he cared for her enough to try and develop her speaking voice and social manner. She was deeply wounded when he told her he could never marry her because of his young son: 'It wouldn't be right for him to be brought up by a woman like you.'

The same film brought Natasha Lytess into Marilyn's life as her dramatic coach. Initially Lytess thought Marilyn was vulgar, artificial, and dressed like a trollop. Then she realised Marilyn's willingness to work hard at acting, and the power of her ambition. Marilyn might present herself as a whore, but Lytess, who would be her drama coach for years, now took her seriously.

Then Johnny Hyde, one of the biggest agents in town, took an interest in her. Thirty years older than Marilyn, Hyde's infidelities to his beautiful wife Mozelle had not damaged his being a good husband and a good father to four sons. But now he became disastrously infatuated with Marilyn. When his son found Norma Jean's nude calendar in the cellar, he showed it to his mother. Soon Mozelle heard that her husband was obsessed by this girl who seemed to her to be a slut. When she confronted Hyde, he made the classic remark of all older men who fall in love with a young girl: 'It's happened and I can't do anything about it.'

Mozelle Hyde filed for divorce, and Hyde asked Marilyn to marry him. He respected her. Already he had refined her manner. He could guide her in what roles to take. He persuaded her to have plastic surgery: the bulb at the tip of her nose was subtly reduced and her jawline slightly altered. He was a millionaire. Interestingly, Marilyn declined. She loved him but she was not *in love* with him. And money as such had no meaning for her. But she moved in with him in the house he bought after separating from his wife.

Then he had a sudden heart attack and died. Within hours his family's lawyer instructed Marilyn to get out fast. She was specifically told by the family not to attend the funeral, but some of Hyde's friends advised her to go. She threw herself across his coffin, screaming: 'Wake up, please wake up, oh my God, Johnny, Johnny.' She was led to the rear of the church.

Joe DiMaggio was the New York Yankees' star and the greatest baseball player of his time. On retiring, he remained an American legend. When he and Marilyn started dating, she was with an American king. Until then she had known only Hollywood kings. He was used to more attention than she had yet received. Neither had an interest in the other's craft, yet he would be her protector. He dressed in conservative suits and his manner was always dignified. She married the idea of Joe DiMaggio.

He belonged to a culture that did not believe a wife needed assurance that he loved her: that he was there should have made that obvious, he thought. Marilyn knew she could always rely on him, but she wanted more than that – she wanted his full attention. When they went out together, he was puritannical about how she dressed. They had nothing to talk about; his conversation was reserved for fellow sportsmen.

The film *Gentlemen Prefer Blondes* established Marilyn as a great comedian. But all that exuberance on the screen was beginning to leave her washed out and insomniac. She started arriving late on set.

The most famous Monroe scene was in *The Seven Year Itch*, when in the hot summer she stood over a New York subway grating to cool off, and each time a train hurtled by underneath, her skirt billowed out from her waist. Among the street crowds watching her was Joe DiMaggio, humiliated by his wife's flirtatious frolicking. He shouldered his way out of the throng and waited for her to come back to their hotel room. That night other guests complained about shouting and noisy weeping. In the morning DiMaggio returned to California. Two weeks later Marilyn announced that they were getting a divorce.

She was now a movie star in search of an education. The man who fitted the bill was the cerebral playwright Arthur Miller. Once again, she was deeply attracted to the idea of the man. As well, he looked like Abraham Lincoln.They had advanced far into their affair when she was asked to go to England to play opposite Laurence Olivier in *The Prince and the Showgirl*. Miller bit the bullet and said he would end his marriage, which meant separation from his children. He and Marilyn married to a cacophony of press hysteria which included a journalist being killed in a car chase. Together the happy couple set off for England.

On set, three men were competing to mould Marilyn's mind. The photographer Milton Greene had put up the money for the film. Arthur Miller was already celebrated for his play *Death of a Salesman*. Lee Strasberg was the inspirational director of the Method school of acting who persuaded Marilyn that she was not just a blonde with sex appeal but a fine actress too. His wife Paula supplanted Marilyn's drama coach.

Olivier was bemused and hostile: he had never worked with a co-star who showed up two hours late, four hours late, or not at all, and who had to be coached by her guru immediately before she undertook each scene. Everyone on location except Marilyn hated Paula Strasberg. Somehow the film was completed, and Marilyn won an award for it. The main criticism was that the prince did not appear to be attracted to the showgirl.

In 1959 she went into hospital for 'corrective surgery'. She had been famously faithful to Miller for three and a half years, and she was trying to have a child. Her twelve abortions since girlhood had messed up some of her organs. Her increasing consumption of barbiturates led her when awake to stumble into chairs before falling into a heavy doze.

They moved to a farm in Connecticut where Miller began the play he was writing for her, *The Misfits*. She was soon bored by the country. They returned to New York while Miller finished *The Misfits*, and because they needed money she filmed *Some Like It Hot*. She had never taken as many sedatives as she did during her years with Miller.

On the set Tony Curtis and Jack Lemmon stood round in high heels for hours, cursing the cause of the delay. On one occasion, when she did finally turn up, 42 takes were required for her to say three words in the right order. Tony Curtis had to bite into 42 chicken legs and would be unable to eat chicken again for a month. The director, Billy Wilder, completed the film with his back in such agony that he couldn't go to bed at night and had to try and get some sleep in a chair. Yet *Some Like It Hot* was a triumph for actors and director, and is considered Monroe's greatest film.

Miller was still working on *The Misfits*. Marilyn complained that she had a better brain than the great intellectual, but they still enjoyed periods of tender love. On their return to Los Angeles, Marilyn began filming *Let's Make Love* with Yves Montand. Montand was successful in France, but to become internationally known he needed notoriety. What better way to get it than with Marilyn?

His wife, the distinguished actress Simone Signoret, whom Marilyn adored, was summoned to France to make a film. Miller went back East to see his children. 'What am I going to do?' Montand asked a friend; 'I'm a vulnerable man.' A two-month affair with Marilyn followed. For Miller the marriage went stone cold.

At last filming of *The Misfits* began – make or break time for Miller who had written nothing but a few magazine articles since he fell for Marilyn. Clark Gable thought it would be the best role of his life, and John Huston was the director. It started badly: Marilyn was taking a high count of barbiturates and still couldn't sleep until the early hours. Filming developed into a pattern: Huston shot around Monroe. When she turned up, her scene was slotted in.

She was now more ill than she had ever been, but her increasing hatred of Miller acted as a charge to keep her going. On location in the desert, she slammed a car door in his face and told her driver to go on. It was the last time that Miller shared a car with her. The cameraman told Huston it was hopeless: 'Her eyes won't focus.' Huston shut down and Marilyn went into a clinic.

Almost at once she sneaked out of the hospital to look for Montand in the Beverly Hills Hotel, but he wasn't there. Nor did he answer her note and phone calls. Instead, in response to the speculation of gossip columnists, he issued a statement: 'Perhaps I was too tender and thought that maybe she was as sophisticated as some of the other ladies I have known. Perhaps she had a schoolgirl crush. If she did, I'm sorry. But nothing will break up my marriage.'

Marilyn came out of the clinic, and shooting on *The Misfits* recommenced. The day after it was at last finished, Clark Gable had a massive heart attack and died eleven days later.

Following the playwright's divorce from Marilyn, her analyst suggested she buy a house in Brentwood just like his own. For a time her life slowed down. Her long relationship with Frank Sinatra was that of friends useful to one another more than lovers. Frequently she went to the alcohol-soaked California home of English actor Peter Lawford, JFK's brother-in-law.

When the President visited the West Coast, he stayed with his sister Pat Lawford and Peter in their seaside house in Santa Monica, where he could count on parties galore. On screen and in his private life, Peter Lawford made a success of his Englishness. At one of his parties, his brother-in-law met Marilyn, and she joined a group of young women known as Kennedy's 'stable'. She and the President often had sex with only a wall dividing them from the Lawfords. All four had a strong streak of voyeurism.

Kennedy once told Prime Minister Macmillan that he got a headache if he didn't have sexual intercourse at least once a day. At that time the American press never alluded to any rumours of Kennedy's insatiable sexuality. Thus when I flew to Washington to interview Peter Lawford, who was starring in a film called *Advise and Consent*, I had no idea that this attractive Englishman pimped for his brother-in-law. When Lawford and I returned at six from the film set to his vast hotel suite, the first thing his Man Friday did was inform the telephone operator: 'Mr Lawford's back in his room. If there are any calls from the White House, he's here.'

The second thing Man Friday did (his name was Tony and he took turns valeting Sinatra and Lawford) was to order ice to be sent up. Lawford told me:

Obviously, if he [Kennedy was usually referred to as 'he'] had asked me not to take the part, I wouldn't have. But it should be equally obvious that he wouldn't have said anything to me about it because:

A. The fact that I was offered a role where I played a bachelor senator who happened to go out with girls couldn't reflect on the President. He's bright enough to see that.

B. He's too busy.

'Tony! For God's sake get that ice up here. I can't stand it another minute.'

He jumped up and paced around in his velvet slippers. In time he resettled himself, two enormous martinis-on-the-rocks adorning the table between us, and we went on with the interview.

Later that evening he phoned me at my sister's house. Would I come with him to the White House to join 'the Man' in watching a film? Alas, I was already tied up. Not until after Kennedy's assassination did his compulsive promiscuity become public knowledge, and in private circles it was thought to be more chic if you had *not* been to bed with the President. I'd like to think that had I gone to join 'the Man' that night, I would have re-emerged as one of the chic.

Kennedy's notorious birthday party in Madison Square Garden in 1962 as good as announced his affair with Marilyn Monroe. Jackie had been warned that Marilyn was planning a performance so outrageous that no wife could have endured being present. She fled to a family property in Virginia for that evening in May. Marilyn's self-image, always shaky, was hugely boosted by her affair with the most powerful man in the western world. Obsessively she talked to others about it and longed for the world to know.

Some 15,000 people were in the audience when, after a fanfare, Marilyn appeared on stage. Her beaded gown, sewn on her, was skintight and translucent so that her beautiful body appeared naked. Her embarrassingly erotic rendering of 'Happy Birthday, Mr President' was followed by 'Thanks for the Memory' with special lyrics sung so meaningfully that many in the audience squirmed and Kennedy's jaw dropped. Always quick on his feet, he slyly joked to the audience: 'I can now retire from politics after having had "Happy Birthday" sung to me by such a sweet, wholesome girl as Marilyn Monroe.' But he realised her growing possessiveness had become dangerous.

After the party, Marilyn was escorted to a private gathering by JFK and his brother Robert Kennedy. The latter was Attorney-General and a family man, and he knew he was more vulnerable to exposure than the President around whom the press kept a cordon sanitaire. Bobby's wife was also there. Yet even so, Bobby made no attempt to conceal his own infatuation with Marilyn. That evening a transference of Marilyn was made between the Kennedy brothers.

And just in time. For when Jackie returned from Virginia, she told her husband that if he did not end the affair she would announce on the eve of the 1964 presidential campaign that she was filing for divorce. Her sister Lee doubted that Jackie would ever actually have given up her position as First Lady, and the President's multi-millionaire father had already bought her off with two million dollars if she stayed on board.

Nonetheless, Kennedy – more cautious than was often realised and knowing now that Marilyn was a loose cannon – ended the affair by changing his private telephone number at the White House and not returning her calls to his office. She was shattered.

Marilyn's affair with Bobby softened the blow and turned out to be serious – which was far more risky for her than a simple sexual attraction would have been. Bobby *liked* women. He took a personal interest in her; the President's only interest in her was for 'wham, bam, thank you, ma'am' sex – both in his attitude and in his performance.

During the next two and a half months, the Attorney-General took over Marilyn's emotional life. She believed that he would marry her – a dream unwittingly encouraged by Bobby's sister Jean when she wrote to Marilyn: 'Mother asks me to write and thank you for your sweet note to Daddy.' Old Joe Kennedy had suffered a massive stroke. 'You and Bobby are the new item!' Jean continued, and she proposed that Marilyn 'come with him when he comes back East.'

On 20 July, using an alias, Marilyn went into Cedars of Lebanon Hospital. One of her publicists was told she was having an abortion. She telephoned Bobby. No one else knows what they said to each other, but when she came out of hospital, she slid into a profound depression. From then until her death her analyst, Dr Greenson, saw her daily.

Marilyn still thought she could rely on Bobby to stand by her, but he too changed his private number. When she went to Peter Lawford's house, Bobby was no longer there. On Friday 3 August 1962, Marilyn phoned him at his office and was told that the Attorney-General had taken his family for a holiday in California. She realised that the Kennedy clan was now shoving her back into her place. That afternoon she obtained two prescriptions enabling her to buy a lethal amount of Nembutal and chloral hydrate to add to the barbiturates already in her bathroom.

Saturday, three months after Marilyn's triumphalist display at Madison Square Garden, according to her housekeeper, Mrs

Murray, Marilyn lay resting in her house in Brentwood, trying to sleep while a stack of Frank Sinatra records were playing. Later, still trying to sleep, she said goodnight to Mrs Murray and closed her bedroom door.

At some point Marilyn must have sensed she had overdone the sedatives, for she called Peter Lawford and told him her fear. As she could not reach her lover, she asked Lawford to contact him so that Bobby could save her. How Lawford responded remains among the mysteries and welter of rumours that followed. One thing was certain, he was concerned by her slurred voice but decided not to go to her house.

When she phoned her masseur, who was her confidant, he was in bed with a girl he had picked up; much later his answering service reported a call 'from a woman who sounded fuzzy-voiced'.

Around 3 a.m. Mrs Murray went to check on Marilyn and discovered the bedroom door was locked – something Marilyn was forbidden to do. She phoned Dr Greenson who came at once and climbed through Marilyn's bedroom window. When he opened the door he told Mrs Murray: 'We've lost her.'

Marilyn lay on her bed, naked, dead, the telephone still in her hand. Not until 4.25 a.m. were the police called, by which time her erratic diary and handwritten notes from Bobby had disappeared.

An unusual document in Bobby Kennedy's Justice Department file records that on that same Friday 3 August, he and his family arrived at a ranch not far from San Francisco. What was unusual about the document was that it detailed times of arrivals and departures from Friday to Sunday – though nothing other than a holiday was taking place. But it established *officially* that Bobby was not in Los Angeles during the critical hours surrounding Marilyn's death.

For a long time, the FBI, under J Edgar Hoover, had tapped both JFK and Robert Kennedy's phone lines. Now speculation about the Attorney-General's role in Marilyn's death was rampant – including that she was murdered to prevent political embarrassment.

A different scenario was that frantic medicos attempted artificial respiration – which would account for why the bra she always wore at night was missing. Then again, it was possible that a stomach pump was used to remove evidence of what did kill her, though a pump would require a doctor, and no doctor made such a report. The original police report and the original autopsy were never found.

Joe DiMaggio took care of all the funeral arrangements. Sinatra, Lawford and the Kennedy brothers were not asked, and Arthur Miller declined to come. Lee Strasberg gave the eulogy. DiMaggio was chief mourner.

25

JACQUELINE BOUVIER KENNEDY ONASSIS

1929–94

Jacqueline Bouvier was born on a Long Island estate that had the trappings of considerable wealth. Her grandfather wrote one of those books in which some Americans indulge, *Our Forebears*, claiming that the Bouviers were descended from French nobility. It was described by Jackie's first biographer as 'a work of massive self-deception'. Such books are known as 'wishful history'.

In fact, the French Bouviers were drapers, tailors, glovers, farmers and domestic servants. The name Bouvier means cowherd. The first immigrant to America in the nineteenth century did well as a cabinet-maker and importer, his son increasing the money by successful operations on the stock market. *His* son invented the aristocratic background, which was swallowed whole by Jackie's father, whose two daughters, Jackie and the younger Lee, grew up with the social confidence bestowed by this yarn. By the time the fantasy was unmasked by an historian in the sixties, Jackie was so celebrated that only the Bouviers cared, though no doubt it gave some amusement to East Coast WASPs to whom the story had been peddled.

John Vernon Bouvier III, commonly known as 'Black Jack', was Jackie's adored father, a lapsed Catholic, wonderfully attractive, vain, and a drunk. His fortunes in the stock market fell after huge losses in the 1929 crash. That and his compulsive womanising led to his wife Janet divorcing him in 1940 – though his elder daughter, then eleven, admired his success with women. His mantra was: 'All men are rats.' Jackie's experience of marriage would not contradict that refrain.

Two years after the Bouvier divorce, Janet married into really big bucks. Hugh D Auchincloss II was a stockbroker with an inherited fortune in Standard Oil, who had weathered the Great Depression. He lived on two magnificent estates – Merrywood in Virginia, and another in Newport, Rhode Island. The Bouvier sisters were sent to smart East Coast schools. 'Hughdie' Auchincloss might be boring, but my he was rich.

At this juncture, Gore Vidal came into the girls' lives as stepbrother. Subsequently he would become a celebrated writer, polemicist, television star, international socialite and general mischief-maker – as well as a self-appointed authority on the Kennedy clan. He too had lived at Merrywood, his divorced mother having become Auchincloss's wife until she divorced a second time and he went on to marry Janet Bouvier.

In 1973 I went to Ravello to interview Vidal for the *Sunday Times*. He lived – and still lives – in La Rondinaia, a handsome villa perched on a mountainside with sensational views over south-east Italy. Our conversations touched on his connection with the Bouvier sisters. His novel *Two Sisters* is based on them. He dedicated it to his brainy half-sister, Nina Auchincloss, whom he loves dearly.

'As if being my sister was not sufficient burden, she is also step-sister to the two most successful adventuresses of our time,' Vidal said. 'They'd been brought up to be adventuresses. Their father had it in mind for them – Black Jack Bouvier, dark, handsome, alcoholic.'

At Vassar, Jackie did well academically and was popular with both sexes. Her happiest and most carefree time was her junior year spent in Paris, and she was bilingual by its end. Rather than returning to Vassar for her final year, she switched to the less dashing George Washington University, whose saving grace in her eyes was its location in the capital.

Although Auchincloss was seriously rich, he wasn't keen on pass-ing his money along to his various stepchildren. As Vidal told me,

The American magnate says, 'I'll give you everything until you've finished your education and training. Then you must live on what you make.' There might be a little trust fund, but nothing of consequence. The Bouvier girls got nothing at all. So they had to marry well.

Having grown up with the benefit of their stepfather's wealth, yet having none of their own, both girls were fixated on acquiring money for themselves. It was Jackie's number one priority through-out her life, and when her children were born, concern for their future security reinforced the obsession.

After graduation in 1951, through her stepfather's connections Jackie got a job as a photographer on the *Washington Times–Herald*, became briefly engaged to a stockbroker, and at a party in May 1952 met John Kennedy who was about to capture a Senate seat for Massachusetts. And he was rich. His Irish Catholic father, Joseph Kennedy, was a crook. He needed the Mafia during Prohibition when he made his immense fortune cornering the bootleg Scotch whisky market. To his dying day, he enjoyed visiting with his friends in the mob.

When Kennedy began dating Jackie, things moved rapidly. In 1953 when she was in London on assignment, he phoned her and proposed. Their engagement was not immediately announced, because the Kennedys feared it would head off a flattering article due to appear in the *Saturday Evening Post*, entitled: 'JACK KENNEDY – SENATE'S GAY YOUNG BACHELOR'. (This was, of course, before homosexuals appropriated 'gay' for themselves.)

Two weeks after the *Post* piece, the engagement was announced. In September, the wedding took place at the Auchincloss estate in Newport. As Vidal described the scene:

There was a great crisis when Black Jack arrived in Newport for the wedding. He wanted to give his daughter away, quite naturally. The late Mike Canfield [Lee's first husband] was delegated by the family to head him off – at least from the reception. Black Jack got drunk and didn't make it even to the church.

Auchincloss took over. Jackie later wrote a long letter to her father, forgiving him.

Jack Kennedy was not in love with Jackie. Indeed, he claimed he was never in love with any woman. She was not even his type physically: lean, dark and nearly flat-chested. But he was intrigued by her elusive quality. She had wit and shared his own interest in literature and history.

Sexually she was inexperienced, more interested in romance than in sex. Certainly she was unprepared for her husband's total lack of interest in romance or foreplay: it was like going to bed with a rabbit. Yet at that stage she was very much in love with him.

In the early years of their marriage, she realised that her husband's compulsive promiscuity was unabated, and she embarked on a few affairs of her own, not from sexual desire but as a means of retaliation. These ended when JFK won the Democratic nomination for the Presidency in 1960. 'We're going to sell Jack like soap-flakes,' said Joe Kennedy, the patriarch, whose great ambition was to found a political dynasty.

Even though Jack did not alter his daily doses of extramarital sex after he became President, his wife had a strong feel for the dignity of the White House. She was now committed to his career and his image, and would do nothing that might tarnish them. His ability to inspire led her to believe he had Churchillian greatness.

With her taste, sense of culture, understanding of art and fluency in French, not to mention her beauty and chic, Jackie cast a spell over France on the Kennedys' 1961 state visit. Returning by way of London, she received more adulation. For the first time the President realised the full aura and mystique of his 'asset' (as he and his father had referred to Jackie when weighing her up before the marriage). As soon as they were back in Washington, she embarked on her grand project of restoring the White House to its former elegance.

She kept to a minimum the dullest tasks expected of a First Lady. Not liking women as a species, she flatly refused to host official entertainment solely for politicians' and ambassadors' wives. But she always made time for her children, Caroline and John. And her banquets for visiting presidents and prime ministers were spectacular. The celebrated Spanish cellist Pablo Casals, playing with a string quartet, and whole orchestras filled the rooms with glorious sound. The expense of Jackie's gowns, indeed of all her clothes and jewels, irritated the President. But she brushed aside his complaints of extravagance gone mad, for she knew he shared her pride in her appearance.

When his stepsister became the First Lady, Gore Vidal quickly made himself one of the clan, hugely enjoying his new role. 'I was charmed by Jack,' he told me, 'as indeed I was until the end. I was pleased that Jackie came back into my life.' Who could have guessed that he would be the first of the insiders to debunk the Kennedy legend?

'Jack was limited by the family which produced him,' Vidal said to me. 'I don't think he had a commitment to much of anything except getting elected. On almost every important issue he gave at least one *very important* speech that made perfect sense. Then, of course, nothing happened.'

By 1962, Vidal's period of intimacy in the White House was coming to an end. The fly in the ointment was Jack's brother, Bobby Kennedy. The two men found it difficult to be in the same room. 'It was chemical,' explained Vidal. 'I'd want to kick him.' He nearly did so at a White House party where Bobby took umbrage when Vidal put his arm around the First Lady.

'The final break came over the piece that I wrote in *Esquire* in 1963.' Dismissing Bobby-the-civil-rights-crusader as calculated image, Vidal depicted the man as an instinctively anti-liberal authoritarian, closer to the right-wing senator Barry Goldwater than to John Kennedy. 'I felt it was time that Bobby's character was drawn large for the electorate. That was the end of my relations with the Kennedys.'

Even with his stepsister?

I've not seen the woman since. She adored Bobby. I think she probably liked him better than Jack. I mean this with no innuendo. Bobby was genuinely good with women. My sister Nina always felt she could go to Bobby when she was having a difficult time. Jack only liked women for sex. Jackie would obviously be angry with me for attacking Bobby. But if it hadn't been one thing, it would have been another in that hubristic family.

Vidal's friend, the poet Stephen Spender said: 'Gore genuinely sees through all that life, so he was not too disappointed when he was rejected. It's perfectly consistent to want to be part of a way of life, but to regard yourself as superior to it if it rejects you.'

August was a favourite month for Jackie: she could go to Italy and forget about American politics. In 1963 she stayed with Lee and her second husband, Prince Stanislaus Radziwill, in their villa at Ravello. All three enjoyed four weeks of party-going with the international set. Jackie particularly liked showing off her skilful water-skiing with her daughter Caroline for the photographers.

She and the camera had a love affair, so long as it was on her terms. Making a late entrance at a banquet, she would stand unmoving in a doorway for several minutes, so those already seated could have a good look and, more important, the cameras could do their work. She was a superb actress in any situation.

Asked by Gore Vidal's sister, Nina, 'What's important to you?' Jackie replied: 'Being attractive to men.' 'It's really quite odd,' said Vidal, 'because it's not sexual at all. It was to create an *aura*.'

It was in 1963 that Jack Kennedy began brooding about assassination. The civil rights movement was burgeoning. Jackie made certain there was no racial segregation at the White House. On 12 February, Lincoln's birthday, Kennedy gave a reception at the White House for black leaders. The country was sharply divided on his advocacy of liberalising state laws that compelled blacks in the South to live in ghettos, plus a hundred other state laws designed to diminish non-whites. Extreme right-wingers' threats against the 'nigger-loving' President were taken seriously.

On 7 August, Jackie was rushed to a Cape Cod hospital for the early birth by Caesarian section of a baby boy, Patrick Bouvier Kennedy. The President was called from a meeting about ratification of the Nuclear Ban Treaty, his foreign policy triumph. Hurrying to Cape Cod, he found his son gravely ill, the seriousness being kept from Jackie. The President accompanied the doomed infant to a Boston Hospital where two days later Patrick died.

A child's death can produces opposite effects on the parents, bringing them closer together or driving them apart. Their newborn son's death brought Jack and Jackie closer than they had ever been. She thought she had finally won his heart.

At this time, Lee Radziwill was enjoying an affair with Aristotle Onassis, the boorish, yet magnetic Greek shipping magnate, a pioneer in the construction of super-tankers. His most longstanding mistress was the internationally celebrated Greek-born diva Maria Callas. In exchange for Lee, Onassis made her husband, Prince Radziwill, a director of Olympic Airways. Lee invited her grieving sister to join them on a cruise on Onassis's opulent yacht, *Christina*, which featured bar stools covered with the suede-like foreskin of the great white whale, and other less than charming vulgarities. Onassis used his yacht to impress and seduce.

Because of his bad reputation with the US government, as well as his international notoriety for caddishness with women, the White House concealed the name of the person who would be the First Lady's host for eight weeks, referring only to a visit to Greece with her sister and brother-in-law. Onassis, of course, had every intention of basking in the glory of having the First Lady on his yacht. As he walked with her through the streets, spellbinding Jackie with the story of his life (while she imagined him as Odysseus), photographers appeared from nowhere, and next day the world's newspapers carried the pictures. Loathing the publicity, the President considered ordering her home, but in the end let her stay until 17 October.

Meanwhile, Kennedy's presidency was falling apart. Congress remained unmanageable. A crisis in Vietnam hopelessly divided his advisers. The response to his emotional appeal for civil rights at Vanderbilt University in Tennessee was the murdered body of Medgar Evers, a black civil rights activist.

The electrifying peaceful civil rights march on Washington, which I attended with my brother-in-law, climaxed at the Lincoln Memorial with Martin Luther King's overwhelming speech 'I have a dream' – and caused deep disquiet to many white voters. As well, reports about the President's ongoing and often blatant entanglements with women began – at last – to reach a larger public, even though the press still protected him. And the 1964 election year lay not far ahead.

Soon after Jackie's return in October, happier and relaxed, plans were firmed up for the presidential visit to Texas, home state of Vice-President Lyndon Johnson. Taking advantage of his wife's guilt about the Onassis trip, Kennedy asked her if she would reconsider and come to campaign in Texas with him. Affectionately, she agreed – 'I'll campaign with you anywhere you want' – and wrote the dates in her diary: 21, 22, 23 November 1963. The closeness between the couple after Patrick's death continued.

Texas has more than its fair share of extreme right-wingers. When Lady Bird Johnson campaigned with her husband in the 1960 election, both were jostled and she was spat upon. The purpose of Kennedy's visit was to woo the Texas populace and try to heal political rifts between Vice-President Johnson and Governor Connolly and Senator Yarmouth, all Democrats. As 21 November approached, Kennedy sat in his rocking chair whenever he could, trying to ease the pain of his back which had always plagued him, sombre and withdrawn, too often thinking of assassination.

The first day was spent in San Antonio and Houston. After the President's speech at the evening banquet, Jackie said a few words in Spanish which went down a treat. Then on to Fort Worth for a short night's sleep.

Before they set off for Dallas the next day, one of the President's aides showed him the *Dallas Morning News*. A full page was bordered in black, like a funeral announcement. The message, ranting and sarcastic, was headed: 'WELCOME MR KENNEDY TO DALLAS'. The paper's publisher had already told Kennedy to his face that he was 'a weak sister'. Grimly Kennedy handed the paper to his wife. 'We're heading into nut country today,' he told her.

It was nearly noon, the white sun blinding, when Air Force One landed at Love Field. The motorcade route had been published in two newspapers to make sure that people were there. In the Presidential Lincoln, top down, the Kennedys sat at the back, Governor Connolly and his wife in the seats facing them. Jackie in her shocking pink Chanel suit and pillbox hat waved to the left, the President waved to the right.

Some of the crowd carried hostile placards; others screamed: 'Jack! Jackie!' People in the Mexican quarter shouted: 'Jack-eee'; parties of schoolchildren hissed.

Jackie put on her dark glasses against the sun's glare. Her husband told her to take them off, and she put them in her lap. The motorcade was moving at 11 miles an hour as it passed the Depository Building. The sun was so dazzling that she put on her shades again. 'Take off the glasses, Jackie,' were the President's last words. Then the sharp crack of rifle fire.

Governor Connolly was yelling, 'Oh no, no, no!'

Jackie turned to her right and saw her husband's hand was up, a quizzical look on his face. He seemed to have a headache. The second crack of gunfire. A piece of his skull flew past her. He pitched over, his head in her lap. Then blood, masses of it, spouted everywhere. She sprang to her blood-soaked knees and shouted: 'My God, what are they doing? My God, they've killed my husband, Jack! Jack!' She crawled out and on to the sloping back of the car where an agent grabbed her and held on as the car gathered speed.

Lyndon Johnson was sworn in as President on Air Force One, Jackie standing beside him, her husband's body in a coffin at the back. She resisted all efforts to persuade her to change out of her clothes stained with her husband's blood and brains. 'No! Let them see what they've done.'

In the moonlight, the plane landed near Bethesda Hospital, Maryland, where a mandatory autopsy was to be carried out. She refused to avoid the press and TV cameras. 'We'll go out the regular way,' she said, and again, 'Let them see what they've done.'

Bobby Kennedy rushed past the Johnson party to meet her: 'Hi, Jackie, I'm here.' Hand in hand they stood at the top of a ramp in the spotlight, the bronze coffin glinting close by. Looking up was a crowd of some 3,000 people, standing in unbroken silence. Kennedy's biographer William Manchester wrote that she had made the effect she wanted.

It was Bobby who told her the assassin had been caught – Lee Harvey Oswald, shortly to be murdered by Jack Ruby who shot him while he was in police custody. For Jackie the shock was that Oswald claimed to be a Communist: like Bobby, she wished to believe that the President had been martyred for his liberal policies. She said to her mother: 'He didn't even have the satisfaction of being killed for civil rights – it had to be some silly little Communist.'

What kept her going was her sense of theatre, her mind already planning the funeral of a hero. This acted as a stimulus. She wanted to talk to Theodore White who was writing a long piece for *Life* about the assassination – to make him see Jack Kennedy as she now saw him. She was about to create the myth of Camelot.

Theodore White recalled:

I realised it was a misreading of history, but I was taken with Jackie's ability to frame the tragedy in such human and romantic terms. There was something extremely compelling about her. All she wanted was for me to hang this *Life* epilogue on the Camelot conceit. It didn't seem like a helluva lot to ask. So I said to myself, Why not? If that's all she wants, let her have it. So the epitaph of the Kennedy administration became Camelot – a magic moment in America's history when gallant men danced with beautiful women, when great deeds were done and when the White House became the centre of the universe.

It would be several years before reality pushed aside the myth.

From now on Jackie had two overwhelming passions: to glorify Kennedy's Presidency and to secure her children's future. Lady Bird Johnson told her she could remain in the White House as long as she liked. Among the house guests for the funeral were Lee and Stanislaus Radziwill and Aristotle Onassis.

In early December, Averell Harriman and his then wife, Marie, moved out of their house in Georgetown so Jackie could live there with her children. Ethel and Bobby Kennedy accompanied her from the White House to her new home. Jackie had never forgiven Ethel for being so popular with JFK: he always enjoyed her outgoing fun and humour. Once when, in front of Jack, a friend was extolling Ethel's attractions, Jackie took the man aside and told him to shut up.

In her widowhood, Jackie's preference for married men – without their wives – alienated former habitués of the White House; she could not have cared less. Trying to control every sentence written about her husband, she quarrelled with his biographers. With Kennedy she seldom had sex in the White House years. Now she had affairs, though Bobby advised her to desist with one of them because it was too soon after Jack's death – not to mention its effect on his own political career: an unsullied Jackie was a priceless asset for a Kennedy running for office.

Although Bobby was a family man with six children, he and Jackie became inseparable. He was the centre of her life and her rock. Gore Vidal believed he was the only man she ever loved. When Bobby moved to New York to pursue his campaign to become Senator, Ethel remaining with the children in the family's home at Hickory Hill, Virginia, Jackie too pulled up sticks and moved to New York.

At the same time, she travelled compulsively, with or without an admirer. Just as Jack Kennedy's daily womanising was ignored, so she was protected by the press. A chain-smoker, she was never photographed with a cigarette in her hand. But in 1967, reports began appearing in the American press that she was to marry Lord Harlech, an intelligent and attractive aristocrat who had been British Ambassador to Washington and was now a widower. Harlech, however, told a close friend that he and Jackie would never have married because: 'A I'm not rich enough for her and B it would have been like having a sixth child because she had to have the kind of adoration a child asks from you and the constant attention . . .'

When she was in London at this time, I met her at a small dinner party given by the famous solicitor Lord Goodman. Arnold Goodman frequently donated his services to Labour figures (or their spouses), who wanted to sue for libel. His usual advice was: 'Don't. It will draw everyone's attention to it.' Once a friend informed me that the prominent artist John Bratby – whom before our marriage Tony had commissioned to draw a nearly lifesize charcoal portrait of me seen from the back, looking in a mirror and wearing nothing but a string of pearls and stilettos – grossly libelled me in the catalogue of a provincial museum's exhibition:

'Erotic Art'. Lord Goodman advised me to forgo the damages, and instead he dispatched a minion to buy up all of the exhibition's three hundred catalogues.

It was curious: throughout the evening at Lord Goodman's flat, Jackie's wide-apart lustrous eyes remained unchanging. She scarcely spoke. No one of either sex appeared to find her all that enticing. Her public allure sprang, it seemed, not just from her glamour and the Kennedy power. It depended on her revealing little of herself. Habitually, she declined to give press or television interviews. She held the fascination of an enigma.

By 1967, Maria Callas's eight-year passionate affair with Onassis was like a rollercoaster. He had never been faithful to her, but the woman who caused the most tumultuous rows was Lee Radziwill. Callas refused to be on *Christina* at the same time as Lee. Onassis gave Maria a million-dollar necklace to appease her. Now she learned that Onassis was preparing to acquire a woman even more famous than herself – the Kennedys' 'asset'. Bobby was horrifed at such a prospect, as were all the Kennedys. And Jackie, adoring Bobby, did not want to damage his political career.

In 1968, Senator Robert Kennedy won the Democratic nomination for President. To some Americans he was an opportunist, to others an idealistic reformer identified with struggling minorities. In high excitement, Jackie exclaimed to the Kennedy clan: 'Won't it be wonderful when we get back in the White House?' Ethel said sharply: 'What do you mean, *we*?' Jackie made a hasty exit.

In May, she spent five days cruising on *Christina* in the Virgin Islands with Onassis. Joan Thring, Rudolf Nureyev's personal assistant, was on the yacht as a front in case Callas got wind of the trip. Thring was convinced that there was nothing sexual between Jackie and Onassis. What little time the two spent together was devoted to discussing business agreements.

The Onassis–Bobby dilemma was resolved on 5 June. In the ballroom of the Ambassador Hotel in Los Angeles, Bobby Kennedy announced that he had won the California primary ballot for the Presidency. To make a quick getaway, he and Ethel went through the hotel kitchen. A shot rang out and he fell to the floor, dying, Ethel across his body crying 'My baby, my baby . . .' He had been shot through the head by a 24-year-old Jordanian immigrant, Sirhan Bishara Sirhan, acting alone.

In New York, a friend lent Jackie a private jet to fly to Los Angeles. She reached the hospital not long after midnight. Bobby, brain dead, was being kept alive on a life-support system by doctors afraid to turn it off. Ethel was lying on the bed beside him, moaning. Teddy Kennedy was on his knees praying. When Jackie arrived and saw no one in any shape to take the decision, she told the doctors to turn the machine off.

Air Force One brought Bobby's body back to New York. Jackie was calm, making plans with Ethel for the funeral at St Patrick's Cathedral. When the plane landed, the cameras showed her leading the way down the steps of the aircraft. At the service, Ethel and her children slipped in quietly. Jackie, all in black and heavily veiled as if she were the widow, walked regally down the aisle with her children; seeing her, President Johnson and the entire congregation rose.

Once the public appearances ended, she went to pieces. Frequently she referred to Bobby as her husband. Unlike the aftermath of JFK's death, Bobby's disappearance from the scene left a gaping void. As well, Bobby had been the principal obstacle to Jackie marrying Onassis, who now flew to New York to comfort her.

She took Ari Onassis to meet the Kennedy matriarch, Rose, who, surprisingly, was able to accept him, despite his not being a Catholic. The rest of the Kennedy clan were aghast, though not for religious reasons. They thought she should remain JFK's widow – in which they had their own political interest. Her mother was distressed by Ari's crudeness. And Lee? She was shattered that her sister had taken her lover – though Lee had always been a pawn in Onassis's long-term plan to take over the wife of the President of the United States.

Four months after Bobby's assassination, the *Boston Herald Traveler* announced the coming marriage. The American public could scarcely believe it. They felt betrayed. Their idol was wedding a coarse foreign tycoon who looked liked a toad. Equally distressed was Ari's Greek rival, Stavros Niarchos: the two men were bitter competitors in their shipping empires and their women.

Probably persuaded by Onassis, Jackie did not have a pre-wedding financial agreement. Ari had given her $2 million in bonds as a wedding present, and she seemed to think that he would always treat her generously.

The ceremony would take place at a chapel on his private Ionian island of Skorpios, where he kept a palace with more than seventy servants on call. He maintained four other homes elsewhere, but the one on Skorpios was the most important to him. As he owned Olympic Airways, all the scheduled passengers were bumped off a flight to make way for Jackie and her children, her mother and stepfather and their daughter and son-in-law, several Kennedy women, a nanny and Secret Service agents. The plane landed at a Greek air-force base.

The Orthodox evening service took place by candlelight. Jackie looked happy in her ivory lace dress by Valentino, ivory ribbons in her dark hair. Ari's children, Alexander and Christina, aged twenty and eighteen, did not even try to put on a brave face. They hated Maria Callas for taking their father away from their mother, the lovely Tina, and they hoped that their parents would get together again. Now, out of the blue, 'the American woman', as they called Jackie, was marrying him. They made not the slightest effort to become friends with her. The only Greek to approve of the marriage was Ari's older sister. In the candlelight, just one face was radiant – Jackie's.

Whatever their separate motives for marrying, they made it apparent in the first months that they were in love. Ari liked to grab Jackie and take her into the nearest room, leaving the door open so he could show off his prowess to guests. Like many very short ugly men, he had made himself expert in sexual techniques. He enjoyed demonstrating them to Jackie, and she delighted in being the recipient.

For a time she was more outgoing, trying hard to assimilate Greek customs. She learned Greek and insisted that Caroline and John speak the language too. Thanks to Vassar, she was already well informed about Greek art and literature.

On Skorpios there was an early-nineteenth-century house – the Pink House – which Ari never used. As he based his life on

Christina, Jackie made the Pink House *her* house, engrossing herself in its redecoration with all her perfectionism and taste. Ari seemed happy to pick up the bills, so long as she made no attempt to alter *Christina* in any way. Usually he chose to eat and sleep on the yacht, Jackie increasingly remaining on the island.

When the Pink House renovation was complete, she had little to do except during school holidays when her children were with her. By the following year, reports were circulating of noisy arguments. Jackie made long visits to New York where she went around freely with other escorts. Ari was again frequenting Paris, dining at Maxim's with Maria Callas, the singer bedecked in the jewels he still showered on her.

He did nothing to discourage the rumour-mongering of marital discord when he issued a public statement:

> Jackie is a little bird that needs its freedom as well as its security and she gets them both from me. She can do exactly as she pleases – visit international fashion shows and travel and go out with friends to the theatre or any place. And I, of course, will do exactly as I please. I never question her and she never questions me.

In fact, he had wearied of her sexually. Jackie's biographer, Sarah Bradford, describes how Onassis complained to his Greek friends that she was cold and spent too much money. She had not been cold at the beginning, Ari told Callas, but going to bed with her now was like going to bed with a corpse.

When Ari and his wife were with his friends, her capacity to 'tune out' drove him wild. As with all the women before Jackie, he began to humiliate her publicly. Bradford tells of one evening when he and two Greek drinking companions had been talking for hours, Jackie sitting at the same table reading a book about Socrates. She broke her silence to ask one of the guests whether he thought Socrates had really existed or been a creation of Plato to represent Athenian philosophers. As the man began giving a serious answer, Onassis jumped up and screamed at his wife: 'Why do you have to talk about such stupid things? Don't you ever stop to think before you open your mouth? Have you ever noticed the statue of a man with a moustache that is in the centre of Athens? Are you too stupid to know that is a statue of Socrates?'

In tears, Jackie left the room and came back wearing a raincoat and walked out into the wet night. When she returned she sat down without a word at the table. Onassis muttered about 'idiotic conversations' and closed his eyes. Yet she had won. She had an actor's sense of how to steal a scene. With Jack she had perfected the art of silent withdrawal. Instead of making an apology, Ari bought her an expensive bracelet.

To his fury, he found himself in a humiliating position. He had courted her and married her as an egotistical coup. But because everyone now knew she married him only for his money, he looked like a prize dope. The best way to demonstrate that he still ran the show was to divorce her. The first thing was to get his chums in the junta government to pass legislation to prevent Jackie from getting the one-eighth portion of his estate that Greek law stipulated. And Ari's fortune was estimated to be more than $500 million.

In October 1972, Jackie celebrated their fourth wedding anniversary with a superb party in New York. In November, Onassis sent a lawyer to her apartment to trick her into signing a document waiving any claim to his estate. (In the event, this piece of paper had no legal validity.) By now he was obsessed with depriving his wife of her statutory rights.

At 66, Onassis began to age dramatically. The Greek belief in curses – along with his daughter Christina – had convinced him that Jackie was the bearer of ill luck. Her first husband had been murdered while he sat beside her. She had pulled the plug on her brain-dead brother-in-law. She had brought a curse on the Onassis family. Olympic Airways was failing. The family's two favourite pilots, the Kouris brothers, had died in a mysterious crash. Eugenie, the gentle sister of Ari's first wife Tina, had married his detested rival Stavros Niarchos and committed suicide. Then Tina, whom Ari still loved, had married Niarchos. There was more to come.

At the start of January 1973, Ari had a momentous dinner with his shy son Alexander, who was afraid of his father. Even though Ari had given his son Olympic Aviation, a branch of Olympic Airways, he was tyrannical with Alexander, belittling him in public and threatening to disown him if he married Fiona Thyssen, the famously beautiful ex-wife of Baron Heinrich Thyssen. She was sixteen years older than Alexander.

Over dinner he told his son that he was divorcing 'the American woman', as the Onassis children still called Jackie. Alexander was, of course, delighted. He did not spoil his father's agreeable mood by telling Ari that he was going to marry Fiona Thyssen willy nilly. On 22 January, Alexander took up a pilot on a training flight in a plane that he had already told his father was a deathtrap. Immediately after take-off it crashed.

The Onassis family and Fiona Thyssen, all at the time on visits around the world, rushed back to the hospital where Alexander lay dying, his face pulped and his brain crushed. To the grief-stricken Fiona's disbelief as she waited in agony for the end, Jackie came over to ask Fiona if she knew what Ari intended to offer her as a divorce settlement.

Onassis was inconsolable. Nearly a month passed before he could bring himself to bury Alexander beside the chapel on Skorpios where he had married Jackie. His health was on a steep downslide. His long neglected, chronically sad daughter, Christina, sat by his hospital bed. Jackie knew he was dying, but as the doctors told her that the end was not imminent, she flew back to New York to host a party. At last Christina had the father she worshipped to herself. She alone was with him when he died on 15 March 1975.

Teddy Kennedy escorted Jackie to Ari's funeral. They both climbed into the lead car where Christina sat in misery. They had just set off to where Ari's body waited, when the lead car stopped abruptly and Christina jumped out and ran back to the next car where her aunts rode. The reason was that as they set off, Teddy said to her: 'And now, what about the money?'

Lawsuits followed and eventually Jackie received $20 million from Ari's estate – not to be sniffed at, yet a far cry from the eighth of the $500 million fortune and more than she expected at the outset of the marriage.

At 46, she divided her time between her New York apartment and a 19-room ocean-front home standing in 400 acres, which she built at Martha's Vineyard. For a while she worked three days a week in a New York publishing house. She supported Teddy Kennedy in his unsuccessful Presidential campaign.

Of her various male admirers, the one she made part of her life was Maurice Tempelsman, a far-sighted, highly successful diamond trader. He was born in Antwerp, Belgium, of Orthodox Jewish parents. They had fled from the Nazis to New York where, in the close-knit refugee community, he married Lilly Bucholz. They had three children, and although Maurice left his wife for Jackie, he and Lilly remained on good terms.

For the first time Jackie had emotional security as well as riches with the number one man in her life. He might not be a ball of fire, but he was reliable and kind, shared her cultural tastes, and seems to have made few sexual demands. They were the same age and very fond of each other.

Gradually Caroline and John came to like him. They by now were leading grown-up lives. Jackie remained close to them, while accepting they had to make their own choices. For John she had a special mother–son passion, and was gratified when he turned out to be a heartbreaker. She worried about his ability at the controls of his plane and had nightmares in which the plane fell from the sky.

When, at 64, Jackie was dying of cancer, Maurice was with her throughout. Four years after his mother's death, John was piloting a small aircraft with his wife and her sister as passengers. As they neared Martha's Vineyard, clouds closed in. He lost his bearings and the plane plunged into the Atlantic Ocean. The wreckage washed up on the beach a mile from Jackie's ocean-front home.

Were I a Greek, I would conclude that Onassis was right. Just as women are the carriers of haemophilia, which afflicts men, Jackie was the carrier of a curse.

26

JEREMY THORPE

1929–

In the last months of 1973, the *Sunday Times Magazine* commissioned me to write a profile of The Rt Hon Jeremy Thorpe MP, Leader of the Liberal Party. Before interviewing Thorpe, I saw a considerable number of men and women who had long known him. As with most people in public life, some admired him, others denigrated him.

Only one mentioned that he had homosexual tendencies. This did not seem to me to be particularly remarkable. The Kinsey Report on American sexology records that 37 per cent of all American males have a significant homosexual experience at some stage in their lives. Among Englishmen who went to all-male boarding schools, the proportion is almost certainly higher.

I wrote much of the profile by candlelight: in defiance of the government, the miners' work-to-rule led to a three-day working week and regular power cuts. On 7 February 1974 (just after my profile went to press), Prime Minister Edward Heath called a general election on the question: Who rules Britain? He narrowly lost, but did not concede at once.

The election left Jeremy Thorpe riding high. Six million people voted Liberal, though this was reflected in only fourteen MPs, an increase of five. His majority in his North Devon constituency increased from 369 to 11,072. Two days after the election, Heath was still holed up in Number Ten where he invited the Liberal leader to discuss a Liberal-Conservative coalition. Thorpe went to Downing Street but turned Heath down.

One of the things that Thorpe's friend, Lady Gladwyn, wife of a Liberal grandee, told me: was 'Jeremy, the scintillating joker, masks from us a complicated personality, sensitive, deeply serious, even sombre.' When I put this to him, he agreed that his showmanship misled: 'People think that what I expose is the whole. There are things that one passionately wants to keep private, things that are no one's business. What isn't realised is how professionally I don't expose what I don't want to.'

At the same time as he was telling me this, a youngish man called Norman Scott – 'He is a spineless neurotic character addicted to hysteria and self-advertisement,' said Mr Justice Cantley a few years later – had moved into Thorpe's constituency and made himself a saloon bore retailing over and over how twelve years earlier he had been seduced and buggered by Jeremy Thorpe.

Thorpe's election triumph made plain that Norman Scott's sordid account did not impress his captive audience. In *The Last Word*, Auberon Waugh wrote that photocopies of Scott's tale had already arrived in *Private Eye*'s office where nobody liked the story.

> Its unsolicited appearance had a faint smell of blackmail, it was defamatory, unprovable and, above all, more than ten years old . . .
>
> A further reason why *Private Eye* – and, for that matter, the whole of Fleet Street – decided to leave the story alone was that Thorpe had married, fathered a child and been widowed in the meantime and was, in fact, on the point of remarrying. A bachelor might have been fair game, but a reformed homosexual, whose only apparent crime was to have had an unfortunate affair with a neurotic many years earlier, was safe.

In 1976, the Thorpe–Scott scandal broke wide open.

*

Jeremy Thorpe's father was a barrister and sometime Conservative MP, Irish, rather exquisite-looking. His mother, a baronet's daughter, much younger than her husband, had their two daughters before she was eighteen. Then came Jeremy.

He worshipped his father. When the child was six, tubercular glands were found in his stomach. In that pre-penicillin age, he was on his back for seven months in a spinal carriage, away from his family. 'He was very philosophical,' his mother told me. 'He had his own cottage at Littlehampton with his little menage – his cook-housekeeper and his nanny.'

Thorpe said that this period had little formative effect emotionally, though it left him with a bad back:

The last time I was electioneering in Barnstaple, my back suddenly went. Agony. There was no osteopath around to wrench it. I said to two ambulance drivers in a garage: 'Look. You see that beam up there? I'm going to hang from it by my hands, and when I say *pull*, each of you wrench down hard on my legs.' 'Lord help us,' they said [here he switched to the broad Devonian accent]. 'It's all right,' I said, 'I won't come to bits.' 'But what will Matron say?' they said. 'It's all right, *pull!*' They did and I jumped down good as new.

Following his illness, Jeremy resumed the normal life of a comfortably-off Surrey schoolboy. His mother was formidable. She wore a monocle. In 1939, with the advent of war, the senior Thorpe's lucrative practice began to crumble, and he gave it up altogether to concentrate on war work.

Mrs Thorpe had three wartime functions: she was a billeting officer, she delivered groceries, 'and she cut up those green horses'. Here I must have looked unnerved because her son explained:

Horse carcases intended for dog food were painted green so humans wouldn't eat them. Nobody in Surrey wanted the unpalatable job of cutting them up. So this enormous table was set up in the Thorpe household, and there my mother would stand, wearing great rubber gloves, chopping up these green horses.

In 1940 the two younger children were sent to live with an aunt in America. Jeremy returned at the height of the doodle-bug period. 'We were anxious to get him back to go to Eton,' his mother said, 'and also my husband felt he couldn't bear being without him much longer.'

Within months Mr Thorpe had a massive stroke. He couldn't talk. His eyes would follow his son around the room. Desperately unhappy, Jeremy found a faith-healer somewhere, but in vain. After Mr Thorpe died, his brother made it possible for Jeremy to stay at Eton. He now began spending time in the Lloyd George household, and to his Tory mother's annoyance, he was a Liberal by the time he went up to Oxford.

In 1949, Oxford was predominantly made up of ex-servicemen who had seen national service if not a war. Thorpe, invalided out of the Rifle Brigade after a few months, was younger than these others. This brash, slightly-built schoolboy orated radical views while dressed in posh suits with cuffs on the jacket and a double-breasted waistcoat and gold watch chain. He played the violin and was a devastating mimic. He was a *figure* – some said a two-dimensional figure.

Endless stories were told about his alleged 'immoral pursuit of office'. Being President of the Union and of the Liberal Club *and* of the Law Society was too much. After every election there was always a row about how he got to the top. He seemed slightly on the wrong side of ethical behaviour.

After he came down from Oxford, he practised as a barrister. In 1955, he contested North Devon as a Liberal and came in second. In 1959 he came in first. He was thirty years old. When he walked down the main street of Barnstaple in his brown bowler hat, he knew the name of *everyone* there.

He left home and took a flat in London, though his mother regularly came up to make sure everything was in order. Thorpe was perfectly aware that in this country, men are not expected to retain close relations with their mothers after the age of twenty. 'They think you must be a raving queer,' he said.

'For a period,' he went on, 'she dominated all her children. That monocle. We were frightened of her. I have overcome the domination, and I damn well am not going to be dominated again.' Though they continued to fight like cat and dog, he found his mother's company entertaining.

In the autumn of 1961, at a friend's stables, Thorpe met an attractive twenty-year-old stable lad named Norman Scott – who at that time called himself Norman Josiffe. He had been in and out of psychiatric institutions and changed his name at various times to claim relationship with a famous public figure. Each man was struck by the other. Thorpe told the young man if he was ever in trouble he could turn to the MP for help.

Within weeks Scott turned up at the House of Commons with his Jack Russell terrier, Mrs Tish. Denied entrance, Mrs Tish had to wait at the Anti-Vivisection Society nearby. Scott told the MP a long hard-luck story about how he had been sacked by the stables after being accused of stealing a horse. As he was always in trouble, I do not know how Thorpe, even in those early days, was not driven mad by Scott's perpetual whining.

The episode that follows was described by Scott at Thorpe's trial seventeen years later. As was intended, the story was so lurid that it remains foremost in the public perception of Jeremy Thorpe. Scott had not learned his tale by heart, and it varied as he told it in bars and at Minehead where the MP would later be formally charged with conspiracy and incitement to murder. Thorpe always denied in its entirety the alleged episode at his formidable mother's house. Here is the version made famous when Scott told it at Thorpe's trial at the Old Bailey:

After Scott first appeared at the House of Commons, he and Mrs Tish were driven by Thorpe to his mother's house, Stonewalls, in Oxted, Surrey. On the way, the MP suggested Scott should pose as a cameraman going with him to Malta the next day. After dinner, Scott retired to the guest room, taking with him a homosexual novel, *Giovanni's Room* by James Baldwin, which Thorpe had given him. After he had been reading the book for about 45 minutes, Thorpe came into the bedroom in dressing gown and pyjamas and sat on his bed.

They discussed Scott's problems with his stable employer. Thorpe remarked that his guest looked like a frightened rabbit and Scott, overwhelmed by this kindness, broke down and cried. Thorpe put his arm around him and said, 'Poor bunny.' Later he produced a towel which he put underneath Scott and some Vaseline from a tube in his pocket which he put on his penis, rolled Scott over and buggered him or, as Scott put it, 'made love to me'. While this was happening, Scott bit the pillow for fear of screaming and upsetting Mrs Thorpe.

Scott had had relations with both men and women before, but had never previously been buggered. After this act, Thorpe wiped himself, patted Scott's thigh and went out. Scott lay in bed crying with Mrs Tish for company. (Scott's version at Minehead was that Thorpe returned two hours later and buggered him again. As I say, he produced various stories as the mood took him.) Next morning, at about 7.30, the MP sauntered casually into the guest room and asked Scott how he liked his eggs cooked. Then Scott had breakfast with Thorpe and his mother.

Thorpe, Scott went on, gave him money for a room in Draycott Place, Chelsea. On the MP's return from Malta, he visited Scott and sexual intercourse took place. Thorpe visited him most evenings when he was in London. And so forth and so on. That was Scott's story.

In February 1962, Scott was charged with stealing a suede coat from a woman he met in a psychiatric clinic. Thorpe insisted that the police conduct their interview in his House of Commons office, telling them he was 'more or less' Scott's guardian. At that, the police dropped the case.

If he did not know already, this incident would have convinced the MP that Scott was a loose cannon. Thorpe got him out of London by finding him a job tending horses in Somerset. The letter he wrote to Scott a few days later dealt largely with practical matters, but ended, 'Bunnies *can* (+ *will*) go to France. Yours affectionately, Jeremy. I miss you.' Years later, the 'bunnies letter', as it became known, would come back to haunt him.

As Scott left one job after another, Thorpe's affection for him cooled. Scott returned to London, where Thorpe had nothing to do with him and wrote to Scott's new employer, disclaiming any responsibility for him. Scott soon moved to a farm owned by a Dr Lister who was treating him for his nerves. While he was there, his dog Mrs Tish killed all Dr Lister's ducks and had to be put down.

Returning to London, Scott told a woman friend that he was going to kill Thorpe and commit suicide. She told Chelsea police who took him to the station to make a statement. He said he wanted to tell them 'about my homosexual relations with Jeremy Thorpe, who is a Liberal MP.' The flabbergasted police summoned a police doctor who examined Scott and confirmed he practised anal intercourse. Scott gave them two letters from Thorpe including the bunnies letter, but as these proved nothing about the MP, the police filed the letters away and took no action.

All of this ongoing saga has been chronicled in detail by Auberon Waugh and Matthew Parris and others, so I am confining my account to what I knew of Thorpe's personality up to 1974 and a summary of the revelations that began two years afterwards. As well as wanting to avoid unnecessary repetition, and despite the occasional comedy and poignancy, I found I wearied of the unrelenting squalid histrionics of Norman Scott.

In March 1965 Scott wrote to Thorpe's mother:

For the last five years as you probably know, Jeremy and I have had a 'homosexual relationship'. To go into it too deeply will not help either of us. When I first came down to Stonewalls that was when I first met him – though he told you something about the programme and Malta. This was all not so true. What remains is that through my meeting with Jeremy that day, I gave birth to the vice that lies latent in every man. . . . I think that was the day I realised that Jeremy did not care for me as a friend but only as a — — Oh! I hate to write that!! It upset me terribly and I was rather sick because, you see, I was looking for a friend in the real sense of the word.

Mrs Thorpe posted on the letter to her son who was seriously shaken by it. How shaken his mother was we do not know. Thorpe's life now seemed to be operating on two levels. On what might be called the upper level, his career was advancing. Simultaneously, the lower level was clouded in an alleged conspiracy to get rid of Scott.

Thorpe showed Scott's letter to his best friend in Parliament, Peter Bessell, the Liberal MP for Bodmin. Bessell was, among other things, a Congregationalist lay preacher. He proceeded to work rather clumsily on his friend's behalf, making threatening sounds to Scott about blackmail. When Scott said he would make no more trouble, Bessell began paying him small sums of money, which over the years came to £700.

Meanwhile on the upper level, things were more straightforward. In 1967 Thorpe was elected Leader of the Liberal Party. In 1968, at the age of 39, he decided to go a-wooing. 'I passionately wanted my own children,' he told me. 'I decided that this lonely bachelor should get married.'

Having initally sought his bride in this somewhat chilly fashion, Thorpe fell deeply in love with her, and she with him. Caroline Alpass worked in Sotheby's Fine Arts Department. Ten years younger than Thorpe, she was described by one and all as a fresh, lovely, unaffected girl.

Thorpe threw himself into organising the nuptials with an intense absorption which irritated his colleagues, conveying the impression that he was more concerned about who was coming to the reception at the Royal Academy than what was happening to the Party.

During their honeymoon on the island of Elba, the new couple saw an English newspaper headlined 'LIBERAL MOVE TO OUST THORPE'.

'I was bloody angry,' Thorpe said, 'but I was *determined* not to break off my honeymoon and go back.'

On his return, he attended a meeting of the Party Executive. He had organised his defence brilliantly. The meeting was packed with his supporters who normally did not attend. His leadership was endorsed 48 to 2. I asked David Steel, then a young Liberal MP, why only two of the rebels held out.

'Thorpe has this *presence*,' Steel replied. 'He defended himself fiercely. You have to be very bold to stand up against him. He may be a brilliant mimic, but he is very much more than that. That meeting was one of the nastiest I have ever sat through – almost fascistic in the way the loyalists attacked anyone who had criticised the leader.'

After that there were only the normal carpings that any leader can expect. Thorpe's authority seemed to grow with the happiness of his marriage. Probably it was more important to him than marriage is to many people. It undoubtedly gave him a security that reflected itself in more relaxed relations with his colleagues. When he made a good platform speech, his wife stood up and kissed him quite spontaneously. If he asked her at eleven to provide lunch for eight people, she loved doing it for him. He adored their baby son, Rupert, who looks just like Caroline Thorpe. Their cottage in North Devon allowed them some private life together.

In the General Election of 1970, Thorpe's mother went down to run the cottage and look after Rupert. Caroline went everywhere with her electioneering husband. Then came Mr Heath's victory and the moment of truth for Thorpe's belief in a Liberal revival. While he held on to his seat, the number of Liberal MPs was halved: thus there were six.

'After that *ghastly* election – I'll never forget it,' his mother said, 'they had to stay down for three days to thank everyone who had helped them.' She cooked some food and went back home and left them alone. 'Caroline was marvellous to him. A week later she was dead.'

Thorpe had gone ahead of her to London to be in time for the opening of the new Parliament – taking the baby with him on the train. Driving up to join them, his wife's car went into a lorry. It is a long drive from Devon, and by the time she reached the Basingstoke bypass, she must have been utterly exhausted. It seems probable that she fell asleep at the wheel, or lost her concentration. She died instantly.

At one time it was fashionable to suggest she had committed suicide after a vile call from Scott, but there was not a shred of evidence to suggest she killed herself. Friends who saw her in the fortnight before her death said she casually discussed Scott's telephone call to her and his allegations. As well, scattered across the road with the blood were the flowers she had cut that morning from their Devon garden to take back to London.

For more than a year Thorpe had the obsession that some bereaved have – unable in private to speak a sentence that does not relate to the dead loved one. He had declined his mother's offer to bring up Rupert. He wanted to have the child in his London flat, looked after by a friend of Caroline's.

'Publicly,' said David Steel, 'he managed to organise his life so that political affairs could continue in a fairly normal way. He made no concessions except when he dropped out during the day to see Rupert. But his recovery took a long time. And it showed a tremendous inner strength that I hadn't known was there. He emerged as a much larger person.'

Just before the August 1971 Assembly, Thorpe received a letter from a Liberal MP saying he would be loyal to Thorpe as long as he led the Party. But wasn't it time he started leading? His wife was *dead*.

'This shook me,' Thorpe told me. 'I hurled myself with intense fury into completing the memorial to Caroline.' It is a column of Portland stone which stands on a prehistoric burial hill behind the cottage in North Devon. 'It was like a miniature Taj Mahal, there for ever. With its completion, I was able to disengage from my total absorption.'

In 1973, Thorpe married Marion, the Countess of Harewood. Born Marion Stein in Vienna, she was a professional pianist when she wed the Earl of Harewood, a cousin of the Queen; they were divorced when their children were half grown so that he could marry someone else.

'In different ways,' Thorpe said, 'Marion and I have been through the fiery furnace.'

Marion Thorpe was not long, I fear, out of the fiery furnace. Norman Scott moved into Thorpe's constituency. To anyone he could buttonhole, he told one or another version of his incredible story. A postmistress made to listen wrote to her Liberal MP, Emlyn Hooson, about Scott's claims.

A secret inquiry was set up under the Liberal peer, Lord Byers. Scott, sensing that his tears were making a suspect impression, called Byers 'a pontificating old sod' and stalked out. Thorpe made a robust defence. The committee checked claims that Scott made about the police and found them to be false. The Byers inquiry found no evidence of wrongdoing or a relationship with Scott. Thorpe was judged to be the victim of a spiteful and unbalanced blackmailer.

My personal knowledge of the upper level of the Liberal Leader's life ceased with the February 1974 General Election, when he was returned with a much increased majority, and rebuffed Mr Heath's attempt to stay in power by forming a Liberal-Conservative coalition.

Interest in Thorpe's tangled affairs subsided until the night of 24 October 1975 when a passing motorist found Norman Scott on Porlock Moor in a terrified and hysterical state beside the corpse of his Great Dane, Rinka, who had been shot through the head. Scott's story was that he was the victim of a murder attempt by a man whose gun had jammed.

Thus it appeared that there had been much activity – some sinister, some barmy – taking place on the lower level of Thorpe's life. David Holmes, a banker and best man at Thorpe's first wedding, was named by the would-be hit man, an airline pilot called Andrew Newton, as the person who had hired him to murder Scott.

Two of Holmes's associates, George Deakin and John Le Mesurier, were alleged to have arranged payments to the hit man – £5,000 for the contract, another £5,000 when Scott was dead.

The hit man proved incompetent. First he went to Dunstable instead of Barnstaple. Eventually he caught up with Scott and persuaded him to get into the car with his Great Dane, Rinka, on the pretext that he, Newton, was saving Scott from some mysterious hit man.

At a lonely spot on Exmoor, Newton feigned fatigue, and Scott got out to go around the car and take over the wheel. The dog jumped out too. Newton produced a Mauser and shot Rinka in the head. Shouting: 'It's your turn next,' he aimed the gun at the petrified Scott. It appeared to jam, and Newton leapt back in the car, cursing, and drove off, leaving Scott sobbing over Rinka's body.

Newton was sent to prison for two years for using a pistol with intent to endanger life. But whatever the press knew or deduced was unpublishable under Britain's strict laws of libel. Then in January 1976, Scott appeared in court in Barnstaple for defrauding the DHSS. To the magistrate's puzzlement, the press and public gallery was packed with journalists. To his further astonishment, Scott began raving about his sexual relationship with the Leader of the

Liberal Party. The allegations made in court could be reported under protection of absolute privilege. Journalists stampeded from the courtroom and the Thorpe–Scott story broke.

By this time Peter Bessell had emigrated to California. In debt and smelling money, he changed sides and sold his turncoat story to the *Daily Mail*. In exchange for immunity from prosecution, he gave the police an *11,000* [*sic*]-word statement implicating his one-time best friend Thorpe. Bessell had employed two investigative journalists, Mssrs Penrose and Courtier (in a move which Matthew Parris caustically described as 'unusual, to say the least') to help him write his statement. This would become the main part of Bessell's subsequent book, which included the claim (for what it is worth) that in 1968 Thorpe told him, 'Peter, we have got to get rid of him . . . It's no worse than shooting a sick dog.'

The *Daily Telegraph*, I am sorry to say, then got in on the Bessell act, offering him $50,000 serialisation rights for his book – to be paid in full *only* if Thorpe was convicted! The former Congregationalist lay preacher returned to England, eager to bear witness against his old friend.

Scott, also realising there was money to be made, hired a solicitor who retrieved the two letters Scott had handed over to the police in 1962. Thorpe, on the advice of *his* solicitor, decided to pre-empt Scott by himself publishing the 'bunnies letter' in the *Sunday Times* on 9 May 1976, alongside an article written by himself denying a sexual relationship with Scott and involvement in the retainers or the dog-shooting. The *Sunday Times*, who believed Thorpe a victim of blackmail, had agreed not to publish adverse comment of its own.

Nonetheless, the 'bunnies letter' gave some credence to rumours of more than affection with Scott. The next morning, on sale in Oxford Street were T-shirts emblazoned: 'Bunnies can and will go to France.'

Later that day, Thorpe resigned the leadership. His bitter letter to David Steel, acting Chief Whip, blamed the press for a sustained witch-hunt.

With Steel the new Leader and Thorpe on the backbenches, things settled down again until April 1977 when Andrew Newton was released from serving his prison sentence. At once Newton headed for the *Evening News* and began negotiating payment for his story: 'I was hired to kill Scott.'

In August 1978, the police warned Thorpe's solicitors privately (an unusual courtesy) that Thorpe would be charged in a few days for conspiracy to murder, along with his alleged henchmen, Holmes, Le Mesurier and Deakin. All four presented themselves to Minehead police station where they were formally charged with conspiracy and incitement to murder. Thorpe had already written a lengthy detailed statement protesting his innocence of the charges, and thereafter declined to give evidence in court, thus avoiding cross-examination of his entire life.

In the May 1979 General Election, Mrs Thatcher and the Tories routed Labour and the Liberals. The North Devon Liberal Party had re-selected Thorpe as their candidate, despite the conspiracy-to-murder charge hanging over his head. Thorpe's public meetings were catastrophic, attended only by a few party workers and the ever-loyal Marion and platoons of journalists. His 6,700 majority was over-turned by his Tory opponent who won with a majority of 8,473.

Auberon Waugh, who until then had nothing against Thorpe, made himself candidate for 'The Dog Lovers' Party' in protest that intimidation and attempted murder had been introduced into British politics. His election address had already appeared in the *Spectator* and the *Guardian* when Thorpe's counsel, George Carman QC, sought to ban it and commit Waugh to prison for prejudicing a jury at Thorpe's pending trial.

Waugh's sardonically thoughtful election address had ended lightheartedly: 'Rinka is not forgotten. Rinka lives. Woof, woof. Vote Waugh to give all dogs the right to life, liberty and the pursuit of happiness.'

The Lord Chief Justice dismissed the application, but on appeal from Thorpe's counsel, the election address was banned. Waugh remained at large. After the election, he acknowledged Thorpe's large personal following in North Devon, for he lost only 5,000 votes despite the intense publicity given the committal proceedings in Minehead. Subsequently Thorpe was elected President of the North Devon Liberal Association.

His failure to hold his seat came as a grave shock to Thorpe. He still wore an air of dazed surprise when four days later he took his seat in the dock of Number One Court at the Old Bailey before a jury of nine men and three women.

It had been billed as the trial of the century. The judge was 69-year-old Mr Justice Cantley. (One of his previous cases concerned a 23-year-old plaintiff who had been grievously wounded in a bulldozer accident which affected his sex life. The judge asked if he was married. 'No,' replied counsel. 'Well, I can't see how it affects his sex life,' said the judge. The Thorpe-Scott story abounded with eccentricity.)

Thorpe's QC, George Carman – who made his name at this trial – when cross-questioning Scott asked:

'Why did you say Mr Thorpe was a friend of yours when all you had done was speak to him for less than five minutes?'

'Because I had had the therapy at the hospital,' said Scott. 'I was going through a delusion, and I had these letters. I was using them to say I had a relationship with him already . . .'

'You were saying you had a sexual relationship with Mr Thorpe before you went to the House of Commons?'

'Yes.'

'Quite obviously, that was not true?'

'No, it wasn't.'

'You were suffering from a delusion?'

'Yes.'

'And you had suffered from other delusions, had you not?'

'Yes, sir.'

Carman also took to pieces the chief prosecution witness, Peter Bessell, demonstrating Bessell's pronounced unreliability and personal treachery. His financial interest in a conviction was what particularly discredited him. Mr Justice Cantley had a deep suspicion of persons (other than lawyers) making money out of a conviction.

By conceding that Thorpe had homosexual tendencies at the time of the events under discussion, Carman strengthened the argument for Thorpe's consistent denial of a sexual relationship with Scott.

The jury at last brought in an unanimous verdict for Thorpe and his three co-defendants to be acquitted of conspiring to murder Norman Scott. (One woman thought Marion Thorpe had suffered enough.) Thorpe was standing motionless in the dock, without expression. When he heard the not guilty verdicts, he threw the cushions which had supported his back high in the air and embraced his wife from the dock.

At a tiny eleventh-century church on Exmoor, the Sunday of 1 July 1979 was devoted to a 'Thanksgiving Service for Marion and Jeremy Thorpe'. In the Reverend John Hornby's sermon were the words: 'My dears, don't you think if it had been you or I in Jeremy's and Marion's shoes, that we'd be either round the bend or in the madhouse, or had a couple of coronaries long since with all they've been through in the last year?'

Thorpe yearned for a return to public life, but his party remained unforgiving. For many years he has endured Parkinson's Disease, but mentally he is as quick and amusing as ever, and keenly interested in modern politics. During the week, he and his wife still live in her house in a fashionable London square. At weekends they go to the North Devon cottage. He remains President of the constituency Liberal Democrat Association.

27

WILLIAM JEFFERSON CLINTON

1946–

He was a child of the sixties: a Rhodes Scholar who dodged the draft and smoked pot, the first to laugh when claiming he had not inhaled. Above all, he was into sex, infatuated with his own penis which he called Willard. Back in the days when he was an Arkansas poor boy with an alcoholic stepfather and a big ambition to make it in politics, he was already taking good care of Willard, giving it endless treats from girls on their knees, while himself giving the girls zilch of his emotions. What he did give was charm, quickly followed by manipulation in getting his own way. He would pursue this double act throughout his life.

Hillary Rodham was something different. She was smarter than he was. They met at Yale University Law School. Each charmed the other, and soon they joined forces to get him elected President. (In America, you learn at your mother's knee that you can become President of the United States.) It was natural that they should be Democrats: she had a liberal education at college; he would never forget his wretched childhood in Arkansas. They married in 1975 when he was 29.

With her comfortable upbringing in Illinois and her East Coast education, Hillary was not crazy about Arkansas, one of the poorest states in the Union, but she knew it was a necessary stepping stone. Their law practice brought them financial opportunities which they exploited by being economical with the truth. In 1977 Bill became the state's Attorney-General. Two years later he was Governor. That was his springboard.

Now – except for Gennifer Flowers – the girls on their knees were mere groupies. The Clintons' beloved daughter, Chelsea, born in 1979, knew nothing about that part of her father's life until she was an adolescent. But her ignorance was not widely shared. A cartoon flyer that circulated around Arkansas showed Clinton looking down at the bulge in his trousers and saying, 'Dick, you kept me from being the President of the United States.' This prediction proved wrong. In 1993 he was elected President.

The beginning was inauspicious: he gave Hillary a major post that she could not handle; he blundered into Somalia and Haiti. But once he got going, he changed America radically. He had guts. Against the advice of all those who said it would be political suicide, he forced through an increase in personal taxation. It was this that made it possible to eliminate the National Debt, which had run wild in the Republican eighties. Under Clinton the economy grew stronger than any other in the history of the world. True, he never showed a feel for foreign policy, but that did not greatly matter to Americans who had a limited interest in 'abroad'.

Ordinary citizens were better off than they had ever been. The strong economy allowed expansion in spending on education and welfare. 'Unstoppable' crime was reduced. The public overlooked his pathological lying in his private life, because he rarely broke a political vow. What follows is the story of how he nearly threw it all away.

Prologue. In 1995, a 22-year-old Jewish American princess with an excessively ambitious mother came on the scene. Monica Lewinsky had a privileged upbringing in Beverly Hills. Her father was a cancer specialist, her mother a writer for the *Hollywood Reporter*, which was all about the lives of movie stars. Monica got good grades but was so physically clumsy that she was mocked at school. She was fat. As her parents' quarrels became more venomous, she ate more and more and became fatter and fatter.

At seventeen, she had a job sewing costumes for the drama department at Beverly Hills High. The new drama technician was a good-looking married lothario called Andy Bleiler. He was 25. He told the fat, lonely girl that she was sexy and beautiful and asked for her panties. For a time she refused to have intercourse because she felt guilty about his pregnant wife. But she was happy to go down on him and quickly became expert at fellatio.

Their relationship lasted several years – until her mother, who knew about Andy, got the bright idea that Monica become an intern in the White House, an unpaid six-week summer job. There were 200 interns. It sounded like fun.

Act I. Only days after she started her internship she knew that women called the President 'horndog'. On television she saw he had a big red nose and grey hair. He was old. She couldn't understand his reputation with women. Then a friend of her mother invited them to watch a presidential arrival ceremony. From her side of the rope-line Monica saw that the approaching President was handsome. Her heart began to flutter, she told her mother.

A week later she went to a presidential departure. She wore the tight-fitting sage-green suit her mother had just bought her. Here he came again, walking down the rope-line. While talking to other guests, he glanced at her. He went on talking to them as he held her gaze. Then, smiling, he came over to shake her hand. His smile vanished as he looked deeply into her eyes, then up and down her (what American feminists call 'elevator eyes'). She felt he was undressing her. Then he was moving down the line, looking back at her.

The next day the interns learned they were invited to a party for the President's 49th birthday. Monica hurried home to put on her tight-fitting suit. When he came down the line again, smiling at her, she did her imitation of Marilyn Monroe greeting Kennedy: 'Happy Birthday, Mr President.' As he moved away, Clinton's arm brushed her breast. When he looked back, she blew him a kiss. He threw back his head and laughed.

Conscientious and enthusiastic, she had no trouble extending her internship for a further six weeks. In the basement lobby of the West Wing, she crossed paths with Clinton and two women with him. 'Hi, Mr President. I'm Monica Lewinsky.' 'I know.' He grinned, undressing her with his eyes again.

Act II. The first time she went into the Oval Office, she was not wearing panties and she bent over so he could see the invitation. As soon as he kissed her, her hands were all over Willard. She knew the score. One of the things the President liked best was sitting in his chair talking on the phone to another head of state while below his desk Monica busied herself with Willard.

It was an older woman friend of Monica, Linda Tripp, who proved to be the President's undoing. She knew about the Oval Office, the presents, the lot. Tripp wanted to write a book about presidential peccadilloes that would make her rich. Being a nice girl, Monica refused to help her, little knowing that Tripp was tape-recording all her telephone conversations with Clinton. It was Tripp who stopped on her way to the cleaners with Monica's dress to have the stain on the lap DNA'd: you never knew when a DNA might come in handy.

After the second internship ended, Monica bombarded the White House with phone calls. Sometimes she got through to the President, other times not. She couldn't believe he would not get her another job in the White House. By now the last thing he wanted was big-lipped Monica in his workplace. She wanted to *talk* with him, discuss her ideas about education, chatter to the President of the United States about some jerk called Andy. Her Valentine on the personal page of the *Washington Post* had scared the wits out of him.

She wrote complaining that he would not take her calls. 'Please do not do this to me. I feel disposable, used, and insignificant. I understand your hands are tied but I want to talk to you and look at some options.' Her mother had known about the liaison (which Hollywood moguls call their post-lunch 'manicure'), and then the President learned that Monica had told her father.

By this time Clinton was into his second term. Linda Tripp began leaking to the press to make her manuscript more saleable. The President was cornered. But the boy from Arkansas was determined that his need for afternoon relief should not bring him down. When Monica admitted the Oval Office pastime, he made a public statement: 'I did not have sexual relations with that woman.'

Hillary stood by her man, blaming it all on a right-wing press conspiracy. When that excuse would no longer wash, she became grim-faced and cold. Chelsea, then eighteen, was snapped walking between her parents, hand in hand with each.

Act III. It was like a nightmare: the President had a natural concern for Willard, and now he was being DNA'd and threatened with impeachment. It was the semen on the lap of the dress that did it for him. He kept on fighting.

At the Monica Lewinsky hearings in the House, he protested that while Ms Lewinsky had sex with him, he did not have sex with her. His statement was more than a lawyer's sophistry: he really did believe that blow jobs do not count as sexual relations. He was impeached in 1998 on charges of perjury and obstruction of justice, the second President of the United States to be thus humiliated. (Andrew Johnson was impeached in 1868.)

Salman Rushdie, in his inimitable style, clarifies the confusion about sexual terminology. In his recent novel *Fury*, he compares life in his newly adopted country with that of his previous adopted country. In England, he writes, fellatio is an uncommon and deep intimacy which does not precede full penetration. For teenage Americans, it is an alternative to intercourse. With their well-established tradition of make-outs in the backs of cars,

'giving head', to use the technical term, precedes full missionary-position sex more often than not. Indeed, it's the most common way for young girls to preserve their virginity while keeping their sweethearts satisfied . . .

'Thus when Clinton affirms that he never had sex with that woman Moonica, the bovine Miss L, everyone in England thinks he's a pink-faced liar, whereas the whole of teen and much of pre-and-post-teen America understand that he's telling the truth as culturally defined in these United States. Oral sex is precisely not sex. It's what enables young girls to come home and with their hands on their hearts tell their parents – hell, it probably enabled *you* to tell *your* father – that you hadn't done it.

'So slick Willie, Billy the Clint, has just been parroting what any red-blooded American teenager would have said. Arrested development? OK, probably so. But this was why the impeachment of the President failed.'

It was a near thing. Congress divided on party lines. He squeaked through. But his reputation was in tatters. Willard had kept him from being ranked in history along with Washington, Lincoln and Franklin Roosevelt.

Epilogue. Out in the cold, Monica grew fat. Yet when the chat shows beckoned, the pounds came off again. She proved an appealing subject for Oprah Winfrey and the rest. Without spite or self-pity, her directness and candour disarmed those who had expected to jeer. There was almost an innocence about her.

The next presidential election came eighteen months after the Congressional hearing. As Clinton had served two terms, there was no question of his running again. The Republican candidate, George W Bush, was distinctly unimpressive. (He needed a catastrophic national tragedy to bring out the strength in him.) The Democratic candidate, Al Gore, he of the great stone face, calculated he would win more votes if he barred Clinton from his campaign. He would pay for his misjudgement.

Late in the campaign, with the Democratic candidate flagging, Clinton independently began campaigning for Gore and won swathes of votes for him. He undertook the tricky job of crediting the Vice-President with successes from the past eight years, while freeing him from the Monica legacy.

Apologising again for the Lewinsky affair, Clinton said of Gore, 'He doesn't get enough credit for what we did together that is good, and surely no fair-minded person would blame him for any mistake that I made.' The great stone face should have used him sooner.

Clinton found a way to turn the scandal against his enemies. Many many American men forgave him. What would they have done if they'd had an affair and the wife found out? They too would have lied. His flaw began to seem like something that might have happened to them. His accusers became the malign ones.

If the Constitution did not forbid a President from running for a third term (with the exception of Franklin Roosevelt), Clinton would still be President today. His popularity outlasted the scandal.

As the tacky campaigns of Bush and Gore turned off the voters, increasingly the American people wished that a third term was possible. They wanted the prodigal son back.

BIBLIOGRAPHY

Among the many books and works of reference I have found helpful, I want to thank the authors, editors and translators of those upon which I have particularly relied:

Anger, Kenneth. *Hollywood Babylon*. Straight Arrow Books, 1975.

Asprey, Robert B. *Panther's Feast*. Jonathan Cape, 1959.

Barnes, Susan. *Behind The Image*. Jonathan Cape, 1974.

Bible. King James and other versions.

Bloch, Michael. *The Duchess of Windsor*. Weidenfeld & Nicolson, 1996.

Bradford, Sarah. *America's Queen*. Viking, 2000.

Calasso, Roberto. *The Marriage of Cadmus and Harmony*. Jonathan Cape, 1993.

Donaldson, Frances. *Edward VIII*. Weidenfeld & Nicolson, 1974.

Drabble, Margaret (edited). *The Oxford Companion to English Literature*. Oxford University Press, 2000.

Eszterhas, Joe. *American Rhapsody*. Knopf, 2000.

Gaunt, William. *English Painting*. Thames and Hudson, 1964.

— *The Restless Century*. Phaidon, 1972.

Grant, Michael. *Myths of the Greeks and Romans*. Meridian, 1995.

Graves, Robert. *The Greek Myths*. Penguin Books, 1960.

Guiles, Fred Lawrence. *Norma Jean*. Grafton Books, 1984.

Halsey, William F and J Bryan. *Admiral Halsey's Story*. McGraw Hill, 1947.

Hickok, Lorena. *Reluctant First Lady*. Knickerbocker Press, 1932.

Jenkins, Elizabeth. *Elizabeth the Great*. Victor Gollancz, 1971.

Keeler, Christine and Robert Meadley. *Sex Scandals*. Xanadu, 1985.

Lash, Joseph P. *Eleanor and Franklin*. André Deutsch, 1972.

Lovell, Mary S. *A Scandalous Life*. Richard Cohen Books, 1996.

Mailer, Norman. *Marilyn*. Grafton Books, 1984.

Maine, G F (ed.). *The Works of Oscar Wilde*. Collins, 1961.

Malory, Thomas. *The Works of Sir Thomas Malory*. Clarendon Press, 1967.

Monmouth, Geoffrey of. *Histories of the Kings of England*. Dent, 1904.

Ogden, Christopher. *Life of the Party*. Little, Brown, 1994.

Ovid: *Metamorphoses*. Completed around AD 10.

Parris, Matthew. *Great Parliamentary Scandals*. Robson Books, 1997.

Plumptre, George. *Edward VII*. Pavilion Books, 1995.

Radice, Betty (trs.) *The Letters of Abelard and Héloïse*. Penguin Books, 1974.

Renault, Mary. *The Bull from the Sea*. Longman, 1962.

Rushdie, Salman. *Fury*. Random House, 2001.

Ruskin, Mrs John. *Effie in Venice*. Unpublished Letters. John Murray, 1965.

St Aubyn, Giles. *Edward VII*. William Collins Sons, 1979.

Skelton, Barbara. *A Young Girl's Touch*. Weidenfeld & Nicolson, 1956.

Smith, Sally Bedell. *Reflected Glory*. Simon & Schuster, 1996.

Stadiem, William. *Too Rich*. Robson Books, 1991.

Untermeyer, Louis. *A Treasury of Great Poems*. Simon and Schuster, 1942.

Vidal, Gore. *Collected Essays*. Heinemann, 1974.

Waddell, Helen. *Peter Abelard*. Constable, 1933.

Waugh, Auberon. *The Last Word*. Little, Brown, 1980.

Weintraub, Stanley. *The Importance of Being Edward*. John Murray, 2000.

Wilson, Christopher. *Dancing with the Devil*. HarperCollins, 2000.

Windsor, Duchess of. *The Heart Has Its Reasons*. Michael Joseph, 1956.

Acknowledgements

I want to thank Jeremy Robson, who proposed this book and has tracked it throughout. In addition, I particularly want to thank Robson's editor, Jane Donovan, and the copy editors, Sarah Barlow and Anthea Matthison, for their care and patience. My agent, Christopher Sinclair-Stevenson, has made invaluable contributions as the stories unfolded.

Robson Books would like to thank Terry Forshaw, Picture Library Manager at Chrysalis Books, for all his hard work.

Picture Credits

Plate One: (p1) The Art Archive/Dagli Orti (Daedalus and Pasiphaë)/Dagli Orti/Corbis (Theseus and the Minotaur); (p2) Michael S. Yamashita/Corbis (David); (p3) National Portrait Gallery, London (George IV)/Hulton/Archive (Frances, Countess of Jersey); (p4) Bettmann/Corbis (Lord Byron); (p5) Hulton/Archive (King Edward VII)/National Portrait Gallery, London (Lillie Langtry)/National Portrait Gallery, London (Daisy, Countess of Warwick); (p6) Hulton/Archive (Oscar Wilde and 'Bosie', Lord Alfred Douglas; (p7) *Illustrated London News* (The Duke and Duchess of Windsor followed by Timmy Donahue); (p8) Hulton/Archive (Robert Boothby MP)/Bettmann/Corbis (Fatty Arbuckle). Plate Two: (p1) Hulton/Archive (The Duchess of Argyll); (p2) PA Photos/Wide World Photos (King Farouk)/portrait of Barbara Skelton kindly loaned from her private collection; (p3) Kobal Collection/MGM (Lana Turner)/Hulton/Archive (Christine Keeler); (p4) Hulton/Archive (Pamela Churchill Harriman); (p5) BFI/Warner Brothers (Sir Laurence Olivier and Marilyn Monroe in *The Prince and the Showgirl*); (p6) Bettmann/Corbis (Aristotle Onassis, Jacqueline Kennedy and Caroline Kennedy); (p7) Hulton-Deutsch/Corbis (Jeremy Thorpe MP); (p8) Corbis Sygma (President Bill Clinton/Monica Lewinsky)/Charles Sykes/Rex Features (Monica Lewinsky).

INDEX